*Asian American Experiences
in the United States*

To Phil and Marilyn,
with love...

Asian American Experiences in the United States

Oral Histories of
*First to Fourth Generation Americans
from China, the Philippines, Japan,
India, the Pacific Islands,
Vietnam and Cambodia*

by

Joann Faung Jean Lee

McFarland & Company, Inc., Publishers
Jefferson, North Carolina, and London

British Library Cataloguing-in-Publication data are available

Library of Congress Cataloguing-in-Publication Data

Lee, Joann Faung Jean, 1950–
    Asian American experiences in the United States : oral histories
of first to fourth generation Americans from China, the Philippines,
Japan, India, the Pacific Islands, Vietnam, and Cambodia / by
Joann Faung Jean Lee.
      p. cm.
    Includes index.
    ISBN 0-89950-585-6 (lib. bdg. : 50# alk. paper) ∞
    1. Asian Americans — Social conditions.   2. Asian Americans —
Biography.   3. Oral history.   I. Title.
E184.06L44   1991
973'.0495 — dc20

                                             90-53504
                                               CIP

Manufactured in the United States of America

McFarland & Company, Inc., Publishers
  Box 611, Jefferson, North Carolina 28640

Contents

Introduction   vii

I. Living in America   1

Growing Up in Mississippi   *Sam Sue*   3
Then Came the War   *Yuri Kochiyama*   10
Japanese Barbie Dolls   *Mari K.*   19
Born and Raised in Hawaii, but Not Hawaiian   *Andrea Kim*   24
To Be True Hawaiian   *Will Hao*   32
West Side Story   *Sue Jean Lee Suettinger*   38
Visiting the Homeland   *Victor Merina*   45
1.5 Generation   *Charles Ryu*   50

II. Aspects of Americanization   55

Exodus

Khmer Masks   *Kim Huot Kiet*   57
The Success Story   *Lang Ngan*   62
Out of Communism   *Alicia Diem*   66
Where To from Here?   *Kenny and Siu Wing Lai*   70

On the Bumpy Road

Recently Arrived   *David Lee*   76
Greedy about Life Again   *Wong Chun Yau*   78
Still on the Move   *Chin Cai Ping*   82
One More Degree   *Valerie Corpus*   84
Traffic Cops   *Lang Ngan*   88
Traffic Cops II   *Kim Huot Kiet*   94
Traffic Cops III   *Charles Ryu*   96

Americanization

To Be More Japanese   *Henry Moritsugu*   99
To Be More American   *Cao O*   104

Looking American   *Alicia Diem*   107
No Tea, Thank You   *Setsuko K.*   108
Tensions   *Mono Sen*   110
Being Indian in Jersey City   *Hardayal Singh*   112
Racial Hatred   *Madhu S. Chawla*   116
Different by Choice   *Sudershan S. Chawla*   118
On Being Asian American   *Phil Nash, Vivian Hom Fentress, Sam Sue,
    Will Hao, Cao O, Tony Hom, Victor Merina, Carolyn Ayon Lee, Charles
    Ryu, Henry Moritsugu*   121
Minorities Within   *Cao O, Lang Ngan, Alicia Diem*   135

Family

The Power of Duty   *Rose Eng*   140
Permanent Sojourner   *Ng Hing*   142
Men without Women   *Victor Merina*   144
Growing Old   *C. Ng*   146
Life as a Senior   *Katie Lee*   150
Food and Mah-jong   *Tony Hom*   152
Obligation   *Cao O*   154
Bossa   *Valerie Corpus*   155
Company Is Family   *Hideo K.*   157

Religion and Rites within Family

Koreans and Church   *Charles Ryu*   161
Family Gathering   *Sue Jean Lee Suettinger*   164
Ancestors   *Chin Cai Ping, Cao O, Tony Hom*   165
Advance Purchase   *Wong Chun Yau*   168
One God   *Alicia Diem*   169
Immigration Theology   *Wontae Chu*   170

III. Reflections on Interracial Marriage   172

Twenty-five Years   *Jim and Kate Mishra*   175
Biting the Bullet   *Vivian Hom Fentress*   181
Chinese Wedding   *Mark Fentress*   186
So He's Not a Jewish Doctor   *Jody Sandler Hom*   194
It All Worked Out   *Tony Hom*   203
Never Rebecca of Sunnybrook Farm   *Betty Ann Bruno*   208
A Male Human Being   *Phil Tajitsu Nash*   216
Eurasian   *Joann Patricia Prosser*   220

Index   227

Introduction

In the totality of American perception, all Asians are somehow lumped together into one racial group, devoid of distinctive ethnic and cultural differences. As one person said to me, it doesn't matter what you are—Chinese, Korean, or Japanese—you'll always be seen as a "chink" in this country. What started me thinking about a book on the Asian American experience was a realization of how different the various Asian cultures really are, even in the face of American transplant.

Asian Americans are the fast-growing group in the country. Today there are six million Asians in the United States. By the year 2000, the Asian population could jump to ten million. Chinese are the largest group, followed by Filipinos, Japanese, Indian (Asian), Koreans, Pacific Islanders, Vietnamese and other Southeast Asian groups.

We are in a historic period in Asian American immigration: Asians have been resettling in the United States at an unprecedented rate over the last two decades; this the direct result of the elimination of national origins quotas in 1965, allowing a large number of Koreans, Chinese and Japanese to enter the country. In addition, during the late seventies, a large influx of Southeast Asian refugees relocated to many corners of the United States.

By virtue of being a minority in this country, the various Asian groups have much in common. A Chinese from Canton or a Korean from Seoul would not describe himself first as an Asian. But in the United States, the trend is increasingly to do just that—to define ourselves as Asian Americans, rather than of a particular Asian country. Advocates see this as a way to build stronger group identity; turning historic animosities into Asian solidarity. But others have spoken just as passionately against this, totally dismissing the Asian American concept. The argument over group identity symbolizes the cultural conflicts that Asians confront.

Once in the United States, Asians, regardless of their nationality, are first seen as members of the same racial group. It is this overriding distinction that has shaped their perception of themselves, their lives and their experiences — be it first, second or third generation Asian American. Language further compounds the problem. As Cao O said, in reflecting on his status in this country, "No matter how many years I am here — even till I die — I will always speak English with an accent. That is a fact that I cannot deny. That is a fact that I cannot escape from. And people would never see me as an American because the conventional wisdom is that if you are American, you should speak with no accent."

In talking to people, in listening to the way they see themselves, how they grew up, their views, I was struck by the power of the larger society in influencing Asian American thinking and behavior. Asian attitudes — how Asians see themselves, how they feel they are seen by the larger society, how they want to be seen — are in large part a product of environment. These interviews are not definitive and certainly do not represent the full experience of any particular Asian group. But what is present throughout the recounting of their lives is a measure of the values of their time. For instance, one Korean woman remembers while growing up in Hawaii, that all her friends used to go to Japan to get their eyelids cut and reshaped to look more western. " A lot of my friends in the summers would go to Japan because their families were there. They would have an operation to make their eyelids double," she said. "It was not an unusual thing. More people would dye their hair lighter — instead of black, they would make it brown." She also said her sisters would never go out with an Asian man because the image of an Asian man was tied closely to her father — who, despite her description of him as exceptionally bright, always spoke English with a heavy accent, and was therefore treated less than equally.

Henry Moritsugu's family was interned during World War II in Canada. He talks of how Japanese schools were closed, and the desire to learn about Japanese things was discouraged in general. "It was more important to be accepted," he said. Not until the next generation, through his son, is there a return to the study of culture and language. "I was always afraid to go to Japan, because I don't speak adequate Japanese. I expected to be ridiculed. So my wife and I went when my son was studying in Japan; we actually made it easy for ourselves by staying with him. We were very sensitive to what we considered our inadequacies."

Then there is the power of duty within family. Eighty-two-year-old Rose Eng came to this country as a picture bride. During the 1930s life was difficult in China, and her mother had arranged for her to marry a laundryman. But they had no children, so after the war, her husband went back to China, he said, to see his mother. He never returned. A year later, he died, leaving behind a daughter by another woman. For over thirty years, Rose worked alone, in her laundry, and then in a sewing factory, to send money back to China for this little girl. That little girl eventually came to the United States. "My life (fate) was not a good one," Rose said. "I was never able to have children. Still, it is good that I have a family again after so many years. . . . My heart is content now. As long as I have enough to eat and live on, and don't have to go begging in the streets."

The chapters that follow are not tied to historical events. They are told by the individuals but may refer to a particular time in America. Whenever an historical context is relevant to the understanding of the times I have included background information such as dates or the passage of certain acts. For instance, in the section on interracial marriage, I noted the progress of American legislation on the issue. In 1922, Congress passed the Cable Act stripping an American woman's citizenship if she married an alien ineligible for U.S. citizenship. (The law was highly discriminatory against Asians, in that Chinese, Japanese, Koreans, Filipinos, and Indians, under the then existing law, were not eligible for naturalization. Chinese were not allowed to become citizens until 1943, Filipinos and Asian Indians in 1946, and Japanese and Koreans in 1952.) Only if the woman (if Caucasian) ended the marriage, would she regain her citizenship. Asian women had an additional barrier: If they divorced, they would not be eligible for citizenship since Asians at the time were not allowed to become citizens. This all happened at a point in American history when an overwhelming number of Asian males moved to the United States to become laborers. They were not allowed to bring their families. Female companionship was not a part of the immigration picture.

Until the end of World War II, thirty-one states had laws against mixed marriages. It wasn't until 1948, for instance, that the California Supreme Court struck down the state's antimiscegenation law. In the 1990s, interracial marriage may still be considered controversial in certain segments of our society, but it has become a social issue, and no longer a legal one. Given this historical perspective, the interracial marriage issue has changed rapidly since *Loving v. Virginia*, a 1967 case in which the U.S. Supreme Court ruling essentially made laws against mixed marriages unconstitutional. Most interracial legislation barred marriages between blacks and whites. But certain states, such as Georgia and California, had laws aimed at Asians.

Growing up as a child of an interracial marriage today is also quite different than thirty years ago. Joann Prosser said, "I'm glad I'm Eurasian, as opposed to pure Chinese or pure Western, because I like the mix. . . . Some of my friends regard me as almost better because they say the prettiest mixes are Asians and Americans." Betty Ann Bruno, who grew up in the 1950s said, "I had been taught that the direction to go towards to be successful was in the direction of the Caucasians. I look very ethnic. I have brown skin, brown eyes, brown hair. And it was a terrible thing to look that way at the time."

It is not the intent of this book to provide a set of conclusions about the Asian American experience. It is clear every group has its own set of cultural values. But within the context of being a minority in the United States, there are certain parallels which become evident with acculturation.

As much as Asian immigrants identify with the culture of their homeland in the first generation, by the third generation, Asian Americans will have developed values inherently Western. This is in part because of the strong desire to do well in American society and an emphasis on education. The vocabulary of success is defined in Western terms: from language to cultural symbols. Second and third generation Asian Americans may retain some of their parents' Asian values, but by virtue of having grown up in the United States, their overriding identity and experiences are shaped by American things.

Also by the second and third generation, the dominant and in many instances only language spoken at home is English. Asian Americans tend to lose the ability to understand, write and read in the language of their immigrant grandparents unless there is a deliberate effort to maintain it (either by schooling, or speaking it at home). This has created gaps in the ability of American-born Asians to communicate with elders who cannot speak English.

For American-born Asians who are monolingual (speaking only English), and have little or no ability to speak their parents' Asian language, many said they desired to have more knowledge of Asian things. Some felt cheated that Japanese or Chinese, for instance, wasn't emphasized more at home, and wanted a greater understanding of their roots. That they did not have this was a deficiency in their lives.

Not all American-born Asians shared this view. Others felt they were Americans, period. Knowledge of an Asian culture wasn't important beyond the point that it would be enriching just to have a greater understanding of a second language and culture (one not necessarily tied to their heritage).

As for the American Dream: everyone I talked to was proud to be an American. Most were happy living in the United States, but not everyone felt they belonged there in the sense of fitting into the larger society.

First generation Asian immigrants believed strongest in the so-called "American Dream." The United States is a place where, as long as one worked hard, there was always the opportunity to live well — even get rich. And the future can only be better than the past. This is not too far from how most immigrant groups see this country. Being in the United States means the freedom to pursue a better life. And indeed, for them the United States is a wonderful country — especially because it symbolizes opportunity for their children.

Beyond the first generation however, a different set of issues surface. While success and overall achievement are still the goals for many, questions of the Asian's place in this country have become much more apparent. There is no longer the handicap of language. There is also a different set of expectations just by virtue of growing up in the United States: beyond working hard, and causing no problems, where does the Asian fit in the larger society? This question crops up in many arenas: politics, civil rights, the media, race-related crimes, even the differences between being accepted as an Asian and a woman, versus as an Asian and a man. It is clear that later generation Asian Americans tend to address these issues more than the first generation.

All the interviewees were chosen randomly. The majority are people I didn't know; names I gathered from friends and colleagues. Beyond this, I also talked to members of a senior citizens' center, and newly arrived immigrants at a social service training program in New York's Chinatown. Some of the interviews were obtained in California, but the majority were collected in the New York tri-state area. In a very few cases I interviewed friends or family members, as I felt their profiles typified a slice of the Asian American experience. Even though several of the subjects are surnamed Lee, only one is related to me. Lee just happens to be a very common name, among both Koreans and Chinese. I deliberately stayed away from celebrities or well-known success stories. In interviewing people, I aimed to come as close as possible to Asian American attitudes and lifestyles as defined by their cultural past and American present. With but four exceptions, all forty subjects are identified by their true names. Since these four felt they could speak more freely if their names were not used, I replaced their surnames (as noted) with others common to their nationalities. Several of the interviews were conducted in Cantonese or Mandarin, as some of the subjects spoke only minimal English.

The focus of this book remains American/Asian throughout. Within these two cultures there exists a hybrid of socialization as manifest in values, families and interpersonal relationships. Much has been published in the last fifteen years about Asians in this country, but mostly in terms of specific nationalities. Where this book differs is in the pulling together of the various nationalities – Chinese, Korean, Japanese, Indian, Filipino, and Pacific Islander. Through these oral histories, issues critical to Asian Americans, such as violence, language, immigration, education and resettlement, are all explored.

Among the numerous media references to Asians today are stories having to do with the model hard-working minority or with gang-related crimes. But there is far more to Asian Americans. Inherent in every ethnic group is cultural baggage of a sort that is seldom looked at, compared or acknowledged in the mainstream media. Certainly the pull of custom is far greater in the first than the fourth generation Asian American. For Hardayal Singh, who arrived in this country ten years ago, not only is it a given that his eleven-year-old daughter will one day marry an Indian, it is natural that the marriage be arranged by her parents. "We plan to send her back to India next year," he said. "She will take all her education there. We wish her to adopt Indian culture. We don't hate American culture, but we like our culture. We will choose a husband for her, but we will give her the freedom to see and talk to him first. This is an old tradition."

But Betty Ann Bruno, a fourth generation Asian American, had no such expectations — either for herself or her children. Her first husband and the father of her children is Italian/Scot, her second husband, an Estonian Jew. Her children are one-eighth Hawaiian, one-eighth Chinese. "They like it," Betty Ann said. "They think it's terrific that they're six different things."

The subject of racism in varying degrees of intensity was a recurring theme among the Asian American interviewees. This came out in discussions not only with those who had difficulty with language, but even for monolingual Asians who spoke perfect English. Education was another topic which surfaced constantly. It's seen as a bedrock, either as motivation for immigrating to this country, or as a channel to opportunity. Every group I interviewed placed a premium on education.

The book is divided into three parts: Profiles, which through the individual experience give insight into such matters as culture, economic lifestyles, family, and relationships; Aspects of Americanization, on specific topics and events; and Interracial Marriage.

I would like to thank those who shared so willingly their lives and feelings with me. From the outset, I wanted to write a substantive book on Asian Americans, but one with broad based appeal. Since, as a journalist, I am drawn to the work of Studs Terkel, the oral history form seemed the best way to do this.

I often wonder what my life would be like if my father had not fled China with my mother and sisters in 1949. I may have spent my teenage years as a Red Guard; or perhaps my children might be among those arrested for demonstrating against the Chinese government on Tienanmen Square. But geography is destiny, and my destiny — along with those of all Asian Americans — changed forever with my family's act of coming to this country in search of the "American Dream."

I. Living in America

The first Chinese to come to this country came, lured by rumors of gold in California. Documented accounts list three Chinese arriving in San Francisco Harbor in 1848. By 1852, twenty thousand more had arrived.
— *Guide to the Chinese American Experience*

Growing Up in Mississippi
Sam Sue

Sam Sue is in his mid-thirties. He is Chinese American and was born and raised in Mississippi. He speaks bitterly of his childhood. Today he is a lawyer in New York City.

"There is this shot in the opening scene of the movie, *Mississippi Burning*, where you see two water fountains. One is broken, and chipped, and water is dripping from it. The other is modern, and shining. A white guy goes up to the nice one, and the black kid goes up to the old one. I remember saying to myself, 'If I was in the scene, where would I drink?'

"As a kid, I remember going to the theatre and not really knowing where I was supposed to sit. Blacks were segregated then. Colored people had to sit upstairs, and white people sat downstairs. I didn't know where I was supposed to sit, so I sat in the white section, and nobody said anything. So I always had to confront those problems growing up. So these experiences were very painful.

"I guess I was always considered marginal with whites and blacks, though I think I got along better with blacks. I really didn't have any childhood friends. I just felt I had nothing in common with them. And I guess I felt there was this invisible barrier. I stayed mostly with my family – I have two older brothers, and one older sister.

"I lived in a town called Clarksdale. At the time, there were twenty-five thousand to thirty thousand people there. In the sixties at the height, there were maybe forty to fifty Chinese families in town. Quite a number. They used to have Chinese parties, and gatherings, and the funny thing about it was they all sort of came from the same village, or district.

"Chinese church was more of a social, rather than a religious event. I always hated the gatherings. I was basically ashamed of being Chinese. I think that's probably true for a lot of Chinese Americans – on the east and west coast. Whether they will acknowledge it is something else. But I think

3

there is a lot of self-hatred, induced by society, culture, and circumstance. So I hated to go to these Chinese parties. Besides, it's not like you could date any Chinese girls, because they were all your cousins.

"I was lucky, in that the school I went to was mostly white, because our store was near the center of town, and the school was across the way. But most of the Chinese families lived in black areas so they went to black schools, and the kids got harassed a lot by the blacks. There was a lot of resentment against the Chinese by the blacks, because some of the Chinese families would rip-off blacks, because it was part of giving store credit to the black farmers—they got surcharged excessively. Or they might be charged for things they didn't purchase.

"I didn't date at all—not in high school. It was totally unheard of. I remember very painful experiences of asking white girls to see if they were interested or anything, and them mumbling some excuse about being busy that night. But you knew what was going on. My cousin, for instance, had to take his cousin to the senior prom. I didn't think that kind of thing would be a good thing for me, so I didn't go to my senior prom. My reaction at the time to the dating scene was total alienation. I never considered dating a black girl. I don't know if it was racism, but I just felt there was no commonality. Because even though one wasn't accepted as a white at the time, dating a white was seen as going up—that was the thinking then. And I think Chinese women had it harder. I think it was okay for a Chinese man to date a non-Chinese, but not for a Chinese woman to go out with anything but a Chinese. Part of that was that Asian women are presumed to be exotic and submissive, and that's a common theme that runs through the stereotype images.

"Northerners see a Southern accent as a signal that you're a racist, you're stupid, or you're a hick. Regardless of what your real situation is. So I reacted to that by adapting the way I speak. If you talked to my brother, you would definitely know he was from the South. But as for myself, I remember customers telling my dad, 'Your son sounds like a Yankee.' I think I had a Southern drawl, but it wasn't pronounced. I also mimicked Northern accents because I was so alienated. Maybe I had this deep alienation, even as a kid. I used to read the *Times*. I'd see this stuff on the television. I grew up on the 'Bowery Boys.' The television and the radio were my links to civilization. I'd be waiting for eight PM to roll around, so that I could reach radio waves from Chicago or even New York. It was like Radio Free-Europe for me."

Family: "My role model when I was growing up was my older brother because he was going to college when I was in elementary school. He was bilingual, so he was sort of the link for me between the old and the new country.

"My brother went to Ole Miss (University of Mississippi), and at one

point, he was the first Chinese on campus invited to join an all-white fraternity. He was also in the ROTC. Actually it wasn't many years after that
that they took away my father's and my oldest brother's citizenship. It was
ironic—here he was teaching American government. He was about as
American as you can get, and it sort of opened his eyes. Being denaturalized
meant he was deportable, so he and my dad had to get waivers, and re-
apply for citizenship—doing the test again. So they had to be naturalized
twice.

"There was a confession period for those who came into the country
illegally. Many Chinese confessed, and things were okay. But what bugs
me, is my dad confessed, and he was nailed to the wall. He came into the
U.S. illegally in the 1930s. Later on, he brought my mother and my oldest
brother from China. The government took away his citizenship by virtue
of him coming here on false papers. He was denaturalized in 1965. That
meant what the government gave, it could take away. I mean, Sue in not
my real family name. I think it is Jiu."*

The Family Store: "Dad said he went to Mississippi because that's
where a good number Chinese from his village had moved to. We, like
other Chinese in Mississippi, ran a 'Mom and Pop' grocery story. Anything
from shotgun shells to fresh meats to corn chop and hog shorts. (Corn chop
is feed for chicken, and hog shorts are grain for hogs.)

"My father would open his store about nine thirty in the morning, and
close it about ten at night. We would eat after the store closed. We all ran
the store, seven days a week. Only on Christmas would he close for half
a day. He wouldn't even close the store when my brother got married. I had
to run the store. I didn't want to go to Florida for my brother's wedding and
let Dad stay home. So I let him go.

"It was a very rural area, and a number of Chinese had done well doing
this. I guess economically they fit in to the area because their clientele were
mostly black, rural farmers. I guess the black rural farmers couldn't get
credit from white storekeepers. I guess that they presumed Chinese store
keepers filled a need—providing credit to black farmers who couldn't otherwise get it. I remember for years on end, my father keeping records of
people who owed him money. And that's what a lot of other Chinese did
too. They filled that function.

---

*A series of Chinese exclusion acts were passed as early as 1882, which made it very
difficult for many Chinese to enter the country. Some purchased falsified documents
which showed they were children of Chinese fathers already in the United States;
thus the term "paper son."

The Act of September 11, 1957, established a "confession" program. Chinese who
obtained entry visas by fraud and misrepresentation would not be deported if a
spouse, parent, or child was a citizen of the United States. If their confessions were
accepted, their papers were adjusted so they could stay.

"Our store was a social place, people would hang out on Friday, pay-day. So black customers would be hanging out, drinking beer, and eating sandwiches. It would be packed, with blacks and red neck. It was a place for them to meet.

"My dad didn't have much time to spend with me, so most of the time I would talk to the customers. We would kid around. I'd ask them, 'How'd your skin go so black?' And they would tell you stories to kid you. 'Oh, I rolled down this river bank and got all this mud on me, and couldn't get it off.' And I used to believe that stuff, and I thought blacks were really different. A lot of the blacks in our store chewed tobacco, so you'd think their spit was browner than white people's. But on a real gut level, you knew that people were treated different. And it's sort of weird on my parent's level, because on one hand they would make friends with a lot of black people, then on another, they would say racist things about them.

"Back then, the amount of poverty blacks suffered was profound. It doesn't come close to the experience of blacks in urban centers today. You're talking about people who didn't have running water, or who only got it recently. My father used to sell kerosene because people used it to light their lamps. I remember people using Clorox bleach to purify the water. It had chlorine in it, so they would let it sit in the water and kill the germs. Blacks were at the very low end of the scale, and the Chinese were sort of in between. We didn't really fit in. Very rich, aristocratic whites, were at the top end. Chinese really didn't have a place in society. Economically they were better than the blacks, but on a social scale, they didn't amount to very much. I think blacks saw us as Jews. We were in the same position as Jews were in the town. We all sort of played marginal, economic roles. There were quite a few Jews in town. They weren't accepted by blacks or whites either. I don't think whites knew what to make of us.

"Buying a store in California or some other urban center was expensive, whereas buying a store in Mississippi was cheap, so that's why a lot of Chinese families moved there. But you have to remember that there were still racial restrictions. A lot of the Chinese couldn't buy property, or had difficulty buying it. By the time my father paid off the mortgage, the owner said, 'I am not going to convey the title to you.' My understanding was that we had to threaten to sue him to get it."

Housing: "We had to live in the back of our store. It was tenement-like conditions, though we didn't know it at the time. I didn't know how poor we were until I left. Everyone slept in one big room. There was a kitchen in the back. We used to use the place to store goods too, so there would be boxes all around. If you went into the living room, you'd be sitting on a box of laundry detergent. We lived that way until 1970. It was only then that we could consider buying a house. We thought of buying a house in

1966, but it didn't work out. It was in a white neighborhood, and the day before closing, we received a telephone call. Someone said, 'If you buy that house, we will burn it.' And we knew it was one of the neighbors calling. One of the Chinese families knew who had called – it was a Pepsi Cola distributor. Many of the Chinese families were so upset about what had happened that they boycotted Pepsi Cola for a long while. We didn't buy the house. The attitude was, if we're not wanted there, we just won't move there. Getting a house in a white neighborhood – it wasn't only impossible – there was no choice. You could either buy a house somewhere, if you could find an owner that would sell it to you, or you could buy property on the outskirts of town and build a house – which is what many Chinese families ended up doing. This way, there were no problems from neighbors because there weren't any neighbors.

"Eventually, my family decided to buy a plot of land and build our home on the outskirts of town near some other Chinese families. We had to get a white man to buy the property and convey the title to us because certain property owners would not sell to Chinese families – and this was as recent as 1970."

Parents: "My father came to the United States in the 1930s from the Hoi Ping district of Canton. Like many Chinese of his generation, he went to California first. He didn't bring my mother. She came later. He worked in a restaurant with several other relatives around the San Francisco area. He said he borrowed money to come over, and the people working in the restaurant, including himself, were working to try to pay off his debt. They also wanted to save enough to go back to Hong Kong or China to get their wives. Eventually he did go back to China for my mother and my oldest brother.

"My dad was sixteen when he came to this country. He learned his English from customers, which would be blacks, or white rednecks. He did not finish school. He just finished the third or fourth grade in China. A friend of mine did a documentary on the Chinese in Mississippi, and she stayed with my dad in his home. She interviewed him, but never used the interview. She said his English was so strange that she would have had to use subtitles with it. He is a Chinese man who can speak English very poorly and does so with a black southern English dialect. It's quite difficult to understand. I can understand him, but it is difficult to communicate with him. And the gap gets even further when you want to get beyond the really simple language. Mom was less able to speak English than the others. One common thread that runs through many Asian lives is that parents spend so much tme working for the future of their children, that they don't devote enough time to emotional needs. Either the parents are working and can't be there, or if they are at home, they are so tired they can't devote themselves to the children.

"The thing with Chinese parents is they make you feel like you owe them for the rest of your life — even when they're in the grave. My mother died when I graduated from college in 1977. My father made me feel terrible because he wanted me to work in the store even after I graduated. They had this idea that they were going to pass the store on to me, as stupid as it was. And they knew it was stupid. By the 1970s, the Chinese stores were declining due to mechanization. People used to be cotton pickers and we would sell these leather things for their knees so that when they crouched down they wouldn't have sore kneecaps. But with the advent of such things as cotton-picking machines and large supermarkets, it spelled doom for the Chinese store keepers. Also, kids my age didn't want to stay. Many chose to move to some urban area, such as Atlanta.

"My parents retired in 1978. But two months before the store officially closed, my mom died. It was a double shock for my dad. He not only lost his wife, but also his way of life. He had opened the store at nine AM and closed at ten PM, seven days a week. He did this for thirty years. He never went on trips. He just worked at the store. He felt there was nothing else.

"My dad is still in Mississippi. It's his life. He's been there since the Depression. It is all he knows. We actually tried to move him, but he is so attached to the area — not that he has affection for it, only that he's used to it — he feels it is home. There are still some Chinese there, though most have died, or moved away."

A Monolingual Chinese American: "I didn't learn how to use chopsticks until I left Mississippi. We never used chopsticks at home. I didn't even have any idea of what a Chinese restaurant was until I went to college. My first encounter with a Chinese restaurant was in Cleveland, Ohio. There just weren't any near where I was growing up.

"I can't speak the language, and you feel intimidated by it when you go into restaurants. Like you keep ordering the same dishes because those are the only dishes you can order. You feel that since you are Chinese, you should be able to speak to other people that look like you. Sometimes they have mistaken me for a *juk-kok* (foreign-born Chinese) and started talking to me; I can't understand a word.

"I don't feel Chinese, and I'm not. I identify myself as Asian American. I feel Chinese to some extent, but not necessarily to the extent of knowing much about Chinese culture or tradition. When I was in college, I met these Asian studies majors, and there was a certain amount of resentment, in that they could speak the language and know the culture, but they didn't *know* what it was like to be Chinese in a white society. They may have had a superficial understanding of the culture and language, but at that time I sort of felt they were expropriating our culture, and I felt very possessive about other Asian women. It's like when I walk outside, I know I will be treated differently. It's not something I like saying. It's not even a political statement. It's just seeing reality. I'm not looking for, or am I supersensitive to, being treated as a Chinese person, or a non-white person, but it's there. It's even here in New York.

"One senses it in my profession as an attorney. You're arguing a case before a judge. And the other guy is white, and he's been around. The moment he walks in the office, it's like he says to the judge or the clerk, 'How's so and so?' But when I come in, it's like this stranger walks in – you don't belong here. But when he walks in, it's like family. I feel like I just walked into the wrong club – a place I don't belong.

"I never worked for a large firm. I never had the inclination to do that. It wasn't only a political choice, I really had nothing to talk to them about. There is this sort of Waspish mentality in the profession. I now work in a small Asian law firm. All the jobs I've had since college have been associated to Asian stuff.

"I don't have a burning desire to learn Chinese at this point, though it would be helpful in my work and in certain aspects of my life.

"If I went to China, I would be an American, and that is what I am in that context. So many of my views, as much as I may want to deny it, are American. If I were in a foreign country, I would be homesick. In terms of adopting the American culture and values I'm an American. But in terms of feeling there is a difference, then I'm still Asian or Chinese. I feel different. Ask me what I feel different about, and I can't really say. It's not only that people may or may not treat you differently. It's that I am different.

"I left Mississippi in 1973. There was no future for me there. I was so alienated that even if I thought there was something concrete to be done there, I have such bad feelings for the place I wouldn't go back. Being Chinese in Mississippi was definitely a handicap."

Then Came the War

Yuri Kochiyama

Yuri Kochiyama is sixty-seven, Japanese American, and was born and raised in San Pedro, California. She got married and moved to New York after World War II. She now teaches English to foreign students.

"I was red, white and blue when I was growing up. I taught Sunday school, and was very, very American. But I was also very provincial. We were just kids rooting for our high school.

"My father owned a fish market. Terminal Island was nearby, and that was where many Japanese families lived. It was a fishing town. My family lived in the city proper. San Pedro was very mixed, predominately white, but there were blacks also.

"I was nineteen at the time of the evacuation. I had just finished junior college. I was looking for a job, and didn't realize how different the school world was from the work world. In the school world, I never felt racism. But when you got into the work world, it was very difficult. This was 1941, just before the war. I finally did get a job at a department store. But for us back then, it was a big thing, because I don't think they had ever hired an Asian in a department store before. I tried, because I saw a Mexican friend who got a job there. Even then they didn't hire me on a regular basis, just on Saturdays, summer vacation, Easter vacation, and Christmas vacation. Other than that, I was working like the others — at a vegetable stand, or doing part-time domestic work. Back then, I only knew of two Japanese American girl friends who got jobs as secretaries — but these were in Japanese companies. But generally you almost never saw a Japanese American working in a white place. It was hard for Asians. Even for Japanese, the best jobs they felt they could get were in Chinatowns, such as in Los Angeles. Most Japanese were either in some aspect of fishing, such as in the canneries, or went right from school to work on the farms. That was what it was like in the town of San Pedro. I loved working in the department store, because it was a small town, and you got to know and see

10

everyone. The town itself was wonderful. People were very friendly. I didn't see my job as work — it was like a community job.

"Everything changed for me on the day Pearl Harbor was bombed. On that very day — December 7, the FBI came and they took my father. He had just come home from the hospital the day before. For several days we didn't know where they had taken him. Then we found out that he was taken to the federal prison at Terminal Island. Overnight, things changed for us. They took all men who lived near the Pacific waters, and had anything to do with fishing. A month later, they took every fisherman from Terminal Island, sixteen and over, to places — not the regular concentration camps — but to detention centers in places like South Dakota, Montana, and New Mexico. They said that all Japanese who had given money to any kind of Japanese organization would have to be taken away. At that time, many people were giving to the Japanese Red Cross. The first group was thirteen hundred Isseis — my parent's generation. They took those who were leaders of the community, or Japanese school teachers, or were teaching martial arts, or who were Buddhist priests. Those categories which would make them very 'Japanesey,' were picked up. This really made a tremendous impact on our lives. My twin brother was going to the University at Berkeley. He came rushing back. All of our classmates were joining up, so he volunteered to go into the service. And it seemed strange that here they had my father in prison, and there the draft board okayed my brother. He went right into the army. My other brother, who was two years older, was trying to run my father's fish market. But business was already going down, so he had to close it. He had finished college at the University of California a couple of years before.

"They took my father on December 7th. The day before, he had just come home from the hospital. He had surgery for an ulcer. We only saw him once on December 13. On December 20th they said he could come home. By the time they brought him back, he couldn't talk. He made gutteral sounds and we didn't know if he could hear. He was home for twelve hours. He was dying. The next morning, when we got up, they told us that he was gone. He was very sick. And I think the interrogation was very rough. My mother kept begging the authorities to let him go to the hospital until he was well, then put him back in the prison. They did finally put him there, a week or so later. But they put him in a hospital where they were bringing back all these American Merchant Marines who were hit on Wake Island. So he was the only Japanese in that hospital, so they hung a sheet around him that said, Prisoner of War. The feeling where he was was very bad.

"You could see the hysteria of war. There was a sense that war could actually come to American shores. Everybody was yelling to get the 'Japs' out of California. In Congress, people were speaking out. Organizations such as the Sons and Daughters of the Golden West were screaming 'Get the "Japs" out.' So were the real estate people, who wanted to get the land from the Japanese farmers. The war had whipped up such a hysteria that if there was anyone for the Japanese, you didn't hear about it. I'm sure they were afraid to speak out, because they would be considered not only just 'Jap' lovers, but unpatriotic.

"Just the fact that my father was taken made us suspect to people. But on the whole, the neighbors were quite nice, especially the ones adjacent to us. There was already a six AM to six PM curfew and a five mile limit on where we could go from our homes. So they offered to do our shopping for us, if we needed.

"Most Japanese Americans had to give up their jobs, whatever they did, and were told they had to leave. The edict for 9066 — President Roosevelt's edict* for evacuation — was in February 1942. We were moved to a detention center that April. By then the Japanese on Terminal Island were just helter skelter, looking for anywhere they could go. They opened up the Japanese school and Buddhist churches, and families just crowded in. Even farmers brought along their chickens and chicken coops. They just opened up the places for people to stay until they could figure out what to do. Some people left for Colorado and Utah. Those who had relatives could do so. The idea was to evacuate all the Japanese from the coast. But all the money was frozen, so even if you knew where you wanted to go, it wasn't that simple. By then, people knew they would be going into camps, so they were selling what they could, even though they got next to nothing for it.

"We were fortunate, in that our neighbors, who were white, were kind enough to look after our house, and they said they would find people to rent it, and look after it till we got back. But these neighbors were very, very unusual.

"We were sent to an assembly center in Arcadia, California, in April. It was the largest assembly center on the West Coast having nearly twenty thousand people. There were some smaller centers with about six hundred people. All along the West Coast — Washington, Oregon, California — there were many, many assembly centers, but ours was the largest. Most of the assembly centers were either fairgrounds, or race tracks. So many of us lived in stables and they said you could take what you could carry. We were there until October.

"Even though we stayed in a horse stable, everything was well organized. Every unit would hold four to six people. So in some cases, families had to split up, or join others. We slept on army cots, and for mattresses

*Executive Order No. 9066 does not mention detention of Japanese specifically, but was used exclusively against the Japanese. Over 120,000 Japanese were evacuated from the West Coast.

they gave us muslin bags, and told us to fill them with straw. And for chairs, everybody scrounged around for carton boxes, because they could serve as chairs. You could put two together and it could be a little table. So it was just makeshift. But I was amazed how, in a few months, some of those units really looked nice. Japanese women fixed them up. Some people had the foresight to bring material and needles and thread. But they didn't let us bring anything that could be used as weapons. They let us have spoons, but no knives. For those who had small children or babies, it was rough. They said you could take what you could carry. Well, they could only take their babies in their arms, and maybe the little children could carry something, but it was pretty limited.

"I was so red, white and blue, I couldn't believe this was happening to us. America would never do a thing like this to us. This is the greatest country in the world. So I thought this is only going to be for a short while, maybe a few weeks or something, and they will let us go back. At the beginning no one realized how long this would go on. I didn't feel the anger that much because I thought maybe this was the way we could show our love for our country, and we should not make too much fuss or noise, we should abide by what they asked of us. I'm a totally different person now than I was back then. I was naïve about so many things. The more I think about, the more I realize how little you learn about American history. It's just what they want you to know.

"At the beginning, we didn't have any idea how temporary or permanent the situation was. We thought we would be able to leave shortly. But after several months they told us this was just temporary quarters, and they were building more permanent quarters elsewhere in the United States. All this was so unbelievable. A year before we would never have thought anything like this could have happened to us — not in this country. As time went by, the sense of frustration grew. Many families were already divided. The fathers, the heads of the households, were taken to other camps. In the beginning, there was no way for the sons to get in touch with their families. Before our group left for the detention camp, we were saying goodbye almost every day to other groups who were going to places like Arizona and Utah. Here we finally had made so many new friends — people who we met, lived with, shared the time, and gotten to know. So it was even sad on that note and the goodbyes were difficult. Here we had gotten close to these people, and now we had to separate again. I don't think we even thought about where they were going to take us, or how long we would have to stay there. When we got on the trains to leave for the camps, we didn't know where we were going. None of the groups knew. It was later on that we learned so and so ended up in Arizona, or Colorado, or some other place. We were all at these assembly centers for about seven months. Once they started pushing people out, it was done very quickly. By

October, our group headed out for Jerome, Arkansas, which is on the Tex-Arkana corner.

"We were on the train for five days. The blinds were down, so we couldn't look out, and other people couldn't look in to see who was in the train. We stopped in Nebraska, and everybody pulled the blinds to see what Nebraska looked like. The interesting thing was, there was a troop train stopped at the station too. These American soldiers looked out, and saw all these Asians, and they wondered what we were doing on the train. So the Japanese raised the windows, and so did the soldiers. It wasn't a bad feeling at all. There was none of that you 'Japs' kind of thing. The women were about the same age as the soldiers — eighteen to twenty-five, and we had the same thing on our minds. In camps, there wasn't much to do, so the fun thing was to receive letters, so on our train, all the girls who were my age, were yelling to the guys, 'Hey, give us your address where you're going, we'll write you.' And they said, 'Are you sure you're going to write?' We exchanged addresses and for a long time I wrote to some of those soldiers. On the other side of the train, I'll never forget there was this old guy, about sixty, who came to our window and said, 'We have some Japanese living here. This is Omaha, Nebraska.' This guy was very nice, and didn't seem to have any ill feelings for Japanese. He had calling cards, and he said 'Will any of you people write to me?' We said, 'Sure,' so he threw in a bunch of calling cards, and I got one, and I wrote to him for years. I wrote to him about what camp was like, because he said, 'Let me know what it's like wherever you end up.' And he wrote back, and told me what was happening in Omaha, Nebraska. There were many, many interesting experiences too. Our mail were generally not censored, but all the mail from the soldiers was. Letters meant everything.

"When we got to Jerome, Arkansas, we were shocked because we had never seen an area like it. There was forest all around us. And they told us to wait till the rains hit. This would not only turn into mud, but Arkansas swamp lands. That's where they put us — in swamp lands, surrounded by forests. It was nothing like California.

"I'm speaking as a person of twenty who had good health. Up until then, I had lived a fairly comfortable life. But there were many others who didn't see the whole experience the same way. Especially those who were older and in poor health and had experienced racism. One more thing like this could break them. I was at an age where transitions were not hard; the point where anything new could even be considered exciting. But for people in poor health, it was hell.

"There were army-type barracks, with two hundred to two hundred and five people to each block and every block had its own mess hall, facility for washing clothes, showering. It was all surrounded by barbed wire, and armed soldiers. I think they said only seven people were killed in total, though thirty were shot, because they went too close to the fence. Where we were, nobody thought of escaping because you'd be more scared of the swamps — the poisonous snakes, the bayous. Climatic conditions were very harsh. Although Arkansas is in the South, the winters were very, very cold. We had a pot bellied stove in every room and we burned wood. Everything was very organized. We got there in October, and were warned to prepare ourselves. So on our block, for instance, males eighteen and over could go out in the forest to chop down trees for wood for the winter. The men would bring back the trees, and the women sawed the trees. Everybody worked. The children would pile up the wood for each unit.

"They told us when it rained, it would be very wet, so we would have to build our own drainage system. One of the barracks was to hold meetings, so block heads would call meetings. There was a block council to represent the people from different areas.

"When we first arrived, there were some things that weren't completely fixed. For instance, the roofers would come by, and everyone would hunger for information from the outside world. We wanted to know what was happening with the war. We weren't allowed to bring radios; that was contraband. And there were no televisions then. So we would ask the workers to bring us back some papers, and they would give us papers from Texas or Arkansas, so for the first time we would find out about news from the outside.

"Just before we went in to the camps, we saw that being a Japanese wasn't such a good thing, because everybody was turning against the Japanese, thinking we were saboteurs, or linking us with Pearl Harbor. But when I saw the kind of work they did at camp, I felt so proud of the Japanese, and proud to be Japanese, and wondered why I was so white, white when I was outside, because I was always with white folks. Many people had brothers or sons who were in the military and Japanese American servicemen would come into the camp to visit the families, and we felt so proud of them when they came in their uniforms. We knew that it would only be a matter of time before they would be shipped overseas. Also what made us feel proud was the forming of the 442 unit.*

"I was one of these real American patriots then. I've changed now. But back then, I was all American. Growing up, my mother would say we're Japanese. But I'd say 'No, I'm American.' I think a lot of Japanese grew up that way. People would say to them, 'You're Japanese,' and they would say,

---

*American soldiers of Japanese ancestry were assembled in two units: the 442 Regimental Combat Team and the 100th Infantry Battalion. The two groups were sent to battle in Europe. The 100th Battalion had over 900 causalties and was known as the Purple Heart Battalion. Combined, the units received 9,486 purple hearts and 18,143 individual decorations.

'No, we're Americans.' I don't even think they used the hyphenated term 'Japanese-American' back then. At the time, I was ashamed of being Japanese. I think many Japanese Americans felt the same way. Pearl Harbor was a shameful act, and being Japa⌐ ⌐se Americans, even though we had nothing to do with it, we still some.⌐ ⌐w felt we were blamed for it. I hated Japan at that point. So I saw mysel⌐ at that part of my history as an American, and not as a Japanese, or Japanese American. That sort of changed while I was in the camp.

"I hated the war, because it wasn't just between the governments. It went down to the people, and it nurtured hate. What was happening during the war were many things I didn't like. I hoped that one day when the war was over there could be a way that people could come together in their relationships.

"Now I can relate to Japan in a more mature way, where I see its faults and its very, very negative history. But I also see its potential. Scientifically and technologically it has really gone far. But I'm disappointed that when it comes to human rights she hasn't grown. The Japan of today — I feel there are still things lacking. For instance, I don't think the students have the opportunity to have more leeway in developing their lives.

"We always called the camps 'relocation centers' while we were there. Now we feel it is apropos to call them concentration camps. It is not the same as the concentration camps of Europe; those we feel were death camps. Concentration camps were a concentration of people placed in an area, and disempowered and disenfranchised. So it is apropos to call what I was in a concentration camp. After two years in the camp, I was released."

After the War: "Going home wasn't much of a problem for us because our neighbors had looked after our place. But for most of our Japanese friends, starting over again was very difficult after the war.

"I returned in October of 1945. It was very hard to find work, at least for me. I wasn't expecting to find anything good, just something to tie me over until my boyfriend came back from New York. The only thing I was looking for was to work in a restaurant as a waitress. But I couldn't find anything. I would walk from one end of the town to the other, and down every main avenue. But as soon as they found out I was Japanese, they would say no. Or they would ask me if I was in the union, and of course I couldn't be in the union because I had just gotten there. Anyway, no Japanese could be in the union, so if the answer was no I'm not in the union, they would say no. So finally what I did was go into the rough area of San Pedro — there's a strip near the wharf — and I went down there. I was determined to keep the jobs as long as I could. But for a while, I could last maybe two hours, and somebody would say 'Is that a "Jap?"' And as soon as someone would ask that, the boss would say, 'Sorry, you gotta go. We don't want trouble here.' The strip wasn't that big, so after I'd go the whole length of it, I'd have to keep coming back to the same restaurants, and say, 'Gee, will you give me another chance.' I figure, all these service men were coming back and the restaurants didn't have enough waitresses to come in and take these jobs. And so they'd say 'Okay. But soon as somebody asks who you are, or if you're a "Jap," or any problem about being a "Jap," you go.' So I said, 'Okay, sure. How about keeping me until that happens?' So sometimes I'd last a night, sometimes a couple of nights that no one would say anything. Sometimes people threw cups at me or hot coffee. At first they didn't know what I was. They thought I was Chinese. Then someone would say, 'I bet she's a Jap.' And I wasn't going to say I wasn't. So as soon as I said 'Yeah,' then it was like an uproar. Rather than have them say, 'Get out,' I just walked out. I mean, there was no point in fighting it. If you just walked out, there was less chance of getting hurt. But one place I lasted two weeks. These owners didn't want to have to let me go. But they didn't want to have problems with the people.

"And so I did this until I left for New York which was about three months later. I would work the dinner shift, from six at night to three in the morning. When you are young you tend not to take things as strongly. Everything is like an adventure. Looking back, I felt the people who were the kindest to me were those who went out and fought, those who just got back from Japan or the Far East. I think the worst ones were the ones who stayed here and worked in defense plants, who felt they had to be so patriotic. On the West Coast, there wasn't hysteria anymore, but there were hostile feelings towards the Japanese, because they were coming back. It took a while, but my mother said that things were getting back to normal, and that the Japanese were slowly being accepted again. At the time, I didn't go through the bitterness that many others went through, cause it's not just what they went through, but it is also what they experienced before that. I mean, I happened to have a much more comfortable life before, so you sort of see things in a different light. You see that there are all kinds of Americans, and that they're not all people who hate Japs. You know too that it was hysteria that had a lot to do with it.

"All Japanese, before they left camp, were told not to congregate among Japanese, and not to speak Japanese. They were told by the authorities. There was even a piece of paper that gave you instructions. But then people who went on to places like Chicago where there were churches, so they did congregate in churches. But they did ask people not to. I think psychologically the Japanese, having gone through a period where they were so hated by everyone, didn't even want to admit they were Japanese, or accept the fact that they were Japanese. Of course, they would say they were Japanese Americans. But I think the psychological damage of the war time period, and of racism itself, has left its mark. There is a stigma being

Japanese. I think that is why such a large number of Japanese, in particular, Japanese American women, have married out of the race. On the West Coast I've heard people say that sixty to seventy percent of the Japanese women have married, I guess, mostly whites. Japanese men are doing it too, but not to that degree. I guess Japanese Americans just didn't want to have that Japanese identity, or that Japanese part. There is definitely some self hate, and part of that has to do with the racism that's so deeply a part of this society.

"Historically, Americans have always been putting people behind walls. First there were the American Indians who were put on reservations, Africans in slavery, their lives on the plantations, Chicanos doing migratory work, and the kinds of camps they lived in, and even too, the Chinese when they worked on the railroad camps where they were almost isolated, dispossessed people — disempowered. And I feel those are the things we should fight against so they won't happen again. It wasn't so long ago — in 1979 — that the feeling against the Iranians was so strong because of the takeover of the U.S. embassy in Iran, where they wanted to deport Iranian students. And that is when a group called Concerned Japanese Americans organized, and that was the first issue we took up, and then we connected it with what the Japanese had gone through. This whole period of what the Japanese went through is important. If we can see the connections of how often this happens in history, we can stem the tide of these things happening again by speaking out against them.

"Most Japanese Americans who worked years and years for redress never thought it would happen the way it did. The papers have been signed, we will be given reparation, and there was an apology from the government. I think the redress movement itself was very good because it was a learning experience for the Japanese people; we could get out into our communities and speak about what happened to us and link it with experiences of other people. In that sense, though, it wasn't done as much as it should have been. Some Japanese Americans didn't even learn that part. They just started the movement as a reaction to the bad experience they had. They don't even see other ethnic groups who have gone through it. It showed us, too, how vulnerable everybody is. It showed us that even though there is a constitution, that constitutional rights could be taken away very easily."

Japanese Barbie Dolls

Mari K.

Mari K. is an eleven-year-old Japanese American who lives in New Jersey. Japanese is the language spoken at home. Mari's father works for a Japanese firm in the United States.

"I was born in America, so I don't like it when people point to me and say, 'Oh, she's Japanese.' I want to say I'm American, but then they say, 'How come you speak Japanese and everything?' So I think I'm Japanese American.

"I've never heard about the redress movement, don't know what it is. I've never heard about any Japanese being locked up during World War II. I haven't learned about it in school, either. The only thing was in fifth grade. My teacher in American school talked a little about the war, but I felt a little bit uncomfortable, because everybody kept staring at me—so I didn't like that at all. This one kid, he asked one question about the Japanese during the war, and the teacher didn't really say anything that I could really remember, just that we bombed Pearl Harbor. I didn't like that part. I guess I felt funny because I am Japanese. I guess I have heard about the camps and everything but I haven't really understood it.

"I don't think of going back to Japan to live when I grow up. I like it here; I feel comfortable here. When I go away, I miss speaking English to American people.

"I speak Japanese to my mother. She can read and listen in English, but she can't really speak well. Even at home, we use mostly chopsticks, unless we're eating steak or something like that when we use forks. I prefer using forks, because if I hold the chopsticks wrong, my father would always tell me it was wrong. I have trouble holding them sometimes, and forks are much easier. My favorite food in the whole world is spaghetti. I could have Italian food every night.

"For Japanese New Year celebration last year, and the year before, my father brought home this pack, and all you had to do was take the fish, and

19

Mari K. and her "Barbie" doll

other stuff out, and boil them, and open the pack, and slip it on the dish. Then we all sat down and drank a litle bit of this kind of wine, ate, and for a couple of days we ate the leftovers. I look forward to the holiday because in Japan we get money in envelopes. My grandmother just sends it. We get money from my parents too, but we have to remind them about it. This year my uncle and aunt came, and they gave me money too. We would play games, too—the whole family. We would play cards, or we would blindfold each other, and there would be this face and we would have to stick the eyes, ears, nose and mouth on it. It is sort of like pin the tail on the donkey.

"If we have free time at home, we read books, go play outside, or watch television. My mother just sews. When we go on vacation, we drive to a place like West Virginia, look at the view and take pictures.

"I have a few Japanese toys. My favorite is the Japanese Barbie dolls. Some have blond hair, some have brown. The doll is a little shorter, and the eyes are different—maybe just a bit smaller. The hair is different too— it's not stringy—it's silky. My grandmother bought me one, and a neighbor in Japan gave me one. Then a friend left me one when she left to go back to Japan. I don't have a favorite toy. I guess these dolls are my favorites.

"One year my grandma sent me a kimono, but it's too little for me now. My mom used to have a red one, but she doesn't know where it went. I wore my kimono twice on New Year's Eve, and once on Halloween. That's it. It's kind of heavy, and not really one of my favorite things. I've never seen my mom in a kimono though we do have pictures of her in one. I think it was at her wedding. She doesn't wear one around the house. Even in Japan I never saw anyone wear one, except for my great-grandmother, but she stayed in the house most of the time.

"My best friend and most of my friends are American. As for my parents, I have a lot of respect for them. Sometimes I don't agree with them, and I get mad, but after a while, I get over it and I can't help but hug them again. I don't know if there is a Japanese word for respect, but to me it means caring for a person, listening to them.

"Learning Japanese is important, because my grandmother doesn't speak any English, so I have to know Japanese to talk to her. And knowing two languages is nice. Some of my friends can only speak one, so it is kind of neat."

Japanese School: "I started going to Japanese school when I went to kindergarten, but I like American school better. I have my own locker there and more friends. The teachers are also funnier. In Japanese school, the teachers are more strict. They ask questions and are kind of boring. They speak in Japanese, and that is how the classes are conducted, every Saturday, nine through twelve thirty.

"We have this book and learn new words. Sometimes it's not fun because my American friends can play, but I have to go to school on Saturday. I would rather be bicycle riding and playing outside. I used to have one friend from American school that went to Japanese school with me, but her mother transferred her to a Japanese school that meets Monday through Friday. And another friend left for Japan.

"I ask myself sometimes why I have to go, but then I guess it's because my mom forces me to. We have tests and report cards from Japanese school. On the report cards, the teachers write something, and your parents have to write something back, that they will do better next time or something like that. But they don't have to sign it. I treat my teachers the same in both Japanese and American school. My parents don't talk about respecting teachers, but my parents just expect me to do it. My parents want me to do well in both American and Japanese school, though my mom wants me to study harder in Japanese school. She is afraid I might get left back. But sometimes I just get sick of it, and leave it for the next day. I guess I have to study Japanese another four to five years. By the eighth grade, you're supposed to know how to read and write pretty well. I can't say I look forward to going to that many more years of Japanese school. I've never told my mom that I don't want to go to Japanese school, because then she'll yell at me. She expects me to go, and I go pretty much to please her. My parents tell me all the time that I have to do well in school. They tell me to do my homework. In our Japanese class, we have this piece of paper where we have to write down our homework, and there is this little place that your parents have to sign that you did your homework. Then there is this list, where if you forget to do something, you get a triangle. Then if you get three triangles, it becomes a circle. So it adds up to an X. The worst is getting an X.

"Then we have plays at the end of the year where our parents come to see us. This year's play is about two people – one is very greedy and one is very kind. They find this stuff at the bottom of a lake, and the greedy guy doesn't want the other guy to have any of the gold, so he makes this fake dragon carved out of wood and he puts it on the bottom of the lake and tries to scare the nice person. But the lake has a lot of waves, so the dragon looks like he's opening his mouth, so the guy who made the dragon got scared. At the end, he told the truth to the nice guy and they became friends. There are a lot of different roles, and I play the greedy guy."

Japan: "I went back to Japan three times. In first grade I went back and went to Japanese school for two months in the summer, and they kept asking me all these questions there, like what is it like to live in the United States, and how do you say this, and how do you say that. I remember always getting sick because we had to walk a very long way to school everyday. It was all very strange. The only fun thing was going to the pool and gym. As for learning the stuff, in Japan they go a little slower so I had no trouble with the class. But sometimes I got mixed up and would speak English. Switching over to speaking Japanese was pretty hard. I got used to speaking English, and the only one I could do that with was my brother. And then my grandmother wouldn't know what we were talking about, so we had to say everything over again to her in Japanese.

"The thing I liked best was there was a river going around our house, and there were these ducks that lived in the front of our house, so every morning they would quack for bread and we would feed them. There were so many mosquitos. And the beds — I didn't like them at all; we're not used to sleeping on little mattresses. The bathtubs and the bathrooms — I didn't like them at all. The bathrooms were like this oval-shaped thing with a hole, and you had to squat down all the time — it wasn't a toilet — it was on the floor. And the bath was in a shack attached to the house, and there used to be all these bugs in there so I didn't like that. It was my grandmother's house. There wasn't any carpeting. We watched a lot of television. The paper would come everyday, and my brother and I would choose the programs to watch from the newspaper. I kind of felt I belonged in Japan, because I can speak the language. I guess if I didn't tell them I lived in Northvale, New Jersey, people wouldn't know it. The last time we went, we stayed two months again but we didn't go to school there. We just went shopping and played with my cousins, and that was pretty fun.

"My mom has been thinking of sending me back, because she feels I'm not doing enough Japanese here. But I don't like the idea. I like it here better. And I don't really have any friends there. It feels more comfortable here because everybody there asks you a lot of stuff about living in this country. I tell them what it's like to go to school here. They do have McDonald's there, though. Sometimes we went to Kentucky Fried Chicken and got some chicken and biscuits."

Born and Raised in Hawaii, but Not Hawaiian

Andrea Kim

Andrea Kim is a thirty-two-year-old journalist. She is third generation Korean American. She left Hawaii to attend Bryn Mawr, and has not lived permanently in Hawaii since. The name Andrea Kim is a pseudonym at her request.

"My Asian background is Korean, and even in Hawaii, Koreans are a minority. The group that dominated my sense of culture the most are Japanese Americans. It pervades everything. In high school, my friends would talk about going to the YBA — the Young Buddhists Association. It's the counterpart of the YMCA. A lot of them went to the Buddhist temple — but it was nothing special. It was just as normal to hear someone say that, as for someone to say, 'I'm going to the YMCA or the Catholic church.'

"You eat sushi, you pick up Japanese words, and there are Bon dances in the summer. Ever since I was little I had Korean clothes but I would be just as familiar with a kimono. It's just as natural as if you were living in New York, and you were familiar with pretzels, roasted chestnuts and Central Park.

"There are certain stereotypes — such as Chinese are very prudent with their money, and that Koreans gamble a lot — but I found the Asian stereotypes to be stonger here on the mainland than in Hawaii. There wasn't a Japanese stereotype, because they were the norm.

"If you were white, you really stood out. I know in high school people would hang out in groups. It was like senior corner, Hawaiian corner, and for the whites, we called theirs Haole (means foreigner, and usually applies to white people) corner. We didn't regard the whites as a minority. They sort of had an exotic appeal. I thought white people were very attractive. In fact I used to wish I had blue eyes and blond hair. In my high school, it was

24

a fashionable thing for people to use scotch tape, and make their eyes look more like whites. You can do it so that you make your lids have another fold. A lot of my friends in the summers would go to Japan because their families were there. They would have an operation to make their eyelids double. It was not an unusual thing. More people would dye their hair lighter — instead of black, they would make it brown. Actually, a fairly popular hairdresser in Hilo dyed her hair blond. Looking back at that it's really pathetic. But Hawaii is really an odd little world. If I hadn't gone away to college, there is so much I never would have realized.

"I would never call myself a Hawaiian because there is an ethnic group that is racially Hawaiian. I say I am from Hawaii or I grew up there. You have an identity with the Hawaiian culture. That's the exciting thing about growing up in Hawaii — you're exposed to not only the Asian influence, but the Hawaiian influence as well. There are obvious signs of Hawaiian culture, such as hula dancing or luaus.

"As for the locals — the Hawaiians — you have to feel sorry for them, because they weren't doing well at all. There are special programs and housing for them, but in general, native Hawaiians do not do well academically and that affects their whole lives. If they don't do well in school, it becomes very difficult to succeed. It is not a perception that the Hawaiians are an underclass — it is a truth. For instance, it is also true to say that, in general, blacks in this country make up the underclass. I mean, we all know blacks who are educated, have gone to Ivy League schools, and are doing terrifically well. But in general, if I had to choose, I would never choose to be born black in the United States. I don't care what my advantages are economically, there is just so much discrimination. It is such a burden to handle, that I wouldn't willingly choose to be a black person. Similarly, in Hawaii, I wouldn't choose to be a Hawaiian person. You can overcome all of that. But if you come from an environment where education is not a priority, it makes it difficult for you for the rest of your life.

"I didn't really socialize with people who are Hawaiian. One of my friends who is Japanese, married someone who is Hawaiian. That must have been a big shock to her family. It's a class thing. It's as if you're marrying someone who is a janitor, or something. I feel it's kind of marrying down when you marry Hawaiian. I mean to me, it's inconceivable. Why would I marry someone who is Hawaiian? They don't have my interests — they're not in my class. They're not in the top classes. I was the salutatorian in my high school class of seven hundred thirty students. I was in the top of all my classes in school. There weren't any Hawaiians in any of my classes. Maybe there were in my gym class but that wasn't based on ability. So the only Hawaiians I saw in high school were hanging around in their corners. In May Day programs you would elect a court — a king and a queen — and they were usually Hawaiians. A lot of the Hawaiians are very good looking.

"I shouldn't give you the wrong impression. There is a great deal of ethnic pride in Hawaii. People are proud of being Japanese, Korean, or whatever. But the whole ideology is that this is a melting pot, and people get along fine. The overriding identification was being American."

Family: "My father was born in Korea, and my mother's mother was born in Korea. My father and grandmother were very active in the Korean Christian Church. The services are in Korean, and they are basically for those who are recently arrived to Hawaii. I played the piano, so for about two hours on Sunday I would be in this totally Korean environment. In the service, I knew the Korean word for psalm so that when I heard that word, I knew it was time for me to play the piano. And other than that I would sit there and daydream. My father was the lay leader. So for two or three years, I would hear Korean, but not really understand any of it.

"It would have been nice if we had spoken Korean at home, but there was no way that could have happened. Because on my mother's side, the feeling was you were in America, so it is important to speak English. My grandmother came to Hawaii as a picture bride, and so on my mother's side we are third generation Korean American, which is quite old. My mother's parents weren't well educated at all. They had a farm in a very small town. It is even smaller than Hilo. They supported themselves by raising chickens. My grandmother also had a kimchee business which my uncle is still running.

"The lifestyle she grew up with was a marked difference from the lifestyle she and my father were able to give us. My mother was a schoolteacher — she's retired — and we went to the school where she taught. It was great to have your mom work at the school, because other kids wouldn't mess with you. After school, we would study in the classroom and the library. All the teachers were Asian — predominately Japanese American. In our family, where my mother is one of eight kids, we are seen as very successful. I went to Bryn Mawr. My sister went to Swarthmore and has her PhD from Johns Hopkins. Her husband also has a PhD from Hopkins. My brother went to Berkeley. He's now in Hawaii and working for a top engineering firm. The fourth sister did miserably in school. This is the sister that is very good looking. Academics is not something you questioned. It was important to do well in school. It's like accepting the fact that the sun comes up in the morning in the East. It was just important to do well in school. But there was no conscious effort on my parents' part to make us study. They made it very easy for us to do well. One thing I will say is that they devoted a lot of time to us. In the summers we had school at home. My mother assigned us compositions. We had workbooks and my father taught us math. We were at least one or two years ahead of our grades in math.

"I felt we were growing up in an all–American way. The whole family used to watch Lawrence Welk every Saturday. I thought we had a very typical upbringing, because the television is a major homogenizing influence. You see the same commercials as some kid in California sees. I decided I was as American as anyone else. We recited the Pledge of Allegiance every day before class. We sang 'America the Beautiful' before class began, from first to sixth grade.

"We ate very American things — spaghetti, hot dogs. But whenever we had a family get together, we would have Korean food. My mother would make Korean marinaded beef, and it would be charbroiled. I learned how to make that by going to the family gatherings. We always had my grandmother's broiled beef, and of course, kimchee. So now when I entertain, the greatest compliment I can show my guests is to serve Korean food. It is food that is very nourishing to me. I was very close to my grandmother, and she taught me how to make it."

On the Mainland: "It was great growing up with Asians all around me, but I didn't appreciate it until I left Hawaii. When I was seventeen, I graduated Hilo High School, and went to Bryn Mawr. It's a good school, but I remember the first day on campus, I thought I was in a time warp because the school had gothic architecture, and I had never seen so many whites in one place at one time.

"But it wasn't until I started my professional career, as a journalist — my first job was in Worcester, Massachusetts., a very white community — that I became really conscious of being Asian. If I went to a major department store, I would be the only Asian person on that floor. I worked at the paper for five years. Toward the end of that time, there were Southeast Asians that were moving into the area. Catholic charities were very active in settling Vietnamese refugees or the Hmong refugees into the area. But in terms of educated, professional Asians, there were very few.

"We covered everything — fires, town meetings, school boards. As I was leaving city hall one day, one of the workers — a very nice elderly woman — said to me, 'My you speak English so well, where did you learn it?' Her assumption was that I was not an American. That kind of attitude was something that really made me quite angry at first, because I am very proud of being an American, and to me, that people would assume that I wasn't, really was very upsetting.

"The first apartment I got in Worcester was in poor section of town. I didn't know it at the time. It was just that the rent was cheap. The landlord was in my apartment fixing something one day. He wasn't very educated. He ran an auto body shop and the rental units were a side business. He asked 'What do people like you do?' I felt like I was an animal in a zoo. But I guess he was actually well intentioned. He just meant that in his daily work, he didn't see any Asians, and he wondered how we spent our time because he never saw us. I responded by being very polite. I said, 'People like me do the ususal things. It's just that there aren't many Asians here in Worcester, so you probably won't see them.' I mean if he had gone to some classical concerts, he would have seen some Asians there because there were some professionals in the area.

"Usually if men ask you to go out with them, it's because they have some interest in Asians — they have taken karate, or something like that. But your standard white-bred male wouldn't think of asking me out at all. I'm not something that would appeal to them. I mean if they had gone to school with some Asians, or attended karate class, or if their teachers were Asian, they might be curious and ask me out, out of pure novelty. Other than that, most had not grown up with someone who's Asian, and this really hit home to me when I was working in a small town."

Dating and Marriage: "Since I am a journalist and move around a lot, the social life isn't that good. But let me tell you about my sisters. They would never go out with an Asian man. I have two sisters younger than I. One is married. Her husband is very handsome. He has dark hair and blue eyes. His ethnic background is Swedish and French. They met in graduate school. He's from California. She's never gone out with someone who is Asian. My other sister is truly beautiful. She would never go out with an Asian either. I think it relates back to my father. He is truly one of the most brilliant people I know. And in many ways I think I take after him because he has amazing qualities of resourcefulness and perseverance. If he is playing table tennis or tennis, and is behind, he can turn that game around and win. I've seen him do it many times. Similarly, he taught himself to fix anything. He has a degree in chemical engineering. He is a chemist. But he can fix washing machines, televisions and cars. He just went to the library and borrowed books.

"However, he does not speak English well at all. He has a very strong Korean accent. Ever since I was a little girl, I have seen how people treated him because of that. They treat him as if he is an idiot. They would raise their voices, thinking that would help him understand them better. They treated him this way just because he sounds like an immigrant. So that was always very painful to me. I resolved that I did not want to sound like my father. So that's why it was important to me not to go to school in Hawaii. When we visited my cousins in California, I heard how differently they sounded, and I wanted to sound like them. I didn't want to sound like an Asian or like my father. So that is why I wanted to go to Harvard or Bryn Mawr. But that also had ramifications. Because my father was seen as the other, or the outsider — my mother is definitely American — there would be clashes between my father and mother on very basic things such as education. Usually my father would prevail, because my mother is a very gentle person. But it's like all of us were American except my father. He was really

Korean. And he's very strict. And even today, he tries to tell me how to run my life, and he is five thousand miles away. So I think that had a very strong influence on why my sisters would never consider someone who is Asian as attractive. My father would embody a lot of unattractive things about Asians to them, he had this accent, he had strange ideas and he just wasn't American. And why would you want to tie yourself to someone who is different and an outsider? You want to be accepted and like other kids. So I think that would explain why neither one of my sisters would go out with someone who is Asian.

"Since I'm thirty-two and not married, and I would like to have kids and stuff, I would just like to find someone who is not boring and someone who would be accepting of the lifestyle I have as a journalist. I belong to a professional association for Asian journalists, and through them I feel I have developed pride as an Asian. I have found that the older I get, more and more of my friends tend to be Asians. In college that wasn't the case. Most of my friends were white. If I had my choice, I would love to marry a Korean American. I would love to have kids who are pure Korean. On my father's side we are descended from royalty. Koreans have a very high rate of marrying other groups, and frankly, if you are Korean and twenty-five, that's kind of old not to be married. It's changing a little now. But traditionally, when I meet old Korean people, and I tell them I am not married, I can tell they feel sorry for me. There are not that many eligible men around my age. Again, I can't marry someone who is fresh off the boat. That wouldn't work. I am very American, and I don't have enough knowledge of Korean to communicate. And being able to communicate is very important to me. So if someone is Chinese or Japanese, that is okay, too. It's perfectly fine for a Chinese to marry a Japanese. But it's nice to marry someone from your own ethnic group, because the kids will have a very strong sense of their ethnic identity. I have cousins who are half Chinese, and it really depends on the mother, as far as how they identify themselves. I'm sure my children will have a very strong identity of being Korean, and it would be nice if they were pure Korean.

"What I find really interesting is that if I had never left Hawaii, I would probably have married a white person because I remember very clearly in high school, that even if a guy was just average, but he was white, I thought he was really handsome. Because there were so few white people, they really stood out. All the subliminal messages to you from television commercials, movies and magazines are that white is beautiful. All the models were white. You develop an image of what is beautiful. Now, I'm really into looking as Asian as I can. My hair is straight. Now I want to see how long I can get my hair to grow. I also want bangs. I would not dye my hair brown. If anything, I would dye it black because I'm getting grey hair.

"Some of my closest and best friends are Japanese. But to be very honest, it would be difficult if I did marry someone who is Japanese, because Japan colonized Korea. My mother once said that in our family, no one married a Japanese. That is true because they married whites, Koreans or Chinese. In one case, one aunt married someone who is Hispanic. They are no longer married. But even that is more acceptable than marrying someone who is Japanese. I would say the likeliest prospect if I were to marry an Asian would be a Chinese American, because they have been in this country longer, and I think they treat their wives quite well. They're used to having independent women. Probably I would marry a Chinese American, or someone who's Jewish. I think people who are Jewish have a lot in common with Asians. They have similar values.

"I have friends who are black. I like them. But I would never marry anyone who is black, because I think it would be a terrible handicap to have children who are half black and half Asian, I very much want to have a family, so it's not an option that I would marry someone for love and not have kids. So I would never marry someone who is black. My parents would be horrified also. They would never understand it. And I think when you marry someone, it is very important that they fit into your family. My parents had no problem with my sister marrying a white. My dad just wants us married. I talk to them every weekend. And recently my dad said, 'Well, I hope this is the year you meet someone and get married.' In this case I don't see it as pressure I don't need. I feel the same way, so it's okay. He's thinking about my welfare. He really thinks I would be better off married."

Physical Appearance: "When I was little, my mother used to always make me curl my hair. I don't do that anymore. I think it's nice to have really straight hair. Another problem is my hairstylist. She thinks it is a sin to curl Asian hair. She's blond herself, and she thinks Asian hair is beautiful. She would not curl my hair anyway. But in Hawaii most people had perms because you wanted to look as Western as possible. So I never considered my black hair anything special. Why should I? Everybody looked like me. Everybody had brown eyes and black hair. It wasn't until college that people would say to me, 'You have such beautiful hair.' They'd say, 'When I was little, I wished I had black hair.' It was a new idea to me that while I didn't have curly red hair with blue eyes, they also didn't have straight black hair.

"If they're Asian, people usually think I'm Chinese, because there are more Chinese and Japanese here in New York. Rarely do people think I am Korean. Even when I go to Korean green grocers, they never think I am Korean. They usually think I'm Japanese. I'm never taken to be Korean. I think it's because they assume that if I were really Korean, I would speak to them in Korean. This is even when I speak my limited Korean to them. Maybe it's because my hair is straight, and a lot of Korean women have perms. Generally Japanese women I notice don't have perms. I also wear my makeup to make myself look more Western. It doesn't matter to me either way, because I'm proud to be Asian. It's okay."

Work: "My Asianness is left at the door when I go to work, because in many ways, I am a replaceable cog. I know if I quit my job, they can find someone tomorrow. But I would like to think that in some small way I make a difference. Little things I can do. When I see something offensive, or egregiously wrong, or stereotyping Asians, I try to edit it before the story goes around the world.

"But some things you can't do anything about, and it's not worth going on the line for. This is a typical example: It is typical that we have stories out of Korea about how people eat dog meat. I hate this story. There is nothing I can do about it. A correspondent in Korea writes a story about dog meat, which is terribly insensitive. There is a huge, long history about why people eat dog meat or snake. In this country, dogs are revered pets, it's just distasteful. The mere idea that another human being could eat a dog, makes Koreans look very barbaric, whereas it's just a matter of culture. I mean, I would never eat dog meat, I would be ill. But I can understand that it's okay. It can be seen as very healthy. But still we have this story that perpetuates this idea. And this story didn't even mention any other Asian groups. It's just Koreans, and how with the Olympics coming up, the government wanted to shut down all these restaurants that served dog meat. So I just edited this story, made sure it was well organized, and passed it along. If I were more militant, or probably dumber, I would make a big issue about it. I can't change it. I'm going to save the fight for something that is really important. But I hate those stories. I would like to own my own newspaper. I would love to be in a position to hire my friends and really make some special product with a special statement. Sometimes people don't have the option or liberty to express that special voice.

"I think I'm very fortunate to be Asian American. Not only do we have a whole realm of Western culture, but we also have this whole world of Asian culture that is part of us. It's a feeling, that genetically, I'm one hundred percent Korean, and my ancestors come from that country. That's why I want my children to be able to say that also. But realistically, unless I compromise a lot about what is important to me, and marry someone just to have Korean kids — and I probably won't do that — my kids probably won't be Korean, they'll be half. And I will be really sorry about that because it's important to me to know that I am pure Korean."

To Be True Hawaiian

Will Hao

Will is in his mid-thirties. He is Hawaiian Japanese and was born and raised in Hawaii. He is now an actor.

"To me, the Hawaiian culture means having great love and respect for nature, for the world you live in, including human beings. It makes me try to understand the forces of nature better. Because of that, I feel I can deal with people a lot better. Growing up, I had friends of different nationalities, so it is hard for me to be prejudiced against anybody — even the white man, whom we call Haoli.

"My father was a fisherman with my uncles. They owned a commerical line. They would go out, and not come back for weeks at a time. One of the great memories I have when I was growing up was going with my brother to the wharf to watch the boats come in. Everyday we would check because we would help them clean the boat once it docked. They would bring back hundreds and hundreds of fish, and take them to the tuna packers across the way. And then they would go off and weigh the fish. So we would go off to the net house. The net house is full of all these old, old men — Koreans, Chinese, Japanese, Filipinos, all different nationalities. They had the most wonderful old faces. And their jobs were as net menders for all the different commercial lines. So you had mounds of fish nets that the commercial boats used. And they were like the keepers of this little special place. It was very sacred. And I always found peace in there because they always took care of you. If you were a little boy, you could sit with them, and watch them knitting peacefully. I remember that so well. It's one of the best pictures in my head, being so young at that time. When you see all those faces, with all the different nationalities, it's hard just to think of the Asian experience, or the Polynesian experience for that matter. It just transcends it, that's all.

"When I say Hawaiian, people get mixed up. Hawaiian is a Polynesian race, like Tahitians, Fijians — people from that locale. People tend to think of Asian people as Hawaiians, but that is not the case. Polynesian is different. I keep telling people that. My father is Polynesian and Portuguese. My mom is Japanese, my grandmother was a picture bride from Okinawa.

"I don't lie when I go out for jobs. There are very few Polynesian gigs I have gone out for. But when I do, I see all these Asian people there, lying that they are Polynesian. Half the time they don't even know where Polynesia is. I guess when you gotta eat, you gotta eat, so I guess you gotta lie to get the job. But my thing goes deeper than that. I've studied the history of Hawaiian people and I know the hurt and bad things that have happened to them. For instance, the throne was taken unjustly — the monarchy was overthrown by Americans with big bucks who wanted a straphold on Hawaii.*

"The Hawaiians gave missionaries gifts — such as a piece of land, meaning you live off the land as we live off the land, and cherish it — not meaning for them to sell the land for a couple of thousand dollars, or to build a store front where a huge business was set up on the side. Little things like that were happening. Not all missionaries were like that. Many were true to what they stood for, and never tried to take away that Hawaiian side. But it just got out of hand and they just wanted more. And generally, people in Polynesia have this childlike quality. They shouldn't have been so naïve to give away so much. But they are very giving people, and not too smart when it comes to saying 'no.' And the people who owned the big sugar plantations essentially ran the government. I wish we still had the monarchy. I mean, we still could have kept the monarchy and been a part of the United States.

"For awhile, the Hawaiians were seen as the underclass. Economically, they were poor. I think even my father's generation fought against it. And you know how when you fight against something, you get defeated, and your pride gets in the way, and you just don't want to do it. And at the same time, you don't want to take low jobs, like scrubbing floors, so you don't do anything. They have babies, but they don't do anything, so they end up living on welfare, and stuff like that. I'm not saying all of them, but a good majority of them did.

"Now, there's been a big resurgence for the Hawaiian culture, and they are getting more social workers to deal with the problems. And I think the hurt and anger of Hawaiians are slowly subsiding. There are not that many

*During the 1800s the kings who followed Kamehameha V who had advocated Hawaii for the Hawaiians, became increasingly anti-American. In 1887, a group of Americans took the destiny of the Hawaiian islands into their own hands by means of a bloodless revolt, forcing King Kalakaua to proclaim a new constitution. Eleven years later, Hawaii handed over its sovereignty and Congress made Hawaii a territory of the United States.

pure Hawaiians left. Most are mixed. I think now there are more Filipinos and Samoans who are at the bottom of the ladder in Hawaii.

"The stereotype of a Hawaiian is that he is big, lazy, stupid. They call them mokes. It's like the black guys you'd see in the Bronx or Harlem, sitting by the car, except these are by the hilltops or the beach, drinking their booze, smoking, just wasting away the time, goofing off.

"With the resurgence, people instead of hanging out in parks and what not, are trying to get land for themselves—Hawaiian homestead land—and they are trying to live off the land. They are teaching the children the Hawaiian ways, how their forefathers used to go fishing. A lot of things are happening like that in the outer islands, though you won't find much of that on the main island. It would be in the country. There is this big movement to go back to what their ancestors were doing, because now they have pride in what they did. Before, they didn't think it was a big thing. You know, like why wait for six months to get this harvest when I can go buy it in a store? But now there is a deeper meaning of what we are and what our forefathers have done before."

Growing Up: "When I was growing up, you couldn't find one public school that was teaching the Hawaiian language. But they were teaching German, French, Spanish. And there was that very familiar line people would always say, 'you stupid Hawaiian.' My friends and I never really cared about learning the Hawaiian language. If it was put on us fine, but we never sought it out. We didn't have the choice in school, so we never thought about it. In our spare time, my brothers and I would go climb trees, pick mangos, and go crabbing. We'd hang out in the park, or go with the fads—like tuck out shirts, pants, hair grease, the pomade—stuff like that. You know, we were Americans and read American magazines, instead of Hawaiian magazines. We were just too busy being like what they showed us on television. Many parents got caught up in it too. They wanted to be like everybody else, meaning people who were successful, people who were in the mainstream American way of living—someone who lived in a house, owned a car. Our family lived in an apartment.

"There was a time when Hawaiians were out, and being white was in. Then there was a point when being Japanese was in. Of course, it depends what side of the fence you're on. I'm speaking from the Hawaiian point of view. I knew some people when I was growing up who were part Hawaiian, and who were ashamed of being Hawaiian at that time. But I always had a rebellious streak, and I was proud to be Japanese Hawaiian Portuguese. Then too, after a while, I forgot that I was Japanese Hawaiian Portuguese. I was American—just like anyone else. I was just having a good time growing up. Now that I'm an adult, these issues don't matter that much.

"There were seven kids in the family. My dad wanted us to learn the best English we could. He did not want us to speak pidgin English. Two of my brothers and sisters took some Japanese; the rest of us just know some words. We didn't learn that much Japanese because Hawaii is the fiftieth state, and we were learning American ways.

"But every New Year's, we celebrated at my maternal grandmother's. Everyone on that side would speak Japanese. The first thing we did when we got there was go light some incense by the shrine. We'd sit at this long table. All the males would sit down, and all the women would serve us. But I never understood a word that was going on. It was like playing charades.

"My father was a very rowdy Hawaiian — full of gusto. The Japanese side of the family — my cousins, would be very embarrassed because compared to him, they were so inert. My father was the total opposite. So I never got to see my Japanese cousins that much because they would be afraid of my father coming around. Isn't that strange? Years later, we got together to touch bases. But now that I look back at it, wasn't that silly?"

Anger: "I never really went through an identity crisis. In fact when I was out in Los Angeles last year, I never came across so many angry Asians in my life. It was this whole thing about the camps. Not so much the parents who were interned. They seemed to have this facade — that it's over, that's it. But these kids — they were just angry! And I don't blame them. It reminded me of my cousin, on my father's side, who declared war on the United States. She, and twenty-five others, just declared war. Her thing was just incredible. She got married to an (American) Indian fellow. They thought he was white because he was fair skinned. So her Hawaiian family disowned her. But then she went to live with him on the reservation. She had a hard time because they thought she was black. So the hate kept building. Then the husband took a job with the U.S. government that put him near one of the islands where they were testing the bombs, and he caught radiation. He still gets treatments and a stipend from the government to this day. My cousin was pregnant at the time, and every summer she still breaks out. So there is so much hate and anger.

"And I got some of that feeling from these Asians. Once you experience that, it is kind of frightening. Because all of this is happening, and you're living in the white man's land. Are you going to keep all of this hatred until you die? I don't know what to think about it — how one could get peace with it.

"The anger is so passionate, so fervent. Back home, you might say, you don't like the Haoles, because they took the land away. But that's beside the point now, because half of us have white blood in us, so you're actually calling yourselves names. So work something out. The past is the past, so work it out.

"It's kind of a blessing to me to be born of a double race. You get the best of both worlds. I'm just glad to be alive. After awhile, being Asian isn't going to mean anything. Being Hawaiian isn't going mean anything. What is important is being a good human being."

Life As an Actor: "I'm asked to go on Asian calls the most because the Polynesian market just isn't happening in New York. You have hundreds of people that show up, and it's like this Asian village going by you, in a day. Everybody's aunt and uncle is there with the baby, trying to get into this movie as an extra. The pay is only fifty dollars, but it's money, and it's this glitzy thing, so everyone is there and you look around you and say, 'Why am I here?' But everyone is packed into the room. You can tell those who are really serious about the craft, and those who have just heard about it and came from Chinatown to be in this big movie with a big disco scene, with hundreds of extras. They come with their tinted hair, and the Chinese girls with their thick soul boots, and their long fake finger nails. It's just incredible. It's not just black girls and white girls with their hair cut and dyed with Mohican cuts—there are a lot of Asian girls too. There are some Chinese, some Koreans. And there was one call where you had these guys with the mousse abuse—where they use so much mousse to make the hair stand that if you touch it, you could get cut. And it's so funny, because the young Chinese guys were popping up, trying to look real macho, and the girls were trying to be like real—not dumb—but well, sexy, and almost tough, too. And of course there were those girls who acted like they just came from *Vogue*. But here is a job for fifty dollars a day for eight or ten hours. It's just incredible. Everybody going to this happening at the same time.

"After a while, you get to know the Asian acting community. Everybody knows who's who, and who's going to show up. I just don't go to many of these calls, because I don't consider myself in that medium. When they cast for a Chinese, they want a Chinese. A Japanese is a Japanese. They would cast a Chinese person in a Japanese role, and visa versa. But I'm just a little too dark so it doesn't work. Or maybe if it's an Asian who plays in a horror film, I might have a good chance. I did a horror flick in L.A. called *The Vampire on Death Beach*. It's funny because they didn't ask for an Asian. I just went in to audition. It was a terrible B movie.

"The roles for Asian actors in the mainstream—like film work—are still limited. Thank God for Rambo; I'm sure he employed a lot of people. Today, there are more Asian writers, and therefore, more work being produced. There's a little more, but not great amounts. And I know the black people cry a lot, but by golly, there's a lot more happening for them than the Asians, I think, in terms of what's available. Theatre-wise, it's picked up a bit.

"I'm not sure whether I would be further along in my career if I were white. I mean there are a lot of Asians going out for roles, but for whites, it's triple that. There are also a lot more blacks than Asians. So I don't know if being white makes a difference. A lot has to do with luck.

"I did do a whole season of singing all over the Catskills, the Playboy Club, the Plaza hotel. I was singing Hawaiian music which was very nice. And it was very funny, because you meet all these girls who took hula lessons, and they go on gigs and say they are Hawaiians and I know they're from the Bronx, or I know they're from Brooklyn because I just finished speaking to them. The band is almost always the same. But you always get these girls who try to do these numbers, and I just laugh to myself. In my heyday, I probably would have screamed, ranted and raved, but now I figure it's just stuff they are going to deal with—it's a cycle.

"I also do avant garde stuff. I was in L.A., in this big, eight hundred seat theatre. It was a packed house of Asian Americans. I got standing ovations. Then a week later, I was having dinner with some of the Asian actors. My friend introduced me as Will, who just appeared in this play, and someone said, 'Oh, really? I thought the part was played by a black man.' Can you believe it?

"The agency sends me on Japanese calls and they would say I'm not Japanese enough, meaning my skin is too dark. The only thing Japanese about me, maybe, is the shape of my eyes, and my nose. But the lips have to go. You get to understand that after a while, because at first I said, 'Huh? they're saying I'm not Japanese.' The Polynesian thing—for Hollywood anyway—means an Asian with dark skin. It's very strange. I think I basically do avant garde shows because they don't care what you look like."

West Side Story

Sue Jean Lee Suettinger

Sue Jean was born in Canton China and immigrated to the United States with her family in 1952, when she was four years old. She graduated Princeton University in 1970. She now works as a China consultant and is married to a fifth generation German Norwegian.

"I had a lot of fun growing up in New York's Chinatown. I remember the fun of having friends close by, or playing on the sidewalks — hopscotch, handball, tag, roller skating, and going around the block to the candy store. I remember the fun things. I was also aware, from a very young age, of the diversity in cultures that I encountered in school. I remember making very good friends with two Jewish girls. It was probably an odd sight to many, but the three of us did *Havah-Nagilah* on stage when I was in the fourth grade. I got to know their families pretty well, and remember tasting Jewish food. In that sense, it was very rich. It was a very Americanized environment.

"When I was thirteen or fourteen, I hung around with one group called the Continentals, and in keeping with the times, the boys wore black leather jackets, and hung around on street corners being cool, with ducktail type hairdos, and tight black pants. This was around 1963. There was almost a uniform of what the girls and guys who were a part of that social gang wore. Very often, girls would wear white shirts with black shorts. But I remember the white blouses with the initials on them. And we had our dances. The Continental group was a mixture of first, second and third generation Chinese teenagers, many of whom attended the Chinese school. And then there were other teenage groups, whose social life was centered around a church.

"Our idea of rebelliousness was hanging around street corners. Because we were the Continentals we would go around finding Lincoln Continentals and try to rip the little Continental symbols off the cars. That was the time of the movie, *West Side Story*, where teenage gang rivalry was

38

depicted. These were gangs, but not as we know of them today — with access to guns, or extortion. These were social gangs much like the ones in *West Side Story*. They carried switchblades or chains — but that was as far as they would go in terms of weapons. And every now and then they would get into scuffles with Italian gangs, each maintaining dominion over their neighborhood block. And it was cool for us to be a part of that. And it was cool for the girls to watch how the guys would get hurt in those things.

"I look back at my teenage years and think now that I was involved in some pretty off the wall stuff, being part of these gangs. And hearing the elders in Chinatown give us a bad name, and at the same time knowing we didn't do anything wrong — we just looked threatening because we hung around and shared that sense of rebelliousness — of wanting to be independent, grow up, and have an identity. My parents didn't know I was in a gang. They were very strict, and if we went to a party, often it was without the knowledge of my parents. We'd say we were going to the movies, and then we'd go to a party. At these parties, we'd do the twist, the cha-cha, the lindy, or jitterbug as it's called, and the Continental Walk. There were all-Chinese parties, and strictly limited to groups we hung out with. The extended group had forty to fifty people. Dating was certainly not the young man asking shyly whether I would go someplace like a movie or dinner, then having him show up at my door with a corsage or something, and being nervous about talking to my parents. The dating that we saw on 'Father Knows Best' was not the kind of dating experience I had. We didn't really date, one on one. We went out in groups to the bowling alley, ice skating, or to the movies. Then you paired off with someone. I don't remember being asked unless there was a dance or the movies.

"I remember being very insistent about going to Chinese school because my two older sisters went, and I wanted to go too. But I didn't start first grade Chinese school until I was two years ahead of that grade in American school. That was common. You often found older children in the lower grades because of ability. It was just the way the school was set up. We were all there, learning Chinese, memorizing the same lessons, and we were all competing for the same thing. But the social life was different. And the friends I eventually chose to develop a social life with were mostly second or third generation Chinese Americans. There was still that sense of competition, and the ones you competed with were the immigrants.

"School was from five to seven o'clock, five days a week. In my third year I started a Mandarin club because I was very interested in the dialect. I got our teacher to agree. Our Mandarin club would meet at four fifteen so that meant school started much earlier.

"Chinese school was comprehensive. We learned history, science, social studies (but from a Chinese perspective), geography about China, and in some cases, the world. Very seldom would I mix the lessons from

Chinese school with American school. They were two distinct worlds. With only two hours a day, what we did was very selective. We learned composition; we learned how to write. The whole method of teaching was so different from American school. There was a lot of memorization. And penmanship, of course, was using the brush. It was learning how to write Chinese characters, with ink and brush. A very important part of that schooling was poetry.

"The Chinese school also had a tradition of a drum and bugle corps. I was a baton twirler. And I was in it for four or five years. All this time that this was going on, it never dawned on me to think about how much out of the mainstream of society we were. It wasn't until I left Chinatown that I realized what a homogenous community Chinatown really was. What a tight, closed environment we lived in. We interacted with the rest of the city only as far as our activities took us. But in terms of sufficiencies, such as food and social activities, it was very contained.

"I can look back at my teenage years and see that it wasn't so different from other teenagers in other culture groups. It always amazes me how much of a New Yorker I was in terms of the environment. We had our dances, played our 45 records, had little transistor radios we played, and hung out on corners. Friends gathered after school at the local malt shop and had egg creams and french fries. These were all Chinese kids. Because the schools I went to were so close to the Chinese community, many of the students who went to the schools were Chinese, so invariably, I ended up hanging around with Chinese teenagers.

"In my early teens, my parents did not think it was appropriate for us to be seen with guys. So I just didn't tell them. The activities I would do with a guy would be done in a group setting. So there was no need for me to tell my parents I'm going with so and so, because I'd meet up with a group anyway. When my parents said to me, you're too young to be dating, I assumed they meant Chinese guys. There wasn't even a race issue in that, because it was understood that I would eventually end up with a Chinese. They certainly didn't have to warn me not to date Caucasians.

"At that point in my life, it never occurred to me to date anyone but Chinese because of the environment I grew up in. The school I went to had Italians, blacks, Jews, Puerto Ricans, whites — it was a pretty good mixture. But there was a sense of difference. I got along with people very well in school. I had some very good Italian friends — males and females — but it never occurred to me to date them. Or if I looked for cute guys, I'd be attracted to the Chinese ones and not the Caucasians. Although by the time I got to college, I could say my horizons broadened a bit, and I could say there were non–Chinese guys who were cute. You found them attractive, but not to the point where you'd say, 'Oh gosh, I wish he would call me up' or something. Again, I was looking for the Chinese or the Oriental guys. I grew up in a very sheltered environment in Chinatown, and there wasn't the need to look beyond. There were plenty of guys around to date, and enough to have crushes on. And there were some in the school environment as well."

Family:"My father was in several businesses. He owned an import-export trading company, and for a while he worked in a Chinese butcher shop owned by some relatives. He also had his own business of producing monosodium glutamate which he sold to restaurants. And then he started one of the first suburban Chinese restaurants in New Jersey in the 1950s.

"My mother, because she did not speak any English, found work in Chinatown in a sewing factory. But both of them were pursuing ways of supporting a family that were not in line with their original interests. They were both college-educated people who had to essentially give up careers in their fields of interest to come to the States.

"We were a poor family, and when I look back at it now I can see that. There were six of us living in a three-room flat. There were two small bedrooms and one room in the middle which had a sink and bathtub in it. We had to draw a curtain around us every time we washed. The bathroom was in the hall and we shared it with other families. This living arrangement was supplemented by our father's store, whic^l was where we had our kitchen and cooked our meals. In the back of the store was a hallway which we used as a kitchen. There was a living area in the back of this storefront and we spent most of our time there, so all we really did in the three-room apartment was sleep. My youngest sister and I slept in the same room as my parents and my two older sisters slept in a tiny bedroom of their own. As we grew up, there were times when the four of us would sleep in one bedroom. We were poor by middle class standards, but at that time the families around us were living in the same situation. I never felt spiritually poor. I felt the difference when I visited beautiful homes and houses in suburban areas. When my sister and I went away for these summer programs sponsored by inner city churches that matched up city children with families in Connecticut, I remember visiting a family for two weeks, and living for the first time in my life, in a single family house with a big yard and a big kitchen. The little girl who was my age had a huge bedroom of her own, that was almost larger than the three room apartment that we lived in. I became aware of the difference in living standards in a situation like that. But I never really felt that I was poor.

"In looking back at the way my grandparents lived, I would say it was very poor. They lived in a garage that was in a city alley. It was a structure that was behind a building in Washington D.C.'s Chinatown that my grandfather was responsible for. And being a very humble man, my grandfather didn't see the need for a more comfortable environment. It was comfortable for him, so that was what he and his wife, my grandmother, would make do with. There was a bedroom in the upstairs portion of the garage with a little kerosene heater. And downstairs was a concrete floor of the garage. It was not covered with anything — just bare cement. He lived this way for over forty years. About a third of the downstairs was taken up with storage of very old things — like wood and glass. There was a junk pile stored in the garage and they lived in the other half of it. They set up a little living area of benches made out of wood and a wooden platform that my grandmother could lie down on. In the corner there was a two burner gas stove, that probably wouldn't meet anybody's fire codes these days. And they had a small old ice box. There was running water that came out of a pipe sticking out of the floor. There was a commode, but it was not one that you could flush. You had to pour water down there every time you used the bathroom. And that was it. If we took a bath, we had to use a tin bathtub. There wasn't any hot water, so we had to boil it. And there was no drain, so we would have to carry it and dump it down the toilet, or down a drain in the alley. And the running water from the pipe had to be caught by a tin bucket that rested on a cut off stool. So if you were going to wash your hand you had to wash it over the bucket, and then you dumped the water into the commode. My grandparents lived this way until my grandfather gave up his restaurant and retired in the mid–1960s. Then he moved to New York to be with us.

"We cared for family elders, respected them made them a part of our lives. I remember when my grandmother was still alive. There was a time when we had to face a decision of either putting my grandmother in a nursing home or keeping her at home. And it was pretty much unanimous, as difficult a woman as she was, she should stay at home, even in her handicapped state after her stroke."

Leaving Chinatown: "I grew up in a very traditional family setting. I went to Chinese movies just about every week with my parents. As a first generation Chinese, I never even ventured a thought of marrying anyone but a Chinese. So when my older sister married a non–Chinese, I was very, very upset. I was disappointed in her and felt betrayed.

"What changed my world completely was going away to a small college in Vermont to study Chinese in the end of my sophomore year. I had just been accepted to Princeton University for a special program and a summer of intensive Chinese at Middlebury College in Vermont was part of that.

"For the first eight weeks I knew nothing but the study hall, dorm, eating hall and language lab. That was my world in Middlebury. I kind of isolated myself from some of the students, and maybe in a way, I was reluctant to deal with it and rejected that kind of environment because it was so foreign to me. There were some Chinese Americans there — a few who were second or third generation. But the rest of the students study-ing Chinese were not Chinese. They were students from all over the country.

"I was struck by the number of non–Chinese people who spoke the language very well and were studying the Chinese culture. They were studying history to an extent of being much more knowledgeable culturally of my heritage than my peers in Chinatown. I mean, to see a lecturer who acted more Chinese in terms of his mannerism and the way he spoke than some of my friends — when he was in fact Caucasian — was mind boggling. It was a shock. I was immensely impressed, and admired that. It was something that never occurred to me as being possible. I also met a Cauca-sian professor at Princeton, who had the grace, if you will, of a Chinese gentleman. He had more grace than many of the Chinese men I have come across. The image of a Chinese scholar, of a Chinese gentleman that we grow up seeing in the movies — soft-spoken, very intellectual, who knew the social nuances of a Chinese setting, in terms of what to say, how to act, how to respond, patience — this man embodied much of that. He was mar-ried to a Chinese woman. I am sure the way he developed was very much affected by his marriage to this woman. If I closed my eyes, I would have seen someone who was Chinese.

"So it was like all different subcultures of this country converging on this little school. That was the first time for instance, I encountered a Californian — the free spirit of a Californian — who would take off on his Porsche up the mountains of Vermont. You couldn't be in an environment like that without being affected by what was going on around you. And at the end of the eight weeks, I just broke down. I became more social. I was finally able to interact with them on their level, a level that was comfortable with me. It was like the layer of sheltered life I had led in Chinatown just slipped away. It took eight weeks, but I was finally comfortable. I don't know if it was purely a race issue, or if it was exposure to different social groups.

"I met my husband there that summer. He's the first of five generations not to carry on the family business. They had always lived in Wisconsin. He works for the government. He was one of the brighter students at Mid-dlebury who really picked up on the language, and showed a real apprecia-tion for the culture and history. I was very impressed.

"I couldn't have felt more loved from my first visit to meet his family. They were warm, loving, and they were not at all prejudiced against me. Or if they were, they certainly didn't show it. They had some concerns as to why their son was dating a Chinese girl before they met me. But they thought that was part of the weird things he was doing in terms of studying Chinese politics. But once I got there, I felt very much at home. And they were very much in favor of the wedding.

"My family was the complete opposite. My oldest sister married someone who was not Chinese and was the first in the family to do it. My father was very much against her marriage and tried to break them up anyway he could. And in the end, when he couldn't he did not speak to them for a long time. In my case, I was the second one to get married. He was so disappointed, hurt and maybe disgusted at the idea that this could repeat itself, that he didn't talk to me for a good six months before the wedding. So instead of doing everything he could to break us up, he just ignored me. It was something I had expected. I had to consider that marriage very carefully because I knew all that I was giving up in terms of relationships with my family. So I was prepared for it, and in a way, respected his decision not to support me, and not to come to my wedding. In the end, about two days before I got married, my father and I had a long talk, perhaps worked out a mutual understanding, a respect for each other's decision, and things were fine after that. Now my relationship with my family is good. I often marvel at how well my husband and my father can communicate — even in Chinese.

"My children, unfortunately, do not speak Chinese. Language is very important to me. It would be very nice if they could. Unfortunately I don't offer them the environment where they can learn it and speak it on a regular basis to retain it. And when they were little I would teach them a couple of Chinese words, and it was confusing — more confusing than helpful. Even when we went to Hong Kong and lived for two years, it was still very difficult for them to learn, again because the kids they interacted with were not Chinese. But eventually I would like for them to make that decision on their own. I would encourage it. I don't go out of my way to force them or make them go to a Chinese school right now. But I hope that they will recognize the rich heritage that they come from and will eventually consider learning Chinese. But I want it to come from them. I don't want to force it.

"I've always seen myself as a Chinese — even today. Though there are times I recognize how Chinese American I really am. The music, the culture, the issues of the time, I can relate to them. So in looking back to the sixties to the things I enjoyed doing and the things that affected me, a lot of us in the States shared that. And I think that is very distinctly American, rather than Chinese."

Visiting the Homeland

Victor Merina

Victor is a Filipino American who lives in California and works as a reporter for the L.A. Times. He is forty years old and is married to a German Irish American. He has two sons.

"I remember the stories my parents told us when we were gowing up, and I try to convey them to my children. The very little Tagalog I know happens to be a song which I sing to my children. I think that it is important to have these little things which we and our children can remember.

"I was born in a hospital on a military base in Manila. So my sister and I grew up as army brats because we moved around a lot. In the Philippines my father was a guerrilla and fought in the mountains during the war. The U.S. Army made those guerrillas Philippine scouts — sort of an auxiliary force — during the war. So after World War II, he joined the U.S. Army as an enlisted man.

"I grew up partly in California, went to elementary school in Kansas, came back to California and went to high school in Kentucky. In Kansas, in a neighborhood where we lived off the base, the Kansan students there thought I was Japanese, so I had some run-ins with students in the elementary schools. This was in the 1950s. My father was really upset about this because he fought against the Japanese in World War II. This was still a sensitive thing to him. We lived on Kiowa Street, and everyone called me the Kamikaze of Kiowa Street. We fought a lot about that.

"Another thing that reminded me of how different I was was going to speech impediment class. Several of us would be taken to the attic of the school. The other people were there for stuttering and other impediments. I went because of my accent. Today, I still recall this vividly. I couldn't pronounce the r's. I grew up in an environment where my parents have strong Filipino accents. For instance, my father would call cockroaches, 'COKE-ROCHES.' I mean, that's the way it was pronounced. I grew up in the house like that.

45

"One time I had an oral report where I used the word, 'COKE-ROCHES,' and everyone burst out laughing. I had absolutely no clue what they were laughing at. I always thought that's the way it was pronounced. I was having trouble saying r words, and so I would have to go to this attic a few times a week and I would have to crow like a rooster, to make the 'er' sound. So I would say, 'er-er-er-er-er, er-er-er-er-er.' I remember sitting there and the teacher would come to me and say, 'Well, how is the rooster coming?' I would say, 'er-er-er-er-er.' Once the kids learned that that was why I was up there, people would greet me with rooster crows.

"I remember going home to my father and telling him how people laughed at me when I said 'COKE-ROCH.' And he just roared with laughter. He said, 'I always thought that's the way people said it.' He took it fairly well.

"But as a child, you are being corrected at school, and you go home and correct your parents. Then you start to wonder if there are other things they aren't saying right. There was so much pressure to be accepted. I think what it did was made me reticent about speaking out in public. I was afraid to volunteer answers in class. I guess what struck me so about that oral report was that I stood up there and was proud of what I was saying, and the laughter just took the floor out from under me. Everyone just zeroed in on that.

"Looking back, my resentment went beyond having a physical impediment. They were telling me the way I pronounced things which was exactly the way my parents pronounced words, was wrong. So on one hand we were corrected, and then turned around and wanted to correct our parents.

"In the South, when I was there, (we were on the Kentucky-Tennessee border) it was okay for me to date and go out with Anglo women in the small town nearby. And that was fine. I was sixteen and going to high school. My father was stationed at the military base, and I had a girlfriend in town. But then one time I was walking in the town with a black friend of mine from the army base, and all of a sudden, the girlfriend of this girl I was dating was telling me I would have trouble going out with her again. So I said, 'Why is that?' She said 'Because you were seen with a black guy, and her family is really upset.' I was shocked. At the time, I didn't feel I was objectionable, but all of a sudden I have a black friend, and suddenly I became objectionable. So in that sense, there is a feeling that there are whites, and blacks, and Asians. Filipinos are somewhere in the middle.

"There was much more pressure for blacks to pair off with their own kind. I remember there was a black football player and a black cheerleader in high school. People were trying to get the two of them together. But the football player didn't feel attracted to her. I could understand how he felt. It would be like people saying to me, 'Hey, Vic Merina, go out with a

Filipino girl.' There were only two other Filipino families in town at the time, and one of them had all boys, so it would have been like saying, 'You can only date this one Filipino girl.' The thing that was discriminatory and affected me much more than the racial issues was class rank. My father was an enlisted man, and the girl I was seeing was a colonel's daughter. That was much worse than any racial issue.

"My parents encouraged the Filipino culture at home. The one thing we all regret now — and it stemmed from language problems like the 'COKE-ROCH' incident — they didn't want us to learn Tagalog, (the main language of the Philippines), or a dialect from their islands, which is called Ivatan. At first they spoke both dialects at home with my sister and I. But after the incidents of language in school, they made a conscious decision not to mix the languages. So they didn't speak any Tagalog to my sister or I when we were growing up. In retrospect, we all regret that now.

"One of the things in the Filipino culture is 'Utang na loob.' In the crassest form, it is like quid pro quo. But it really means that you owe a debt to someone who helps you. And it is a very strong cultural and traditional trait there. If someone helps you in schooling or to get your education, you owe that individual. It's not that if you help someone, you expect them to pay you back. But in the culture, that's what happens. You feel the need to reciprocate.

"Even when it comes to eating a meal, there are certain things we still practice at home. What we saw readily, as we were growing up, and it still happens today in my parents home, is that we would have friends come over, and if you have a meal, everyone takes some food home afterwards. I don't do that in my family now. But we like for our children to visit my parents' house because the vestiges of the culture are present there. I feel saddened that this sort of tradition will be lost after my parents' generation."

Going Home: "When I was in the Philippines to cover the Revolution in 1986, I visited my parents' old home in Batanes (a group of islands located in the northern part of the Philippines). When we were in the airport in Manila trying to get to Batanes, the seats were all booked, and we couldn't get on the plane. So the photographer and I were going around, talking to people, trying to get them to sell their tickets to us. We were willing to buy the seat for however much they wanted, just to get on the plane. So a group of people found out that I was a Merina, and they asked me if I was related to Eloy (my uncle), so I said, 'Yes, I'm Victor Merina from the U.S.' So when they found out that I was related to my uncle, they began giving us their seats to get to Batanes. They said, 'No money, no money. Just go see your family.' And they wanted to share food they had brought with them. Getting off the plane in Batanes, it was nothing but a dirt runway. But all these people were lined up, and I thought somehow the word had gotten out and they were there to see us. But no, these people were there just to greet anybody who came from the plane. My uncle was there, but he wasn't there to see me. They were just waving to people when they arrived. And when the plane left, the same thing happened. My uncle said, 'When ever the plane comes, we just come to greet people and to say goodbye.' Even strangers. It was just the friendly thing to do. That was our first experience in Batanes. And that was the way it was throughout.

"When the word spread that I had come, people would come, and just deposit things at our door. Food, little gifts, the outpouring of warmth was incredible. The people had this big feast for us. They went out in the fishing boats to get fish, they cooked all day, slaughtered a pig and got vegetables from the fields. There were groups of people doing this. It was a real communal thing. At the end, these women in their eighties were wrapping up all these little things of food and giving it out.

"There was no entertainment there, no movie houses. So each of these houses would have kids riding on bicycles holding blackboards saying which movie was showing at which movie house. As it turns out, the movie house was just the family home, with a Betamax, and they would be showing cassettes. And they would come out and give you popcorn and stuff like that.

"When I was there someone had just bought a chain saw. Its price was equivalent to a year's wages. So there was a crowd of people at his home watching him cut logs because it was a big thing. And people had brought wood for him to cut for them.

"There are at most a few thousand people living in the Batanes Islands. In our village, there are maybe a few hundred. My uncle was the village elder, and he settled disputes between neighbors. He also chose people to do public works projects. One time when we were there, a young wife came over and needed my Uncle Eloy because there was a dispute over a chicken. Someone had accused a neighbor of stealing her chicken. He had to go out and mediate this dispute, and then came home to dinner.

"Several of my aunts and my uncle could barely speak English, so my cousins had to translate for us. Then they would try to teach me phrases in Ivatan. Some of them didn't even speak Tagalog.

"I want my children to be exposed to what I saw when I went back to the Philippines. I want them to see, like in Batanes, where people have very little money, where the material goods that we have come to accept and rely on in this country mean much less. They have this feeling of family camaraderie and they've retained the culture. They can see that one of the greatest things about the Filipino culture is the helping of one another; and this blend of old folk ways with a Catholic religion would be tremendous for my kids to see. It made the culture real for me, when I saw it."

Food: "Food is important because it provides a time when the family gathers. For instance, when you make lumpia — it's like a wonton wrapped dish — it is a family thing. I like to have my children go over and help my parents make lumpia. You have to wrap and while you wrap, you sit around and talk. Just chatting and talking and all this, making this meal together. As I've grown up, that's always been a part of the culture. You sit there, and make these dishes, and the family talks, and it extends all the way to the end, when you wrap things up, and send the extra food home with the guests. So food is very important.

"When my wife came to California to meet my parents for the first time, they made this huge, very important meal. When she left to go back to New York where she lived, they packed this huge thing for her, and she was stunned. She asked, 'How much food do you people make?' My folks don't have a lot of money — just the military salary. But no matter where you go it seems this is typical of Filipino families I know. Even the poorest families have all this food. What helps them, like my parents for instance, is they've always had a garden. They grow a lot of their food. They also grow fruit trees. So a lot came from what they grew. It wasn't like buying everything. There was always an abundance. I have never through all the years, felt a time when there wasn't enough: not just enough to eat, but to give away.

"When my college classmates first visited us, my parents were concerned they wouldn't like Filipino food. So they made an entire dinner of Filipino food and an entire dinner of American food. The first couple of times I wondered why they made so much food. And finally my mother told me, it was in case they didn't like the Filipino food. Because my parents were concerned my friends wouldn't enjoy the food, they made extra stuff.

"I think being a Filipino male today helps me professionally, rather than hurts. That is in part because there is a renewed emphasis in my profession, and in the world, on Asian matters — the Pacific rim. And now there is this worldwide interest in what's going on in Asia. Because of the changeover from Marcos to Aquino, and the elections coming up in 1992 in the Philippines — I think all that, and the realization that the Philippines has some bearing on defense, and the growing number of Filipino immigrants in this country — all that speaks to the point that it is going to be more and more important to have people who are sensitive to the culture. I think we're at a point now, where we're starting to have our literature, and a lot of information on the experience of that."

1.5 Generation

Charles Ryu

*Charles is a thirty-year-old Korean American who immigrated to the
United States from Korea at age seventeen. He has attended Boston
University, the University of Chicago, and Yale and is currently a minister
for the Korean Methodist Church and Institute in New York City.*

"Sociologists call it the 1.5 generation, but we young ministers don't
like it very much, so we gave it a different name — we call it, transgen-
eration — TG. I'm a TG.

"TG's are those born in Korea, who stayed there until their teens, then
came to America. By the time they come to the United States, they have
already acquired the Korean language, and the cultural behavior that is
uniquely Korean. But they came to America at such an age where they were
still very easily influenced by the new culture, so the latter part of their
teenage life is formed by American culture. Somehow they developed this
mixed identity. They are functionally fluent in both languages, but only
functionally. They tend to speak Korean with an English accent; they
attended Korean school only up to the junior high or high school level, and
left. And English is not their first language. I speak pretty fluent English,
but it's not polished. I still have an accent.

"I used to call the 1.5 generation bilingual, but also, bi-illiterate. We
are bicultural, but we don't belong to any culture, therefore we are
biculturally deprived. Even though English is not the mother tongue of TG's
it soon becomes their lingua-franca, because that's what they use all the
time. You may learn some level of fluency, but you can never use it like
native speakers. At the same time, because you don't use the Korean
language all the time, it recedes. So you are bilingual, but you are not fluent
in either language. We tend to mix things together, so if I meet with 1.5
generation, I don't have to feel strained in my expressions, because I mix
both languages; sometimes using Korean language in English syntax or vice
versa, or making up new expressions which are very lovely, but nobody
understands except 1.5 generation.

"One of the greatest problems of the 1.5 generation is not having a place to belong to because neither social matrixes that of Koreans in America, or Americans in general, know what to do about this group. They're anomalies. In a Korean setting, you have to act like Koreans, yet they see you as not being one of them. You try to fit in the mainstream, and the same thing happens. You're not quite American. The first generation see me as the second generation, and the second generation see me as the first generation. I see myself as being nowhere, and that nowhereness has become part of my struggle.

"The 1.5 generation can be forever lost, and most of them are lost, so they either withdraw from involvement, or join gang activities. Most Korean American gangs are of the 1.5 generation. They came here and had difficulty adjusting. Gangs at least give them some structure.

"The possibility of a cosmopolitan personality in a real global sense can be possible with the 1.5 generation. Meaning, human beings tend to be very parochial with whatever they confront. Because you are forced to move back and forth between two cultures, Korean and American; or we can put it in the larger context of East and West, or we can put in in the context of a neo-colonial power: America, and a colonial subject: Korea — this cuts across all these boundaries, and also generations. So that being a 1.5 generation Korean American at this time in human history poses a unique possibility of seeing all these things embodied in the existence. That's my theological reasoning. Of course, I may be rationalizing too much."

Language: "Language is culture, and culture is language. You are what you speak. So if you have language fluency, that means you can express yourself, and can communicate better. At the same time, in America, there is a kind of chauvinism about language; the way established Americans use language, as a leverage to put you down. I think that is social insecurity, but we do that. That's why we try to get rid of accents, even regional accents of native speakers. Language becomes status. Unless you become fluent, with no accent — which means no individuality, right? — you're nobody. America tends to make everyone nobody, before they can become somebody. If you don't speak English well, then you are stupid. I went through that in high school. So that when I met somebody, he didn't care what I had to offer. It becomes a language lesson. What I said didn't count, because I didn't speak the language the way they did. There's automatic marginalization in everything you do and everything you are. Especially in high school and college, when you're still trying to develop who you are, it's an incredibly depressing situation.

"I think one of the manifestations in our language behavior of racism is the question 'Where are you from?' People always ask me that. I always say, 'I'm from Los Angeles.' And then they have to decide if I was born here and grew up somewhere else with my family or if I was born elsewhere, and grew up in L.A. Then they ask, 'What is your nationality?' Nationality is a legal status, and I say I am an American citizen. Then they really get frustrated and they ask whether I was born in Korea or not. I say 'Yes, I was born in Korea,' and they feel at home. Once they've made me an outsider, they feel at home. They get so angry with me claiming to be American because I've been here only eleven years. And I have no right to talk about America, because I am not a white American. Any analysis I make about American society as an American citizen, even with my educational background, simply doesn't count. Once they've established that I wasn't born here, they say, 'You're an outsider. You have no right to stay in America.' I was bluntly told, 'If you don't like it here, why do you stay? Go back home,' many, many times. I don't get angry. So among Koreans, language anxiety is very, very strong. If you speak good English, you tend to think you are better off than those that don't. And those who don't speak good English, are often envious of those who can. So it is there; we don't speak about it. But I went through this and I felt good about myself because I speak good English. Once I realized I was doing this, I felt sick."

Racism: "There are profound suspicions that you don't count simply because you're not white American. And once you suspect that, everything that happens around you feeds on that. For instance, when I was at Boston University, I was one of the top students. Nobody cared to ask me if I wanted to go to graduate school. The department chair called in my white friend and gave him a chance to go to Oxford. My friend told me that I'm the one who should have gotten it. Then when I got into the University of Chicago, I told my teachers, and they said, 'Oh, you're going to the U of C. Good for you.'

"Lack of help is one thing I experienced. Another is having to prove yourself. I was taking a Western philosophy class. I was the only non-Western person there. And my presence in that class means everything is fair. In other words, America is not a racist country, because, I, an Asian, made it to Chicago, Boston, Yale. But at the same time, there's an assumption that minority students take up a lot of financial aid, and that somehow I would lower the standards for everyone else. So when I was there, a lot of people assumed I got in because I am an Asian, and not because I am good. And they are flabbergasted when I excel, and they get angry and it shouldn't happen. I play the role of token minority so well. I get picked out as the only minority, only Asian, and I make people very comfortable, in certain ways. I have this suspicion that I am always dispensable.

"In taking an ethics class with an Oxford trained scholar, I had difficulty in the way he argued his position. So I made a point against his position, and his response, which shocked me, was not to what I argued.

I challenged him with some difficulty about the system he was supporting. His answer was, 'I think Confucius was a good ethicist, too.'

"I was lucky that my father and mother asked me to take philosophy. But my guidance counselor was profoundly distressed. She said, 'You will never make it.' I mean, discouragement begins in high school. It took a long time to convince my counselor that I could make it because I was from Korea, and they had never seen a Korean make it outside of science. They never thought Koreans could make it in other fields.

"I don't think Asians prefer the sciences. Sometimes it is the only avenue open to them. In the sciences, empirical results matter more than in the esoteric discussion of humanities. So that at least as an engineer, you know how to put machines in, and you can be a useful bolt and nut. And I think the job opportunities for us lie in this field. Having bread on the table everyday is important, so they compromise and work in those fields. A lot of engineers are profoundly unhappy because their work is not good enough to try for such areas as philosophy or literature."

Disillusionment: "The biggest disillusionment I had was that the American dream is a lie. It had a lot to do with growing up. As a kid you tended to see things in black and white. Now you see things in perspective. I did become an American citizen because I transplanted myself here. But all the promises of America are more of a dream and well orchestrated hoax than reality — for most Americans, even. America is not a freedom-defending democratic country, but simply a capitalist imperial force that does whatever it wants to do for its profit.

"I didn't have very many dreams. Coming to America was just another way of living, because survivability in Korea was questioned. Opportunities and the ability to study were the main things. And that I have achieved in some ways. But at the same time, coming to America shattered my self image tremendously. I had to rebuild it. And the rebuilding process, which is still going on, is something good. I like it. But my naïve idealism was shattered. Anything and everything America does promised a lot of idealism: If you try hard, you will make it, it's up to you. If you don't make it, there's something wrong with you, which is not true; America as a Christian country — which was an assumption I had — was profoundly shaken. It's a country that needs to cast judgment on everything, yet we allow economic and political injustice to go by.

"Racism was an eye opener. I didn't know what racism was about, and I couldn't believe that I was part of the racism in certain ways, and that was a very disillusioning experience. And also my assumption that America has been a friend to the Korean people since the late nineteenth century was shattered. I learned that it was never a friend; that Korea was just another Virgin Islands or Puerto Rico to be exploited and used, and controlled, and immigration is a result of that neo-colonial impingement into the Far East.

Once they (Americans) established themselves in the 1960s, multinational corporations came to South Korea, and as a result, the middle class collapsed. Small sized businesses all collapsed. My family belonged to that category, so I had no place to go. Either you become part of this gigantic conglomerate, or you had to leave, and you left. We came to our master's country. Still, a lot of other Koreans continue to come to America with the hope of making it in the American dream, which they couldn't do in Korea."

The Good Things: "I learned to love the way I am. I don't ask which place is good for me to live anymore. I simply ask what I can do where I am. I love my ministry. I'm a workaholic. I find meaning in talking with others. America provides this unique opportunity to meet with all kinds of people, which I was not given while I was in Korea. I am meeting with other Asians, blacks, whites. I don't know any other place I can do that, except in America. There is a freedom in America, that is a blessing, and my will is to use that to make America a more just society."

II. Aspects of Americanization

The six largest Asian Pacific American groups in 1980 were, in order: Chinese, Filipino, Japanese, Asian Indian, Korean, and Vietnamese. By the year 2000, Filipinos are expected to become the largest group, followed by Chinese, Vietnamese, Koreans and Asian Indians. The Japanese, the nation's most numerous Asian Pacific group from 1910 to 1970, will be the smallest of the six groups. — *Asian Pacific Americans Handbook*

In April 1975, the U.S.-backed government of Vietnam collapsed, setting in motion one of the largest refugee movements in the past twenty years. In 1975 alone approximately one hundered and thirty thousand of these refugees entered the United States from Vietnam, Kampuchea (formerly Cambodia), and Laos. By 1984, seven hundred thousand Southeast Asian refugees had entered the country.

EXODUS

Khmer Masks
Kim Huot Kiet

Kim Huot Kiet is in his mid-fifties. He is Cambodian and fled to the United States from Thailand in 1975. I visited him in his home in New York. Three walls of his cramped living room are lined to the ceiling with golden faces, some haunting, others angry, a few smiling. All are frozen symbols of Cambodian culture. There are over thirty Khmer dance masks, all made by him. Their presence is a soothing reminder of happier days in Cambodia.

"In 1975, while on mission in Thailand, there was very heavy fighting in Cambodia. I heard the president of the Republic of Khmer, Pot Pol had escaped from Cambodia, and there was a really serious problem there. I had no way of going back because airplanes and transport by land had been banned, and there was heavy fighting. There was no way for me to go back, and no way to keep in touch with my family. I never saw them again — not my wife, nor my four children. They all got killed. But I don't know how.

"When I was in Cambodia, I was an officer in the Air Force. This was thirty years ago when it was still the Kingdom of Cambodia. The prince, Sianouk, would go around the country to inaugurate hospitals and schools, and I flew escort planes for the royal party. In 1970, I was assigned to Thailand by the Khmer Air Force to train as an airplane commander. I had flown for fourteen years already. I flew mostly light planes to patrol and observe our country in air space, and also a transporter plane. That year, there was a coup. The communists started to invade Cambodia. The uprising lasted five years. The communists finally took over.

"After a few months in Thailand, I decided to come to the United States. I was stationed in the American air base in Thailand at the time. I did not want to stay in Thailand, and could not go back to Cambodia because I was not sure what fate I would suffer. Because of my past position, I felt I would be in danger. But it was hard for me to decide to leave my country. At the time, the United States helped Cambodians who wanted to come here. It was a temporary decision. I decided to come here and wait and see what happened in my country in the next few weeks, the next few months, the next few years. It's been fourteen years since I arrived, and although I didn't plan to stay here this long, I have no choice. My country is still communist, and I can't take a chance on returning.

"In 1979, the Vietnamese invaded Cambodia, and after that the people could return home and look for their family. When my brother found out I was in the United States, he sent me a letter from Cambodia. He told me that only he and my sister were alive. I wrote and asked him about my family. He didn't know how they died. Both my sister and brother are married and have families in Cambodia. They are alive. My father had five children, including me, from our mother. I also have two half sisters, and three half brothers. They are all either dead or missing. I don't know what happened to them. I think they got killed. I don't know how my children and wife died. But I can only imagine that it must have been terrible. At that time, there was no food, no shelter. You had to move along the street, and there were purges. But what can you do? It was the transfer of one regime to another. Everything was in turmoil. Everything was mixed up. It was just terrible. People had no choice, no human rights, no freedom. But what can you do?

"I don't think things are much better today. Our country still remains in the control of Vietnam. So how can things be better? I feel the Vietnamese are terrible. They tried to swallow up the land of Southeast Asia. The Vietnamese have been a traditional enemy of Cambodia since the eighteenth century, when the former lowlands of Cambodia was taken over as part of Vietnam. So most Cambodians in Cambodia dislike the Vietnamese.

"It is very hard for me to talk about the camps today — very hard. You escape from Cambodia. Along the road there are mine fields. When you've crossed the mine fields, there are thieves. And you get to the camps. But you have to struggle to get into the camps. And once inside the camps it is controlled by the Thai authorities. And they are terrible, the camps. Then the Cambodians come to the United States — a strange place — and they put them in neighborhoods they don't know anything about, and some neighborhoods in New York are very bad. I think this is terrible, even to think about.

"There are still a lot of people waiting in camps in Thailand and the Philippines. I know of one lady who just got into a camp in Thailand. She arrived in the Thai camp in November 1988. She has a family of five. She came by boat, and fortunately, she landed safely in Thailand. As you know, many people have had bad luck, met some sea pirates, and refugees got raped. It's hard to talk about this. I don't want to think about it too much. But as long as they survive, I try to help them when they come here.

Kim Huot Kiet and his Cambodian mask.

"Who do you blame for what happened in Cambodia? I cannot blame anybody. The only thing I can blame is the Vietnamese and Thailand, because my country is located between the two. As our country is a Buddhist society, we don't like to have violence. We don't fight much. I think war is terrible — the revenge, the hate. I am still a Buddhist. I am not bitter. I think what happened to me happened because my country got into a war. I miss my country; I miss my legacies; I miss my family, my people. I can't compare this feeling with anything in the world. Since the communist takeover, I feel everything's changed. It's not that all the culture is lost. I hope someday there will be a good leader to restore the country to the peace there was before. I would like to go back when that happens. If I could live there, I would, because it is my country and I love it very much."

Looking Back: "When I was young, we used to sing a song, 'Kampuchea Is a Golden Land.' (Kampuchea is the original name. The English called it Cambodia.) So I feel Cambodia was rich in everything, and it hadn't been exploited yet. I was the son of a merchant — my father was an officer of the census bureau — not of people but of rice. He used to go from town to town to survey the rice, to see how much was produced during the year. And my mother was a sales woman. She sold cake. So I grew up not very rich, not very poor. I felt I was very sociable. I had a lot of class-mates who loved to play together in their spare time. And I felt happy. I didn't think of anything else but being happy. In my hometown there was a river nearby where I could go swimming. My hometown once a year would be flooded, so we would have to make bridges to our houses. Sometimes we would make a small boat to take people back and forth to their houses. I felt very happy. My experience in my childhood was very nice. I try not to think too much about my life in Cambodia anymore. I just remember that when I was growing up, things were very good there."

Life in the U.S.: "Now, here, my life has changed. I have remarried. But I cannot get a pilot's job anymore. I only have a private license so it is difficult to find a job. I tried for about a year. I tried to start from ground school again. Finally, I couldn't get any further because you had to pay more money to go commercial. I miss flying.

"In this country, I worked on a Khmer art project for three years. I made over thirty figures, headdresses and masks of Cambodian dancers. In Cambodia, there is traditional and classical dance with the mask and crown and costume. The dancing is not for everyday life, but for special occasions and celebrations. Once there was an Empire of Cambodia, then later, it became the Kingdom of Cambodia, where there was a king. During the Kingdom period, there was a group of dancers who performed in the palace for receptions, and once a year, they used to play for the population when the water went down. There are rivers stretching through Cambodia, and the capitol of Cambodia was along the border of one of the rivers. So when the water went down, they celebrated what was called the Water Festival. So I learned how to make these masks and headdresses here. I went to the Library of Congress to find a book, and I used to read the art books. I read how to paint and sketch these masks. I went to the stores to see the tools to use. In 1980, I had a friend in the camps in Thailand. He was in the Khmer Air Force, and served on the Royal Air Force. He has six children. His wife knew how to perform the Cambodian dances. So when I knew he was in the camp, I filed an affidavit for them to come to New York. In 1981, when the Cambodian community wanted to celebrate Cambodian New Year, I didn't know what material to use to sew the costumes. So she said she knew how to sew the costumes, but didn't have the material. She knew how to make the costumes, but she didn't know how to make the head-dress. She had some pictures and showed me the form. And I made the handmaiden headdress for her to perform with.

"I didn't know how to do any of this before I came to this country, but I learned. I taught myself to do it. I want to preserve the culture. I want my culture to be alive in this country, not to die out. We've already had many exhibitions here in the United States, from New York to Florida. A lot of people are interested. They say, 'Oh, these are Khmer masks.' It was lost, so that is why I had to learn how to make it — to make it survive again. That's the most important thing: to keep the culture alive. I know they are still dancing in the camps in Thailand, Cambodia, Florida, New York and California. There are people dancing, and keeping the culture alive."

The Success Story

Lang Ngan

Lang Ngan came to the United States in July 1975 by military airlift during the first wave of evacuees from Vietnam.

"On April 25th, near the end of the war, my supervisor called me in, and told me that by six o'clock that evening, we had to meet, to get to the airport by nine the next morning. I had worked for the U.S. embassy in Saigon for seven years. If we had stayed, we would have been persecuted by the new government.

"There was no time to talk to friends or relatives because the evacuation was supposed to be secret, and we were not allowed to tell our relatives. We couldn't even take our money out of the bank. We weren't prepared to come to this country. It was a last minute thing. We had to make our decision overnight. We didn't have any time to think about it.

"I was allowed to take my family, because I was single. My father, my mother, myself and six brothers and sisters — the nine of us. We were so frightened because we didn't have any friends or relatives in this country to help us. We couldn't sell our property. We literally left with the clothes on our backs. I was twenty-nine when I came to the U.S., one brother was twenty-three, and one was nineteen. The youngest was only eight. The rest were in their teens.

"I didn't have the Golden Mountain dream (a Chinese term for America, where making lots of money fast is believed possible). I knew life wouldn't be easy, especially since we didn't receive a high education in Vietnam. I told my brothers and sisters on the plane coming here that I didn't know whether I could support all of them. If not, then I would have to give them up for adoption. They said they understood but asked that before I left, I give them my address so that when they grew up, they could look for me.

"We were transported by military cargo plane. At the time, the evacuation was so sudden the U.S. government didn't have a chance to prepare for our arrival. So we were taken to a military camp in the Philippines for a few days. From there, some of the refugees were sent to Guam. We were sent to Wake Island, and screened for admittance. We left Vietnam April twenty-fifth. We arrived at the camp in Arkansas on May fourth.

"At the beginning, there wasn't enough food. There was a shortage because the U.S. government wasn't prepared for us. But really it wasn't bad. It was actually much better than the first asylum camps in Malaysia and Thailand. We felt we were the luckiest. A month later, the government contracted a company to provide food for us, so after that, there was plenty of food. The living situation wasn't bad. The housing was used by soldiers in training, and the facilities were good like staying in dorms. There were bunk beds. The volunteer agencies — refugee resettlement agencies — started sending people to process us. Some of the agencies, such as the one I work for now, are partially funded by the State Department. Currently they provide five hundred twenty-five dollars for the initial resettlement cost. Part of the funding is also provided by public donations, or foundations. These resettlement agencies and the immigration office sent people in to screen us, to see if the refugees have relatives or friends in the country they could go to, and to process them. Because I could speak English, I started helping many of those who couldn't, translating for them. I met the representative from the International Rescue Committee, and started to work as a volunteer for IRC. I ended up in New York because the IRC offered me a job. Southeast Asian refugees were calling the office, and no one could understand what they were saying. I was so happy that I could get a job right away. I asked my boss if he thought that I alone could support a whole family of nine. And he said, 'Probably not. Why don't I hire your sister, too?' She was only nineteen at the time, and we've worked for the IRC ever since.

"My sister and I left the camp first, and we started work as soon as we got to New York. We started looking for apartments, but at the time, my salary was only one hundred fifty dollars a week, and my sister made one hundred twenty-five dollars. Someone took us to look for an apartment in Flushing, Queens. A two bedroom was two hundred fifty dollars, and a one bedroom was one hundred ninety dollars, and even with a family of nine, we took the one bedroom, because we tried to save as much as possible. Fortunately, the building superintendent was a refugee — from Cuba — and he helped us. He said he wouldn't tell the landlord that there were nine people living there as long as we didn't make any noise, and kept the children quiet. So he helped us get the apartment. He lied to the landlord for us by saying there were only two girls in the apartment — my sister and myself. The superintendent was very helpful. He tried to get some used furniture for us, and used clothes and dishes. He collected them from other tenants and his friends. That is how we started.

"Half a month later, we had the rest of our family join us. Even though there was only my sister and I working to support nine, life wasn't bad. We were quite happy. But the only frustration was our parents. They had a lot of difficulty adjusting. They felt isolated, because there were no Cantonese-speaking people in the building, and in the daytime, when all the children were in school, there was nothing for them to do but sit. In the beginning, I wanted to go back to Vietnam, because life was easier there. Here, we had no friends or relatives, and the lifestyle was so different. Even the mailbox was different. Every evening, we opened it and it was full of papers and envelopes. I was afraid to throw away anything in case it was important, so I would read every word — thinking they were letters — not realizing that this was advertising, junk.

"As for my siblings, they knew that if I couldn't support them I would give them away. So they were very happy when I didn't have to do that. They felt lucky. So they worked hard. They didn't think about many of the things children think about today — expensive toys, expensive clothes, fixing their hair. We wore whatever people gave us. Today I tell my refugee clients, I wore the same used clothes people gave me until two years ago. I finally threw them out because they were so worn.

"The first books we bought were dictionaries. We got three or four of them. We used them a lot. We didn't have any friends or relatives here, but at least we were together as a family. The children studied very hard to catch up in school. We had only one table, and they all had to study together around the same place, and all of them still feel this closeness to this day. We helped each other. I helped the children at that time, but not now. Now they correct my accent.

"We had no furniture — just a few chairs and a used sofa that the supervisor gave us, and broken TV. And the rest were mattresses. We had no beds, only mattresses. In the evening, we had to carry all the mattresses to the living room for the males to sleep. All the females slept in the bedroom. And we lived in this condition for two and a half years, until we were able to get a two-bedroom apartment. We waited till we felt financially secure to do this. We had saved some money over the two and a half years, and because I was getting married, I felt that with my husband's income, we could afford to move. My husband and I got a one bedroom apartment and my family moved to a two bedroom place in the same building. We were very happy. We felt that we were one family unit. We were really together, and sharing. There was no privacy, but we all remembered the times we had gone through together, and we were able to work things out with each other without problems.

"All my younger sisters and brothers have done very well in school. And the teachers and school counselors have shown them what is the best way for them to go. Actually, we didn't give them that much counselling.

They all got it from school. Even though they don't act the same way I did when I was going to school in Vietnam, they still have certain values — such as respect, and obeying teachers, and therefore the teachers liked them, and tried to help them. My sister got a full scholarship to MIT from Bell Labs. I have one brother who got an electrical engineering degree from Columbia, and the other finished at City College. One other brother is going to medical school at New York Med.

"I think the problems we had when we first came to this country helped our success. We're not like other people who were born here, and had everything. We went through all those difficulties, so when we have a chance, we grab it. We now own a two family house. My husband and I live in one side, my parents in the other."

Out of Communism

Alicia Diem

Alicia is forty years old and imigrated to the United States in 1984. She learned English only after coming to this country. Our interview was conducted in English. Alicia is a pseudonym used at her request.

"In my opinion, a lot of people want to live in America because they have freedom, and the opportunity for a future. If you work hard, you can have everything. Sometimes I think life is not fair. But here, in the United States, it is a little bit more fair. If you work, you can have everything. Don't expect to have a lot of money, or to be a millionaire. But you can get things like a car. Right now I think I have enough.

"Everybody wants to come to the United States. Everybody wants to leave Vietnam. Even those who love the country, don't like the communists. The economy keeps going down. I lived almost ten years under the communists. Before the communists, everything was okay. We did not have a rich life like in America, but the lives are satisfied. I had a good life too. I had a good job. I had family and relatives there. I liked to stay in Vietnam. But after the communists came, my future was nothing. I worked hard, but for nothing. My salary for one month was equivalent to one or two U.S. dollars—that is if you exchanged it on the black market. Everybody got sixty Vietnamese pias. My boss got one hundred pias a month. One month you can buy half a pound of meat for the whole family. Everybody had to sell things—furniture, jewelry, gold, diamonds—just to eat. But after our things ran out, there was almost nothing to eat.

"My father had a second wife, so he didn't want to leave his second family. But now he misses us a lot and so we send gifts and money to them every three or six months. If I have money, I help them. My younger sister helps too. My family was basically middle class in Vietnam. My father worked for the Ministry of Economics. All of us went to college, except for my youngest sister, who left Vietnam while she was in high school.

"In a Vietnamese family, usually the husband works, and the wife

66

stays at home. But I am a new generation Vietnamese woman. I like to work and make my own living. After the communists came, the man would still work, but he could barely live on what he made — let alone support a family. So you know, if you have no money, you are often not happy and divorces increase. They tried to escape Vietnam a lot. A lot of people died on the ocean because they escaped by boat. It is very dangerous. I tried to escape twice by boat, but I didn't make it. I had to pay money. Before, I didn't have much money, so I had to ask my sister who lived in America to help me. She sent money to me in a secret way — not directly. She sent me almost three thousand dollars. I couldn't stand being in Vietnam anymore. I wanted to live. But I lost money, because someone cheated me. I tried again the second time with a little money, even though I knew I could die in the ocean, but I didn't care. That time, I wanted so bad to live in America. In 1979, the Vietnam government allowed those with sponsors to apply to leave. My sister sent the papers, in 1979, to try to get me out. But it took five years, I had to do the papers, and to give money under the table, before I could get out.

"I wasn't exactly glad to leave because my father and brothers and friends are there. And here I had nothing and could not speak English. But I felt inside that I could do anything. So I worked as hard as I could when I got here. To me now, I feel lonely. My mom and my brother live in San Francisco. And my older sister lives in Pakistan. I really don't feel very good about this. I live with my younger sister now. We enjoy food every Saturday and Sunday in Chinatown. We go to a restaurant — a Vietnamese restaurant, or a Japanese restaurant. But most of the time, after work, my sister and I cook dinner together, we watch some television, and we go to sleep. At home when we make dinner, it is always Vietnamese food. I work six days a week, and have two jobs, working full time at a publishing house, and part time for a fashion designer. I'm lucky that we have a good clean house in a good neighborhood. When I walk down Chinatown, I see Oriental people, and it looks like Saigon or Vietnam. So it feels pretty good. In my opinion, I like the Chinese. They are honest. They say something, they will do it. They don't try to cheat you; most of them don't anyway. There may be a few, but for the most part, they are honest. And they like me very much.

"I don't want to ever go back to Vietnam to live, even though I love my country, my family and my friends there. If I have money, and the political relationship between the U.S. and Vietnam is good, I would like to go back to visit. For now I just want to stay in this country and work, and send money to help my family in Vietnam. We are not rich here, but I know how much I suffered, and how unhappy I was when I was living in Vietnam. I know what unhappiness is.

"I tell my father not to write and describe in great detail the problems and unhappiness he is going through. I know all about it, and it just gives me a great headache to think about it. If I have money, then I will send money to help. So I tell him not to write to tell me how unhappy he is. I don't look forward to those letters — constantly complaining, telling me of the hardships. I can't stand reading those letters. The Vietnamese are very unhappy people now. People don't like to work, especially for the communists. You cannot complain against the government. If you complained, you would be sent to jail. But now, no one wants to work. You can imagine everything going down. So they can't control the people. There is no money, therefore, no power, no everything. So the South Vietnamese people, they just wait for gifts from outside. Like I send my father, one or two hundred dollars so he can relax for a few months or a year. And they don't need to work. My father is retired already. So we have to help. But not much, because if we help, they get lazy. I talk with my brother. I tell him that he is young and has to work. Even if I send money to him, he still has to work. I don't like a man to be lazy and expect money from his sister. This is what I tell my brother in Vietnam.

"As for America's responsibility to Vietnam, I think maybe some people in government still think of doing things for Vietnam. But as for the American people, they feel it is over. Some Americans don't even know where Vietnam is. Some Americans have asked me, 'You're from where? Vietnam? I don't know where that is on the map.' Some know, but many don't know where it is.

"In my previous job, which was to restore paintings, I just liked to work as an assistant, but I really didn't understand the American way. I had a fellowship. My boss wanted me to keep going up. But I worried about my English. I could barely talk, so all I wanted to do was to stay as an assistant because I loved the work. But my boss wanted to send me to Japan to learn more. Sometimes she wanted me to read art books. But it is not easy for me to read. It is a difficult life for me here. First I have nothing here, and I have to think about money for rent and expenses. And I have to send money to Vietnam to help my father, brother, and friends. So all the time, I just wanted to save money. I didn't want to go away to study. I just wanted to work. But this is not good. So I learned. I lost that opportunity and that job. I just didn't understand the American way which is to keep moving up. You cannot stay at the same level. If you stay at the same level, then people will push you out. I can do everything in restoring paintings, but they don't want only that. After this fellowship, they wanted me to become a professional.

"I could make clothes by myself before, but I didn't know the secrets of doing special work. So I am learning from a designer. I work for her. She likes me, so she tells me how to do many things. But she doesn't know I'm going to leave her. I cannot choose that career for my life. She pays me only thirty dollars a day. I help her a lot. I get no rest for eight hours. It is not fair. But I like to stay, because I like to learn from her. She thinks I cannot find another job and I have to stay with her longer. But I don't. I like to make money to pay rent."

Meeting the Right Man: "It is very tough for me to meet a good man now. Here in New York, there are terrible people. It is not easy to find a good man, the right man. If I want to marry now, it's not easy. I don't want to mix with a bad person. I am old enough to tell who is good and who is bad. And I've seen a lot of bad people. A Vietnamese, or a non–Vietnamese man is okay. I don't hate anybody. I'm not racist. If anyone can attract me, and I fall in love, it's okay. But in my mind, I like Asians, not European or American. In Vietnam, when I was in school, I had some boyfriends. But I didn't want to get married right after college. I wanted to enjoy my life. I played tennis and enjoyed sports. I had a good job. But after a year, the communists took over South Vietnam and it finished my future. How could I want to get married? I didn't want to make a new generation, to have my children live under communism. It was too terrible. If I got married in Vietnam, I had no chance to go to America. Like my brothers in Vietnam, they have kids and they have to stay in Vietnam. They were not allowed to leave. If you're single, it is okay to leave. If you're married, it is not easy to leave Vietnam. It wasn't a question of economics. It was just not easy to go because the government wouldn't allow it.

"You have money, you have power. I learned from America."

Where To from Here?

Kenny and Siu Wing Lai

*Both sneaked out of the People's Republic of China at age twenty-three.
After a few years in Hong Kong, they managed to immigrate to the United
States in 1978. As their English is minimal, they preferred to speak in
Cantonese.*

Kenny Lai, 40 (Husband): "I graduated from junior high school in
China in 1964 and was sent to a commune to farm. I spent nine years there.
You couldn't choose what you wanted to do. The government chose for
you. If you didn't accept their choice, it would be difficult to survive. I was
only fourteen and impressionable. I accepted what people told me. They
told me to go, so I went. We were constantly told that we were the next
generation that the country counted on, and so after a while, you really
believed it. When you're young, whatever the adults say, you followed. So
when they said to go to the farm communes to receive your education, we
went. There wasn't much individual thought. But after a few years, things
got bad. I had lived in a city all my life, and it was hard to get used to working on a farm. Plowing the land was very hard. Farmers and their families
were able to withstand it because that was the way they lived for generations. But for city people to go to work on a farm was hard. I also missed
home. We could only visit once or twice a year. I was desperate. I wanted
to return to the city, but they wouldn't let me. Even if you said you were
going to visit family, you had to apply for permission to leave.

"A lot of people waited and waited to be allowed to leave the commune,
but permission never came. Initially, I never had the desire to leave China.
I always wanted to go back to Canton. But there was no way out. I had
been in a commune six years. I kept waiting for a new assignment, but
nothing happened. No one had been reassigned. Yes, there were some who
were able to leave, but they knew someone important who helped them
arrange it. For instance, party members, who had children in the commune
would arrange to have their children returned to Canton. But for those of

us who had no connections, we could plan on spending the rest of our lives there. I thought that as long as I didn't marry, maybe I could withstand it. I could stand spending the next forty to fifty years on the commune. But I was thinking when I got married, my children would be forced to stay there, and my children's children. So future generations would be forced to be farmers. So there was no way out. If they wouldn't let me leave, the only thing to do was escape.

The commune was sort of between Hong Kong and Canton. Not far from it was the edge of the Pearl River. So the opportunity to escape was there. One night I stole a small boat, and five of us from the commune, (including my future wife) left. We used a sheet attached to a pole as a sail, and a gust of wind started us moving. We left at eleven at night and arrived in Hong Kong Harbor at four AM. We weren't afraid. If we were afraid, we wouldn't have left. We had to watch out for patrols. They were all over the place, but it was dark, and that helped us.

"We got off the boat at the edge of a mountain. It was early morning, and so we walked until sunset the next day before we crossed the mountain into Hong Kong. There was a police station, so we entered. The police were very kind to us. They ordered someone to fetch rice for us to eat. After they took our names, a ship was summoned to take us into Hong Kong itself. We stayed in a police station — it was the weekend — and on Monday, they let us out to look for work. At the time, they didn't turn anyone back. They gave us identification papers and helped us. That was October 1973. Two years later, they stopped that policy. Anyone caught entering would be sent back to China. During the period when we arrived in Hong Kong they were still welcoming people from China. Once in Hong Kong, the lifestyle was very hectic, like New York. My first job in Hong Kong was as a laborer, remodeling and fixing things. I stayed there for six months, and a friend suggested I find a way to come to the United States under refugee status. And so the church helped us to apply without cost. But we had to get someone to sponsor us. It turns out my wife's father's friend was in the United States, so he wrote a letter to him, and he was kind enough to offer help.

"At the time, it should have taken us four months to get the paper work processed. But we waited two and a half years because during this time, there was a large influx of Southeast Asians from Vietnam, who were also seeking asylum in the United States. I was just getting established in my work in Hong Kong, and I really didn't care too much if our application came through. Sometimes I think if I had stayed there, I could have done better in terms of my work. When I arrived in this country, my first job was as a dishwasher. I only stayed at it for a month. A relative got me the job. Then I looked for construction work, because that's what I did in the past. It would mean more money. As a dishwasher, I was earning thirty dollars a day. That was already five dollars more than most dishwashers make. And you can't support a family on thirty dollars a day. If I planned to move from that job to a short order cook in a Chinese restaurant, it would take me two to three years, and it would have been hard to support my family on the wages in the interim. I also didn't want to be imprisoned in a Chinese restaurant. If you work there for ten years, you would still feel the world outside is foreign. There would be no opportunity to speak English, to meet people. I didn't have any interest in it. I hated the idea. I answered an ad in the Chinese newspaper. I became a laborer, fixing up interiors for places like restaurants. I worked like that for three months, then my friend suggested that we strike out on our own.

"Now my life is much better than the past. We own a house and a car. My two children were born in this country. You make friends, you get to know people and build relationships, so that they know you are available for work. Now most of my work comes from Asian businesses, people from Southeast Asia, for instance. For some reason, the amount of Chinese clients has dropped. They're just not building or constructing things as fast as the Southeast Asians or Koreans. Most of my work is remodeling – such as interior work.

"As for my English, I haven't been able to go back to school. When I first got here, I was able to attend classes for about eight or nine months. But every night, I had to get there late. There was no way around it. Classes started at seven PM, but I wouldn't get off work until six, so by the time the vans took us back to Chinatown, it was already six thirty. Then I had to eat. By the time I got to class, it was well after seven. I was late for every class by about half an hour. I was very ashamed. The teacher saw that I was late every day. She probably wonders whether my heart was in learning or not. But I had no choice. The work came first and the hours were just that way. I stopped after eight or nine months. I really didn't learn very much. First, I had no foundation in English, then because I had to work, there was little time to study or to use what I learned in class. Everyone I worked with was Chinese, and so we spoke Chinese. There was little opportunity to speak anything else.

"It's good to work on the outside. You come in contact with more people, and it forces you to speak. I can pretty much understand the English now, but not write very much.

"The worst thing about this country is the sense of racial differences between people. I still don't feel that this is my country even though I am a U.S. citizen. White people ultimately think they are superior to you, and you are a level beneath them. It's not a very obvious thing, but I certainly feel it among my neighbors, sometimes in talking to people. When I buy things, there generally isn't much of that sense of superiority. They welcome your money. But after you purchase it there is something else again. Once you hand over your money, they don't know you anymore. Everything is fake.

"Politically, I feel that this country has equality, but that the justice or legal system is too lax. For instance, even if you capture a criminal in this country, it doesn't count for much because he can go free. Even if someone murdered someone, he can go free for lack of evidence. I think there is something very wrong when lawyers are willing to defend anyone as long as the price is right.

"Communists, you can say, do have some good points. There is a greater sense of social responsibility. People who break the law are all dealt with severely. Here, if someone is arrested for stealing, he would be out in the streets in twenty-four hours. My car was broken into twice last month. I called the police — at least they came — but all they did was report it. In some places, even if you tell a policeman to come, they won't even show. It's just that there is too much crime, and they don't have time to deal with little things.

"There are times when I think I should have stayed in Hong Kong — that my work opportunities would have been better there. At least I wouldn't be laboring such long hours. It is very difficult here. Sometimes people call you boss, but in reality, you're working harder than your lowest paid worker. I get up at seven AM and at eight I leave for work. The practice in the past for this line of work is for everyone to meet in Chinatown, generally in a place where workers can have a Chinese breakfast, and then a van would pick them up. That's because the new immigrants can't drive, and you can't have them wait for you in the street when it is so cold, so the best way to get them to a job is to pick them up. So as a boss, you would have go to Chinatown to pick them up. But now I tell the workers that we meet on site, that the workday ends at the site and not when they are delivered to Chinatown. We will take them to a nearby subway, if there is one.

"I work over twelve hours a day. After working, I still have to do my books and go for estimates. I work from seven in the morning to seven at night. Right now I have nine people working for me. My partner and I bought an old house and are working on redoing it. But it's been hard for the last two years, because we ran out of money, and had to stop work on it. We wanted to sell it, but right now the market is bad, so we are renting it out as an investment.

"I still dream of going back to Hong Kong, to give my luck a try. Everyone seems to be afraid that the Communists will take over Hong Kong. I'm not worried about that. I see opportunity there. The problem is, I can't see myself working so hard for the rest of my life. In this line of work, once it is busy there is no time to think. But once it slows down, I keep thinking about what to do for the future.

"I don't know what I will do twenty years from now. A lot depends on where my children will be. The thing is, this is a good country for children to grow up in. As for myself, I am used to depending on myself ever since I was a child. My mother died when I was four years old. My sister brought me up. So I lack a sense of family warmth. I was without the sense of parental love. Sometimes I still feel lost."

Siu Wing Lai, 40 (Wife): "I insist my children speak Chinese at home. I will not speak with them in English. Every Saturday, they go to Chinese school.

"My status is a U.S. citizen, but in my heart, I can't confess to seeing myself as an American. I still look towards being Chinese more. I am still very concerned about what happens in China, and keep up with it by reading the Chinese papers.

"The good thing about living in this country is that you can be anything. Once you decide what you want to be, then you work hard, and can achieve it. The bad thing is the relaxed laws and the lack of family values. In school in China, they always taught you what is right and wrong. In this country, even if a student does something wrong, the teacher is afraid to correct him or scold him. It's like they don't want to impart strong values to students. Another thing is the relationship between parents and children. In this country, the relationship is very easygoing — not strict enough. In the Chinese culture, it is acceptable for the father to be very strict and to have a stern face in scolding childen. Children need to be corrected, otherwise how will they learn to behave? For instance, we have a neighbor whose son is known on the entire street as a bad boy. This is disgraceful. But not only do the parents allow him to roam about without correcting him, if you say anything, the parents will come to you and tell you off. So I tell my children, they are never to copy him. I just don't understand why Americans are like this. As for schools, there is no discipline. You can see that children start off fine when they are six years old, but over the next few years, they start to learn bad things like smoking or disrespect. But to tell you the truth, I feel teachers are almost afraid of telling students off. Every time you go see a teacher, all they say is how good the student is. They never criticize.

"I always tell my kids never to copy bad people. They must be good people before you can get close to them. My son has adopted the American way. He even dares to question me. 'Why do you always harp on such things,' he asks me. 'Other children's parents don't admonish their children. Why are you always yelling at me?' My son dares to say this to me, but my daughter listens a little more. I believe I am right, I tell my son. So he must listen. Some people raised in the country might think I am too serious about the need for respect, but I feel I am right — that respect for the parent is very important, and I will teach my children this.

"Homework must be done before anything else is done in the house. That is the rule. They have done this since they were little. I hope they will do the best. They don't have to be perfect. Since the beginning, I have not been able to help them in any of their homework outside of a little math. Certainly I have not been able to help with any of their English homework. Everything has to be done themselves. I tell my children, 'If you don't do well in school, society will have no use for you, so you can't blame anyone but yourself.' I tell them to look at us. They know how we came to this country. Look at your father, I tell them—he is working so hard today, because he can't speak English. I tell them there are a lot of things we can't help them with so if they don't work hard, they will not be able to catch up to others."

On Holidays: "We still observe Chinese holidays. Like I still buy moon cakes on Moon Cake Festival Day and tell my children what it is about. When we first arrived, we lived in Chinatown and celebrated Chinese New Year. But now we have a house in an area which is all non–Chinese, so we really don't do much to celebrate. The kids go to school on that day, and I don't make any special dishes. I just tell them that it is Chinese New Year, and that it is a special day. The longer we are here the less we do on the holiday. For instance, just before New Year's there is a special meal to close out the old year. We don't prepare that meal, because we eat chicken, fish and meat, almost every day, so why do we have to have those dishes again as a special meal? There is already so much to eat in this country, that we feel the abundance everyday. You can almost say now that every meal is a holiday meal, because we have so much."

ON THE BUMPY ROAD

Recently Arrrived
David Lee

David is twenty-eight years old and arrived in the United States from Taiwan in 1985. He speaks some English, but was more comfortable talking in Mandarin (a dialect of Chinese).

"I guess my goal is to go as high as I can, and keep aiming for the top and as much money as possible. I am doing it for my next generation. I want them to travel an easier path. But I haven't really found a way to do that yet. Right now, I'm taking fifteen hours of English classes a week.

"My first job in this country was to wash linen for a French restaurant. It was a tough job — seven days a week, twelve hours a day. I did it for three years and then was laid off. The restaurant wasn't doing very well. So I got some odd jobs, such as in a factory, hanging up clothes, and washing dishes in a restaurant. Then I saw an ad in the paper about a training program in setting jewelry. So that is what I am studying now. A friend of mine has a jewelry business in Taiwan, so I'm thinking maybe I can learn this and work out a profession for myself.

"My skills are in shipping — how to restore ships and the mechanical aspects of it. When I first came to this country, I tried to get a job in this area. But I couldn't find any. My life in this country has been very hard. Everyday, you work hard, and you want to do good, to earn a decent living. But after work there is nothing to do, unlike Taiwan, where there are lots of things to do for leisure. For instance, after work in Taiwan, you could call up friends, go have a late supper, take in a movie, or go for a stroll at night. Places are open twenty-four hours a day even. But in this country, things seem to close up by eight o'clock. And then, no one has time. If I have time, you don't have time. When you are free, I am working. So in terms of my existence, I feel it is pretty thin. At most I may call up my friends and chat on the phone. So it is not like the life I had in Taiwan at all, where whenever you were free you hung out or went out to eat. Here, we work long hours, but you can't say we do exceptionally well. We eat, go to sleep, then wake up and go to work. And everyday, it is the same thing. When you wake up, it's go to work. So mentally, the adjustment in lifestyle has been the hardest part for me. Nothing is fun anymore.

"My family is from Shantung, China. But I have never been there. I was born and raised in Taiwan, and that is where I feel my home and my country is right now."

Greedy about Life Again

Wong Chun Yau

Wong Chun Yau is seventy years old, heavy-set, with a deep infectious laugh. She is jovial and loud. She immigrated to the United States from China in 1979. She speaks no English. The interview was conducted in Cantonese (a dialect of Chinese).

"I look back at my life in China and I get scared. Now my life is worth something; it is precious again. In the past, I felt so what if I am shot, I just die. There wasn't anything to live for, anyway. But now, I am greedy about life again. I want to live.

"My daughter lived in San Francisco, so that's where I went when I arrived in this country in 1979. I was sixty years old. There was a social service agency there that provided orientation and training for new immigrants. So I enrolled in the eleven-week program. The first week, I was always sleepy because of the change in time differences. So I would rub my eyes and tears would come out. The teacher saw this and thought I had major problems in my life, and was troubled. By the fourth week she figured that maybe I needed some financial help, so after two hours of classes in the morning, she would send me to a job, where I made three dollars and twenty-five cents an hour for three hours. I said, 'Wow, more than three dollars an hour.' I had never made so much money in my life. I was ecstatic. My paycheck was over one hundred dollars a week. In China, I didn't even make one hundred dollars a month. And then they purged me there, too. In San Francisco I was sent to a hotel to clean bathrooms and pick up cigarette butts. It was work, and I couldn't believe I had such an opportunity to make money. People kept telling me how hard it would be in this country. But I say, this country is great. There is no comparison between China and the United States. One is striking the hot pot (a term for eating mongolian hot pot), and the other, is striking the rear end. Not only did I make more money here, I could also buy whatever I wanted. How great it is. The U.S. government is excessively wonderful.

Many of my friends tell me, 'Only you can get used to this country, many people can't.' I say it is true. I am very content. If I want something, I can buy it. So why not be satisfied? My sons have all prospered here, especially my youngest. He owns over six buildings. So, what is there to worry about? Nothing. My eldest son has three buildings. He gave me five hundred dollars for Chinese New Year this year, and when my daughter-in-law returned from China recently, she gave me a gold necklace for taking care of her two children. So isn't that a fine life? I am absolutely satisfied. My daughter graduated from medical school in China, and knows acupuncture. But she studied Russian in school. When she was going to school, China was friendly with Russia, and she refused to learn English. So now she can't do very much in this country, so she sorts mail for some company. Her husband is a doctor too. but he can't get a job here either. He has a practice in Hong Kong, and visits her once a year.

"I came to New York because my two sons were here. They had opened up a Chinese restaurant. So I took the ten thousand dollars I made in San Francisco and gave it to them to open a takeout place. But the place lost money, and so we closed it. Now my youngest son is doing very well; he's in insurance. The oldest is in renovation work."

Escape from China: "In China, I owned two houses. And if you had money in China, it was a crime. If you were an intellectual, it was a crime. The really poor, who didn't have a thing, they were the average, so no harm came to them. But if you had a cent, they would purge you. If you owned land, they would purge you. I was purged by the Red Guards twice. This was in the 1960s. Every time they had some movement, they would drag me out, and make me the center of the event. They took everything – my money, my furniture. Even now the furniture hasn't been returned. They beat me – took off my jacket and beat me. I was sick for three months after that. They stuck me in a cow pen. And then they kept telling me to list my crimes. In the mornings, when I got up, I would have to write. But what could I say? I didn't kill anyone, or set any fires. So what was I supposed to write? So they told me to write down all the things I did against humanity. But I couldn't figure out what I did against the people. I was never a thief or anything. It was a very painful period.

"I worked as a nurse for over twenty years. From seven to five I would go to work. But then from seven to nine in the evening, I would have to go to class to learn about the Party and communism. I was envied by a lot of people where I worked, because I was making over eighty dollars a month. And those who were new were making maybe thirty dollars.

"My husband swam to Hong Kong in 1962, and then all my children swam out of China into Hong Kong in 1967. Then they came to this country as refugees in 1970. But I didn't leave China until 1979 when my son petitioned to have me join him in America.

"When I was in my forties I followed some local guys trying to make the break. I am a good swimmer so I swam for almost three hours to the outer territories of Hong Kong, and I saw this fishing boat, so I asked to get on board, thinking, I am so close, this must be a Hong Kong ship. But as it turned out, the fisherman was from China, and he took me back because he could get twenty for returning me to the government. So I was purged and beaten, and beaten and purged. They even took a knife and stabbed me in my face. I still have this scar where they split open my mouth.

"Things are fine now in this country. I want to live to be one hundred. In China, I always wanted to die. There was hardly anything to eat and you had to work all day. If you wanted one particular thing, you couldn't get that particular thing. You could get only one dollar's worth of meat a month. And a dime's worth of fish a month. And even with the dime, you couldn't always find fish to buy. So I ate vegetables, lots of vegetables. I would salt them, and then dry them in the sun. Then I would steam them with some sugar. As for the salted fish — it was thirty cents a 'gun' (slightly over a pound), so I would buy the salted fish. For each meal I would just nibble at the fish for flavor, then eat a big mouthful of rice. A small nibble, then another mouthful of rice. If you had money, on pay day, you might go out to the farms and get the meat of some dead pigs or some real old pigs to eat. They rationed the rice — twenty 'guns' a month. Even if they allowed forty 'guns,' I would still be hungry. There was no oil, no meat. But here, I couldn't eat twenty pounds even if you gave it to me, because you have dishes such as chicken to go with the meal. In China, you ate chicken on New Year's Day and would have to wait until New Year's the next year to eat it again. Here, you could buy chicken by the pound. I love chicken so much, I eat it every meal now. Everything required ration tickets. Rice, bread, congee, everything required tickets. What's great about this country is I can buy a whole loaf of bread and even pastries and not need a ration ticket for them. Just the idea of being able to order a bowl of noodles, and not have to give a rice ticket — it's fabulous.

"They gave you just enough cloth to make one set of clothing. If you bought a pair of socks, it would be a few inches of material. All of it was rationed by the amount of material. The saying goes like this: 'A new set of clothes for three years, an old set for three years, and mending it again, you get another three years.' So it wasn't unusual to keep an outfit for nine years.

"My husband, at sixty, found himself another woman. She was thirty-two years old. He was in Hong Kong then and I was in China. He told everybody that I was missing and couldn't be found, so he divorced me and married her. He even had a huge banquet and invited all these friends. When I got to Hong Kong and applied to come to America, he was afraid

I would go after him, so he sold everything and moved this woman and their two children to Canada. Now I can't even locate him there, because no one would give us their address. He's afraid I would come after him.

"At this senior citizen center I go to, I don't have to cook, and there is a meal for me. When I am finished, someone even wipes the table. I go there even though I have to pay thirty-five cents for lunch, because they give me a dollar back for car fare, so actually, I am ahead sixty-five cents. Another place I can eat free, but there is no reimbursement for car fare.

"I even got a picture from President Bush thanking me for voting for him. I don't know which party he belongs to, I just voted for the one who would be most helpful for old people."

Still on the Move

Chin Cai Ping

Chin Cai Ping is in her mid-twenties. She immigrated to the United States from the People's Republic of China in 1984. She speaks little English so the interview was conducted in Toishanese (a dialect of Chinese).

"Being in Chinatown is like being back in the village in China. Everyday I am with Chinese people, I speak the language, and the food is the same, so it's not like being away at all. It's not unless I go into the country that I really feel I am in America.

"I met my husband in my village, and we married in 1982, and then he left for America. He returned for me a year later. We arrived in Seattle, and my son still lives there with my mother-in-law. My husband and I moved from there to Boston because we felt the wages in Seattle were very low. I found a job in a factory where I made belts and accessories, so that was pretty good. But then my brother asked my husband and I to go to New Orleans to open a restaurant. But New Orleans was very hot, and neither my husband or I could take the heat, so after a year, we moved to San Francisco. The restaurant was sold. We all left because it was just too hot there, and there were very few Chinese.

"In San Francisco, we couldn't find work, so we were pretty concerned. Finally, my husband's older brother, who is in the jewelry business, told us to join him in New York. So we moved five times in four years. New York is so hectic, it is hard to adjust to. I tried to learn how to sew and get a job in the sewing factory, but it paid very little money. It is hard to find a way to eat with that kind of job. I only spent half a year at it. Sometimes you got about fifteen cents for a skirt. Sometimes, when the style is hard, I make only seven dollars a day. The most I ever made in a day, working ten hours, was about twenty to thirty dollars. That's on a good day when the pieces are easy to sew.

"My husband works in a restaurant, in the kitchen, six days a week. Including the time it takes to travel, he is gone for about fourteen hours a day. He gets up at about ten in the morning, and is on the subway by ten thirty. He won't be home until after midnight. And on weekends, it is even longer. I studied a little English in Boston and in San Francisco. I really want to get a job with an American firm. But right now, even if I study English, there is no way to practice it at home.

"I like the freedom in this country, the freedom to go anyplace, and to find work. But what I don't like is the crime here. I was robbed when I was in Boston. They broke through a wall in my apartment and took everything. After that, I was petrified, so we moved out of Boston.

"We are planning to go back to China soon to take care of some paper-work on a building my husband's family owns. But I really don't want to go back. I've gotten used to things here. The only reason I do want to go back is to visit the ancestor's graves and make sure everything is okay there. I feel very privileged to be in the United States. I had heard when I was in China how many opportunities you had here. And I wasn't disappointed. As long as you work hard and are thrifty, you will have money. Even if you are thrifty and work hard in China, there is no way to get what you want.

"I have a three-year-old son who was born in America. I plan for him to grow up here because the politics in China is so uncertain. But my husband feels the education is much stricter in China, so he wants to send him back to school there. For instance, my niece is in fourth grade here, and when she writes, she's sprawled out all over the place. She doesn't even know how to sit right. In China, you have to sit very straight to write. You can't lean over and you can't lie down. You can't do whatever you please when writing. There is just too much freedom for kids here. It is not good. It's a bad habit."

One More Degree

Valerie Corpus

Valerie is in her mid-twenties. She was born and raised in the Philippines and immigrated to the United States in 1979.

"I don't consider myself Asian. I am Filipino. When I think of Asian I think of Singaporeans or Malaysians. It's culture. Tagalog is the language I speak and was raised on. That's what I speak. That and Spanish.

"I didn't like it when I first got here. It was April and it was cold. I had just turned sixteen and gotten out of high school. I didn't have any friends. I didn't like seeing bums on the street, or people kissing in the street or in stairways, or these kids selling dope.

"In the Philippines, we had house maids. I didn't have to do my own laundry, shopping, cooking, or washing the dishes. And when I got here, I had to do everything, and I really hated it. I told my mother that she was treating me like a maid. I was so mad at her. I kept calling Manila. I wanted to go back, because my grandmother was finally letting up on me. She was going to let me go out with my friends, and then I come here, and I had to do everything in the house. I kept calling Manila. I kept saying you have got to get me out of here; you have got to take me back. But my mother is sick. She has multiple sclerosis, so I had to take care of her. My sisters weren't here because they were still in high school in the Philippines. I hated everything. The most shocking thing to me when I came to this country was the bums on the street, and having to learn to deal with different types of people. I was on the subway one time, sitting down, reading one of my math books. And this white woman came up to me and told me I didn't belong here, and I should go back to where I came from. She said I had no right to be here and that she should be sitting in my seat. I didn't know what to do. I didn't do anything. There was a white man next to me, and he started talking to her about why she shouldn't say those things. Another time I was on the subway I was offered a seat, and these white women wanted to know *why* they weren't offered a seat when *they* were standing there before. So what I usually do is go to another car because I don't want to get into an argument over a seat. It doesn't happen anymore, because now I know basically when it will happen. You usually can see from the type of person, so I stay away from them. When I first arrived, I didn't know where to look when I was riding the subway, so I would look down because I didn't want to look at other people because I was afraid they might say something to me, and my English isn't that good. I'm really not aggressive so I wouldn't be able to yell back at them, and I'd end up crying. I would get off the subway, and end up crying. I'd say, 'Jesus Christ, help me.' You know what these people look like: They usually look like they didn't get the job they wanted or like there owe money. They need somebody to pick on, to take this out on, and I usually just walk the other way to avoid them. Now I've learned it's a matter of looking like you know where you're going, and know what you're doing. Other than that, I don't want to get picked on, in the subways or streets."

Education: "I have a degree in mathematics, and I want to work on a master's degree in health care administration. The pressure is on for me to get another degree. Most of my cousins are getting master's degrees. Naomi is getting a degree in marketing, another one is getting a degree in electrical engineering. My aunt's in Berkeley; she is working on her second degree. My father has three degrees in engineering: electrical, mechanical, and nuclear. Everybody has a degree in my family. My uncle says an undergraduate degree will soon be like a high school diploma, and a master's degree will be like a bachelor's, so that's why I am rushing. I want to get it before it is worthless.

"Money is why many Filipinos want to come to the U.S. Everybody leaves, everybody works outside the country. There is no future there. Many Filipinos go into nursing because they know they can get work visas to come to this country easier. Usually, when they hire nurses, the nurses look for housing in the area. Like with my aunt, she lives a block from the hospital, and she took three nurses to live with her, so the nurses can be more comfortable in a foreign country. Usually after their contract expires, the employer petitions to have them stay in the country. If not, they go back to the Philippines. I've heard of some cases too, when their visas expire, they might try to hide or maybe go to Canada."

Philippines: "Things are still pretty bad. They just try to cover it up. It's pretty much the same thing. Aquino has only been there for a few years and she has no experience in government. It will be at least ten years before I can feel she's done a lot to change it. Right now, it's pretty much the same. I have a cousin who is a communist. But I never discuss politics with him. I don't want to hear about these people in the mountains hiding or passing little notes to others for supplies. A few years ago, I stayed over my aunt's house in the Philippines. It was New Year's Eve. The next morning there was this dead body right in front of the house. And it was somebody who was 'salvaged.' It means he was killed someplace else, and his body was dragged there and shot again. That's what they did to warn people. Usually they say it was the cops who were responsible.

"I have an uncle, who was a med student. He was already married and had a daughter at the time. He was studying with the window open in one of the provinces. There was this woman who screamed for help in the street because she was being attacked, being raped by this man. And this man was one of the guards. He worked for an influential family. And so my uncle helped her, but she ran and he got shot. She ran away, and the man left. He was calling for help and nobody helped him. People just closed their windows because they didn't want any part of it. I don't want to go back and mess with things like that.

"Everything is who you know over there. That's what I learned. It's not what you know. Everything is done that way. You pay someone under the table to do this or that for you, you hire somebody because they can get things done for you, or you hire somebody's relative because you owe them a debt. That's the way things are done there. Personally I would rather owe people money. Like, if I wanted to become a librarian or teacher there, all I would have to do is go to one of the schools there where my grandfather has set up a scholarship, and tell them I am my grandfather's grand-daughter, then I would get the job. If I wasn't related, then I'd have to go through this whole long process.

"I have an uncle who's a general so whenever his kids or wife come here, or his relatives visit, they even bring their maid along. It is difficult enough getting out of the country, but to bring along the maid! They can get papers fixed from both sides. I have an aunt who was told the list was full, that she had to come back next year, but that when she applies there will be a ten-year wait. She's not on the right side of the family. Everything depends on who you know in the Philippines, and people arranging things for you.

"I like it a lot better here, because I have a future here. I don't have a future there. Because over there I would have to call up my uncle or my uncle's friend to ask him to help me do this or that, such as get a job."

Voting: "I just don't vote. I just don't care. As long as everything is fine in my life, I don't feel a need to. I mean, government doesn't seem to touch me, anyway. It doesn't seem to affect my life personally, so I don't worry about it. I read about it, but I won't worry about it. I don't see it as a respon-sibility. It's one of those things. Things are better now, because I've gotten used to it here. I am a citizen. As for going back the Philippines, it's fun to visit, but I would not go back to live again. I went back to the Philippines last year. I lived with my uncle. When I saw my uncle's maid who had raised him — doing the laundry and cooking — I wanted to help her, but my uncle said, 'Oh no, she can manage that, just mind your own business.' So it feels different, sitting down at the table and having someone serve you. All you have to do is eat and enjoy it."

Traffic Cops

Lang Ngan

Lang Ngan has handled more than five thousand Southeast Asian resettlement cases for the International Rescue Committee for the past fifteen years.

"Over the past fourteen years, the problems I have seen have changed because the types of refugees have changed. The first wave of refugees (two hundred thousand) who came to this country have done well. Most have settled in and joined the mainstream. But many who come today, tend to come from poor, less educated backgrounds. They have that 'Gold Mountain' dream. Part of that is because they get pictures from friends here, taken in a park, or in a nice place. Never would they get a picture taken from the South Bronx. So they think, 'Oh, in America you can get a house, a car, and good clothes.' But they don't realize how hard you have to work for it, or have any idea of Western life. So many are disappointed right away when they arrive.

"I have many clients who say, 'Oh, if I knew how difficult life is in this country, I wouldn't have come.' They had a misconception to begin with. When a few years go by and they've settled down, the emotional problems start. People miss their families. They feel that they are lonely in this country, and they are uncertain about their futures.

"Another thing I have seen as a case worker over the last ten years is a lot of marital problems. In Vietnam, Cambodia and Laos, and the Chinese culture too, the husband is always the head. In many families, women don't go out to work. Their job is to stay home and cook and raise the children, and take care of the older people, such as the husband's or wife's parents. Many families have at least three generations in the household. But after the family comes to the U.S., many of the men can't get a good job, and they are disappointed because they used to hold high positions in government or in the military. They used to be so powerful either in the family, in the community or in society. They are used to ordering people around and being obeyed. These types of families have more problems than white collar or blue collar families.

"Here, they feel useless even for the family let alone the community because of the lack of language. Some women can get jobs in factories, and those with a high school education can go for vocational training so in many families, the woman has become the bread winner. They not only make more money than the husband, they very often have better jobs. And of course, if a woman takes a job, she has a certain amount of a social life. Sometimes she goes to a party in the office or she goes out to do business with men, and the husband becomes jealous. I have many cases where the husband becomes jealous and abuses the wife by beating her. It is very common in Vietnam — a husband beating his wife. They think they have the right. They treat their wives like their children. And those families eventually will break up. Usually, the problems are resolved within the family by talking with the older people. They don't like bringing it out in public, to strangers — especially to American social workers. But I know about many of these problems because I learn of them from my clients. They won't go to a social worker to ask for help, unless they are unable to cover it up. For instance, I have one case where the wife was beaten on the street, and people called the police. The wife finally got protection by a court order. They generally will not come to us for help. It takes a long time for people to ask for help. Once they understand the system better, they start to come."

Generational Problems Between Parents and Children: "I get a lot of complaints from parents. They say they come to this country to give their children the chance for a better education, but now they lose their children. That is the culture shock. The children now think they are free to do anything they want. One child wrote a big number on her notebook. And the mother asked her, 'What is this number?' So she said, 'This is the child abuse number. My teacher told me if you beat me, I should call this number. You have no right to beat me. You will be fined; you will be imprisoned.' So the mother came in and asked if this was true. She now feels she has no right to control her children. It took a long time to explain to the child that her mother still had a right to teach her. The children just misinterpreted the meaning of the word.

"Another mother came crying to me saying that her daughter ran away because she coudn't catch up in high school. She had only two years of education in Vietnam, and because she was sixteen she was put in high school. She said she tried, but couldn't do it. So the guidance counselor suggested she go to a school for vocational training, and she said even for vocational training you need English, and she gave up. She went out and took a job. And now the mother came in to say she ran away with a man, and she doesn't even know where the daughter lives now. She came in, and cried, and asked for help.

"A woman came in with her son. The son has been having a very hard time at City College. He said he just could not understand the language. Even his professor had stayed after school for the past year trying to help him. His mother said he could do it because he was an honor student in math in Vietnam. The boy asked me to find him a foster home so that he could move out and not disgrace his family. He said, 'I don't want the pressure from my mother any more. Maybe if I could live in an American home, I could correct my accent.'

"An eighteen-year-old AmerAsian girl came in because she wanted to leave her adopted mother. Her father was an American soldier, her real mother, a bar girl. Her adopted mother was originally her baby-sitter. The girl's mother used to pay this woman to care for her, but she ran out of money and didn't pay anymore, and left the child with the baby-sitter. The baby-sitter adopted the child. Now the eighteen-year-old comes in to ask for help because she can't get along with her adopted mother and wants to leave.

"In many of the families, the children are now the main voice because they are the only ones that can speak English. Every problem has to go through the child. You know in the Asian family, the husband is the head. He is the only one who can talk for the family. The children used to have to obey all adults and their teachers because the adults knew more than them and they had to take their advice. But here, it's different. They think they know more than the parents because they can speak the language, and they've adapted faster to the American system and society than their parents. And now they think they are doing better than their parents so many of them don't respect the parents as they had before. And they think they are independent. They say, 'I have my rights. You cannot order me to do this or that.' These are teenagers.

"I have one mother who complained that when she asked her son to go with her to act as a translator, she had to bribe him — to promise to give him something. This time, the son asked for a Walkman, which the mother could not afford to buy him. I saw that lady a few days later in the subway, and she said, 'Can you believe it? I refused to give my son the Walkman, and he kept me waiting in this station for almost an hour. Now I have to go to the office by myself.'"

Gangs: "When I see clients I haven't seen in five or six years, I always ask them how things are. Many of them have similar complaints — that about their children. So they say, 'I don't know, at least if they don't join a gang, I'll be happy. But I don't think I can depend on them for anything anymore.' Because in Vietnam, the family unit was very strong, much of the culture was influenced by Chinese customs. But here, it is completely different.

"There are now Vietnamese gangs and Cambodian gangs in New

York's Chinatown. The stores that some of our clients are running in Chinatown or in the Bronx have to pay a protection fee. But the people don't want to talk about it. They are scared to death. And the gangs are definitely expanding. They are even sending people out to the Bronx and Queens. Whenever they know it is a store run by their own people, they will go. I have clients who have been robbed by the Vietnamese gangs made up of children. Many of the children come here without their parents — especially the boys. They are sent out because the new government would draft them, when they are fifteen. Many families can't afford to leave together, so they send one child out with the hope that one day the child in the U.S. will be able to sponsor them to come over. And many of those children are resettled by the foster care agencies, or go live with their relatives. I learned that many of those gang members are children that come from this background. The gangs are very skillful in recruiting these youngsters. They send people to the school to attract them, by giving them money for new clothes, taking them to the movies, taking them to eat good food. And they say, 'Oh, I know you are a new refugee, and I know what you're going through. I went through it too. You can look to me as a big brother.'

"A Laotian gangster said he was fifteen when he came to the United States. He was sponsored by a foster home. But the family had already sponsored another three Vietnamese teenagers. He was the youngest. So he was taken advantage of by the other children, who made him do all the work at home. And he was angry. That's why he ran away with a classmate. That boy and his family moved to San Francisco. He went with them, but when they got there the family had a place to stay, but he didn't, so he ended up in the street. There he joined a gang and said he even killed people. He had a tattoo and long hair. He said he finally dropped out because he was frightened twenty-four hours a day. He said, 'I thought I would come to this country to make a better life. Why should I end up in this situation? Therefore I decided to drop out.' Fortunately, he had a relative in New York, so he came to avoid being killed by the gang. These children end up in gangs without really understanding what happened to them. They often lack love or guidance and they end up going in the wrong direction. We don't have gangs in Vietnam. That's one thing we learned about in this country. There were bad people in Vietnam, but as long as you stayed away from them, you were okay. But here, it is different. You actually have people going to schools to recruit new members. And even for those who do have parents here, the parents don't know enough about how this society works to teach their children. They also have their own problems so they are negligent. They think the children will be like those in Vietnam, depending on teachers to teach them right and wrong."

Education: "I always tell the refugees on the first day when they come for orientation, 'Don't depend on the teachers in school. You have to watch your own children because here the teacher is not responsible to tell them how to be a good person.' In Vietnam, we did that. The teacher had a right to beat a student. There is no child abuse. There is no child welfare office. If the child is beaten by the parents, nobody will tell the police or any organization. Of course if a child is killed then the parents will be arrested, but it is not a crime to beat children. In Vietnam, it is the teacher's duty to teach children ethics and how to be good people. And teachers are very proud to be teachers. When you go out and run into a student, they all bow to you. And one time, I was eating in a restaurant, and I didn't know how to open the clams. My student was a waiter there. He stood there and opened every clam for me. I said, 'You need to do your own work,' and he said, 'No, you don't know how to do it. Let me do it for you.'

"As a teacher, there is a lot of respect, not only from the children, but from the parents as well. When I was a teacher and got sick, parents would make greeting cards and send them to me. And the children visited me with food. It's very different. So teachers feel a greater responsibility to the children. They act like they are the parents of the children in school. So parents don't worry when their children are in school because teachers have the power to control them. We seldom had any violations. And there are no security guards. If the child does anything wrong, the parents would be called up to take the child home, and the child would be dismissed from the school. It is very strict. There is no smoking of course. We didn't even have to discuss drugs. And the hair — you had to cut it really short. If you came to school with long hair and an unclean dress, you would be sent home."

The Gold Mentality: "There are certain types of cases that are more difficult than others. For instance, many Cambodian women come to this country alone or with their small children because their men were killed in war. They have a very difficult time adjusting.

"In one case, a woman was burned out of her apartment (the fire actually started in another apartment). She had been here three years and had no other place to stay and could not speak any English. So we found out about her, and helped her relocate to another apartment. I asked whether she could pay the fifty dollar moving fee to the trucker, and she said she had no money. But she said, 'I do have four taels of gold.' (A tael is a little more than an ounce.) So you can see from that they have a great distrust for banks, and even the value of money. They are scared that they wouldn't be able to get their money out of the bank. In their country, gold was the only thing that didn't change from day to day. The people still carry that culture into the new country. So whatever she saved, she bought gold with it. So now in Chinatown, you can see the gold stores are blooming. We tried to change their minds, telling them, 'You shouldn't take all your money to buy gold jewelry, or wear all that gold jewelry, because it could be very dangerous. You can attract thieves.' But they don't listen to you because that's the way many did it who lived through the war. They just don't trust the currency. Inflation was so bad, everything doubled in price overnight. So they don't keep currency. So now in the U.S., they do the same. When they have enough money to buy an ounce of gold, they go buy it."

Traffic Cops II

Kim Huot Kiet

Kim Huot Kiet is a Cambodian American who immigrated to the United States in 1975. He is one of the founders of the Cambodian American Society in New York.

"Overcoming problems of resettlement is a serious matter, so I don't know how to tell you yet how they will handle them. Some Cambodians are doing fine, but some are not. As I read in a report from the New York State Department of Social Services, about sixty-nine percent of the Cambodians in the state are on welfare.

"According to the 1980 census, there were about one hundred eighty-five thousand Cambodians in the United States. So in 1981 we got a federal grant to set up a mutual assistance association to help them. With my friends, I founded the Cambodian American Society. The purpose is to assist the Cambodian refugees sponsored by volunteer agencies, who have resettled in New York and New Jersey.

"Talking about problems for Cambodians, the Cambodians have a big problem because they don't know how to find jobs. They are afraid to go to work because of the language barrier. A lot are widows. Sometimes parents have a lot of small children and lack Cambodian daycare. Some Cambodians are illiterate. They can't even learn to write or read in their own language, how can they learn another one? So there are problems all along with the Cambodian people. Some have come to me — some Cambodians have a lot of children — they cannot depend on just one person working, they have to go to school, and after they've gone for some English classes, I might refer them to a maintenance job, or a cleaning job, so they can support the family. Some of the jobs pay minimum wage, and it is difficult to survive. And there are a lot of people that are hard to place. I think they have been on welfare so long, they have the welfare mentality and they can't afford to go to work because the jobs pay less money than welfare. This is according to family size. In Cambodia, the average family size is from four to nine children in each family. I have a family in New York. The mother has nine children. But three got killed, so she has six children with her. Three have gotten married. So another three are left. The mother is a widow. She is doing fine, but she is still on public assistance. But she tries hard to get the children to finish high school. Nowadays, one boy goes to college upstate, and two more girls are ready to go to high school this year. Another family is orphaned. There are seven children. The parents were killed during the war. They came to this country from a camp where they stayed for a few years. The oldest was eighteen and the youngest was five years old when they came in 1981. I tried to introduce them to a friend who introduced them to another friend. These people loved the children, and go to visit them every weekend. They try to practice English with them. And now the oldest sister is a medical technician. Another is going to accountant school, and is working. Two other boys are working, one in a hospital and the other in a kitchen. Only one boy and two girls are in school. They were supported by public assistance."

Traffic Cops III

Charles Ryu

Charles is a thirty-year-old Korean American who immigrated from Korea 11 years ago. He is a minister in the Korean Methodist Church and Institute in New York City.

"When we left Korea, each person could carry only four hundred dollars with him. We came to America, bought a little junk car, and we were literally penniless. You work, you save, little by little. That's why some people work sixteen to seventeen hours a day, seven days a week, to do overtime. That's where the savings are made. Now you might have a bank make a loan to you. But in the seventies it was all self-made work.

"In New York, the Koreans run small vegetable and fruit stands because that is the only avenue open to them. Not because they have an aptitude for it. Why do Greeks open gyro restaurants? Or why did the Chinese go into the laundry business? In Los Angeles, Koreans aren't into fruit stores. They open sweat shops. They get the money to open these shops by working and saving.

"If you look at Korean history from nineteenth century on, the term 'leisure' didn't exist. I think Korea, Japan, China, from the twentieth century on, didn't know how to take leisure time off, and they couldn't afford to take leisure seriously, because they had work to do – to catch up, and rebuild society in many ways. Few Koreans see themselves as 'working hard,' some do, but many see it as a sacrifice they're willing to go through, to set up this base for the second generation. In some ways, this working is stifling. My cousins, my uncles, my friends, they all work seven days a week, twelve hours a day.

"In terms of family relationships, this has become a strain. When they first came to America, the family was close so they could afford to do this. But after twenty years, that is breaking down and causing major problems. So now I try to tell them, try to work fewer hours and you still have three meals a day. God will take care of you. Relax and spend some time with the children, your wife and with yourself.

"One of the most serious problems is the lack of parental care of their children. Parents just don't have time to spend with their children and vice versa. See, you can discipline your children to study hard. As long as you can make your children believe you love them, you don't need to spend twenty-four hours a day to affirm it. The basic assumption of caring is part of the Korean culture, which American culture lacks tremendously. So with the lack of supervision, some children can still do well – but not all. Also, the numbers of those not doing well is on the rise. Also for those who do do well – you can pressure the kid, without being there at all. This can have negative effect on the kids.

"Many people of the second generation don't have this spontaneous creativity. They don't seem to speak freely, because they always have this pressure to excel in order to be accepted by their parents, their peers and the American community. It's a fact with them: 'I'm nobody unless I excel or do really well. Then I am accepted by the main society, as a peer, on an average level. Nobody will pay any attention to me unless I do something extraordinary, and then I'm not at the level of extraordinary with Americans, but on the level of commoners.' For survival, the need for overcompensation is very strong. So you just push yourself. And when you do that, you don't grow as a holistic person."

Education: "Koreans are obsessed with higher education. Most Koreans see education as a means of establishing themselves in America. Education does not guarantee it all, but it is one bargaining chip you can have. When it becomes an obsession, it is not healthy. A lot of Korean immigrants who are well educated come here and bag groceries. Some have PhD's. So regardless of whether or not they push it, there is a sense of transference to their children. It is true that a relatively large percentage of Korean children do well in schools, but not all. We somehow expect minority groups to be forever lost. But they come here – suddenly there are over two hundred Koreans at Yale – over one hundred fifty at Columbia – and it shocks people. But this is just a few hundred out of a million Koreans in the country. There are many, many more that are lost, that don't quite make it to the fancy schools. But the fancy schools are perceived as the norm, so the pressure is incredible. Part of my ministry is to destroy the myth that you have to go to a certain school to have a good life."

Who's Coming: "The first Korean came in 1903 as a laborer on a sugar plantation in Hawaii. But the Chinese exclusion acts put an end to Asian immigration. But by 1965, the immigration law changed, and they lifted the barriers against race, and so quotas were set, and starting in 1967, twenty thousand people a year came from Korea. During the seventies most who came were highly educated, the upper class. The fact that they were highly educated, middle class, and urban was an advantage to them in establishing in America in such a short time. Whereas immigration prior to that was poor, rural, Koreans coming to urban America with very little education.

"There are about a million Koreans in this country now. The largest settlement is in Los Angeles where there are four hundred thousand. Second largest is the greater New York City area, then Chicago, Washington D.C., Philadelphia, and San Francisco. They tend to be near big cities. During the late seventies there was an economic boom, and now with hope for democratization that's taken place recently, one reason to come to America has dropped—that is the image of America is if you go there, you work hard, you can establish a good life. That myth is shattered because experience for Koreans here for the last twenty years has been very, very hard, It's still very hard. And you don't have to work that hard to maintain an upper middle class life in Korea. So people who belong to that category don't come to America anymore. Only the lower income bracket, those who don't have much chance in Korea, come.

"So what that means for the nineties I don't know. But the change can be seen now. It might permanently sever two different types of Korean American communities—Korean American ghettos, and those wealthy Koreans, called the upper middle class—kind of like the Chinatown syndrome, and those living outside."

AMERICANIZATION

To Be More Japanese

Henry Moritsugu

Henry is in his fifties, and is a Japanese American. He was born and raised in Canada. He now lives in the United States and works as a newspaper editor.

"There is no way we could teach our children Japanese at home. We speak English. It wasn't a conscious effort that we did this. It was more a question of circumstances, because of the closing of the schools during the war. Certainly some parents discouraged it because of the war, but we didn't make it a point to learn Japanese. It was more important to be accepted. I can speak a little Japanese, but I can't read or write it. My son can speak. He studied the language in college. I feel proud about that. Before the war, ninety percent of the Japanese children went to Japanese school. But that was stopped with internment. I was always afraid to go to Japan, because I don't speak adequate Japanese. I expected to be ridiculed. So my wife and I went when my son was in Japan; we actually made it easy for ourselves by staying with him. We were very sensitive to what we considered our inadequacies. I wish I could speak the language better. I love Japanese food. I love going to Japanese restaurants. Sometimes I see Japanese groups enjoying themselves at karaoke bars, singing to tapes in the background and having a good time. I would love to join in that kind of thing, yet I'm not quite part of that. I feel definitely Western more so than Asian. My children feel that way too. It's the only way. But we look Asian, so you have to be aware of what you are. You go along for days, weeks, months, thinking you are one of them, then something happens to cut you short, so you really have to be on guard. I think we all have identity crises at some point.

"I still feel there's a stigma sttached to being Japanese because of what happened in the war. Sometimes people look at me and wonder. But usually they think I am Chinese. Like when I am in a bar, people ask me if I am Chinese or Japanese. The bartender would say, 'You can't call him

Henry, 8, and Ted, 3, with mother, Shizuko, 43, in front of tar-paper shack home in Tashme internment camp near Hope, British Columbia (1942).

Chinese—he's Canadian.' But underneath all that, there is prejudice there. Half the time people mistake me for Chinese. Generally they don't know to ask. Usually when they do ask, it is out of curiosity. They say, 'What's your background?' And I'm proud to say I'm of Japanese descent. I don't know why I should be proud, but I am.

"When people ask about internment, or my feelings about it, I think first that most Americans are not aware that Japanese in Canada were also interned. That's a big surprise to a lot of people. It's a big surprise to Japanese people too. Of course, many non-Japanese Americans did not know about the evacuation when it was happening. But I would be more likely to tell them proudly about how I was interned as a kid. I've been trying to figure out what my feelings were then. I was seven when Pearl Harbor happened. My family lived in British Columbia. In Canada, it was the Mounties who were in charge of moving us. One hundred miles from Vancouver, there was a town called Hope. We were ordered to go there. From the trains, we boarded stake trucks and were driven to a place called the Fourteen-Mile Ranch. There was a caravan of three trucks. We passed this long stretch of river gorge. It was a really treacherous road. The next impression I had was arriving there. Houses were being put up. There was an open field with grasshoppers. I had never seen so many grasshoppers, flying and jumping all over me, and it was a beautiful spring day. I was only a kid. It seemed like fun. But of course I'm sure I felt some of the sense of shame that my parents were feeling.

"Only half the buildings were built by then, so for the first three months we had to share the house with other families. We strung up some wire, and draped some sheets and blankets over it to separate ourselves from other families. We weren't allowed to leave. That was enforced. Only the men had to go to work camps during the day. My father would come back and stay with us at night. I think the adults in the family were definitely affected by this. My dad was a gardener. My brother thinks my father turned prematurely grey because of the evacuation. He was sent to a work camp with my brothers to help dig ditches and build highways. They were paid twenty-five cents an hour, while the women and children remained in the internment camps. The children didn't know what was really going on. We played; we had fun; we didn't realize we were being deprived of our freedom. We stayed in the internment camps for one and a half years, then we received permission to leave for Ontario. My family deemphasized being Japanese after that.

"I think something like that can happen again to any ethnic group. The whole racial thing is there, and will never go away in America. I think it will be more difficult now because of World War II and what happened, but it still can happen to any racial group. It's nothing you can prepare your children for. They become aware of it on their own. I don't talk about that period to my children at all. Perhaps it's come up when they prepare for a high school project. But we've never made a big discussion about it. That experience taught me a lesson: even in a democracy, there is always some way people can violate your constitutional rights.

"Today I consider myself a Canadian, and not Japanese. My children's

Moritsugu family in February, 1943. Back row: Ken, 18, and Harvey, 17; second row: June, 13, Frank, 20, Eileen, 15; third row: Joyce, 9, Dad (Masaharu), 50, Mom (Shizuko), 43, Henry, 8; in front: Ted, 3.

lives are totally Western. There is no attachment to Japan. Once in a while I'll get into something really culturally Japanese, then my wife thinks I'm really putting on airs, and she reminds me that I'm really a Western person.

"We're interested in Japanese movies. We've seen a lot in the last ten

years in New York. We encourage our children to do the same. My older
boy in Japan is interested, but my younger boy, he is not, and has never
come with us to the movies. The movies would be primarily in Japanese
with subtitles. We can understand maybe a third of the story in Japanese.
We go because we can re-identify with it. Even though we are not that
Japanese. We also think we're somewhat like these people. We sympathize
with their way of thinking, and understand why they react the way they
do on certain things.

"The biggest Japanese holiday is the New Year. We celebrate that.
Everyone celebrates that. But I don't celebrate the emperor's birthday. I
would tend to celebrate Victoria Day, which is a holiday in Canada. I
remember as a child that New Year's was a time for a lot of feasting, and
food would be laid out. Today, we visit our relatives in Canada for New
Year's, and we still eat Japanese foods, such as sushi and sashimi. We would
munch all day. The food would be laid out all over the table, and covered,
and we would eat it whenever we wanted.

"Sometimes I am still reminded in a joking way of the war. For the last
twenty-five years, this friend has sent me a telegram every December
seventh."

To Be More American

Cao O

Cao O is a Chinese who was born in Vietnam. He came to the United States from Vietnam in 1975 when he was in his late teens.

"Confucianism was part of me, part of the culture, and it was part of how my family lived. I have the values — obeying your parents, being a good citizen, taking care of your family. I can't deny the existence of Confucian values on my life. But after being here in this country for a few years, I started to develop my own value system, and I don't necessarily take Confucianism as my Bible anymore.

"When I first arrived, I took some odd jobs, delivering newspapers, and as a janitor in a daycare center. I was also trying to study, understand the language, and the facts of life — like how should I behave — the customs, the habits. At the time, we were living with our sponsor. Every night, he would tell us, that's not the way you should eat — you don't hold up your bowl. He taught us how to use forks and knives. We watched television to learn about the American way of doing things. We learned all the basic things — even doing laundry. We had never used a washing machine before. We had no refrigerator at home. Now there was one, but what do you do with it? Now what I use to eat with, depends on who I am eating with. In a way, I'm in between Chinese standards and American standards. At home we don't use the small rice bowls any more. We use the American soup bowls to eat with. Yet my family would use chopsticks to go with that. We don't pick up the bowl anymore. I guess I picked up the habit of not lifting my rice bowl, and it is a part of me now. I'm also much more conscious about certain living habits — like privacy. Before, my family all lived and slept in one big room. Now I have to have my own room. In Vietnam we had seventeen people in my family, including grandparents and cousins, and we all stayed in the same place. We had no individual bedrooms. We just all stayed in one big area. It was like one floor, and we had sections. One section would have four to five people. Also in America, you have

104

rugs and sofas. We never had those things, so you kind of enjoy that way of living.

"Delivering papers on the west side of the Village, even one day a week, was hard. We spent from six in the morning to five (with no break), going from block to block. They had a van with a few people. they would drop you off in one corner and meet you at another corner. Then my sponsor got a job with a refugee resettlement center, so he got me a part-time job there. Everyday I was supposed to turn on the computer, and connect that with the computer in Washington D.C. Everytime I picked up the phone, the other end couldn't understand what I said. It was a simple statement to connect the computer. But people just couldn't understand. After awhile, the guy at the other end just recognized my voice, and would turn the computer on.

"I moved out of that sort of existence by spending a lot of time learning the language, and by being open to constructive criticism. Basically my sponsor would correct me if I didn't say a word right or if I didn't behave appropriately in the American sense. He would tell me, 'Hey, you don't do it that way – from eating habits, to sitting habits. I guess if I was too proud of myself I couldn't take the criticism, then there would have been a barrier to learning. But it was hard because even though I knew I needed to do this, I wasn't a five-year-old kid anymore. After a while, I wondered why everything I did was wrong.

"I graduated from Cornell with my BA, then got a master's degree in social work from Hunter College. Now I am going for my doctorate in social welfare at Columbia University.

"Being a Chinese male in Vietnam, the expectations from the family were different than for a male in this country. In Vietnam, my role was defined by the family. We were expected to study hard, to get a degree, to get married, to get a job, and to carry on the family tradition – such as the family name, honor and heritage. It was very important for a family to have a son. If a couple didn't have a son, they would be worried about the next generation. Daughters were good, but they eventually leave the family once they are married. So for the continuity of the family name, you need a son. So generally speaking, people valued sons more so than daughters. Being a son meant a little more status in the family. Just like the family will put all its hope on the son. A family business, for instance, would always be turned over to the son, but never the daughter. The expectations were also different for males. You were expected to do well.

"Now I don't want my family to tell me what to do. I control my own destiny. I see myself as having a role in this country. There aren't enough trained Asian social service workers. This is especially so in the Southeast Asian community. You can count on one hand the number of social workers. I see myself as someone who can make a contribution, and I don't care what my family says about what I want to do. My family would prefer me to do something else. Back home, they would have expected me to be a teacher, or to get into some sort of business. At first when I came here and went to college, my major was in computer science. My family was so happy about that. My father (who was in Vietnam at the time) was proud that he had a son in America studying computer science, one of the newest fields, with the potential for opportunity and great success. My mother told me that once in a while the parents would get together and talk about their sons and daughters overseas. So my father would talk about me studying computers, while another relative might say his son was studying engineering, or something like that to compare. But two years after I started college, I changed my major to sociology. Then the talks between the parents stopped. My father stopped talking about me because he was disappointed. When I was a kid, he taught me math, and I was pretty good. So it was a natural transition from math to computer science. But sociology — it just didn't have the same stature because of money. Asian families in general value success in economic terms. They wondered what kind of job I could get in sociology. You can't make any money from it. To them, there is no job you can take to make money in sociology, so you're not successful. When I decided to apply for the degree, I wasn't thinking of a job, it was more for my own intellectual understanding. I want to teach someday, but right now, I would like to work in the field. I believe in action, in helping people. As a refugee, I was really touched by the help I was getting. People giving me food, clothing, some people offered apartments to us, agencies helping us with jobs and language classes, so I think the whole thing about volunteer work, helping others, really inspired me to get into social work. But at the time, I had no idea what social work meant, or that it was a profession.

"I am grateful to be in this country because of all the opportunity this society provides. I think if I were still in Vietnam, I could not have developed to the level that I am at now. I've always valued the learning opportunities here. You can do a lot of things, and you have the freedom that the system provides.

"Now having said that, I am not proud to be American, for the fact that America has done a lot of wrong things in the world. Simply put, the war in Vietnam is one example. I am not proud to go around to other countries and brag about the glory of America. So in that context, being an American is a necessity, and is not something I am proud of."

Looking American

Alicia Diem

Alicia is forty and Vietnamese. She arrived from Vietnam in 1984. Alicia is a pseudonym used at her request.

"How can I feel I am American? If you say you are American, you must look American, and speak English perfectly. That means being white. No, even if I live here ten or twenty years, I cannot say I am American. Even if I get citizenship, I cannot say I am American. I am still Vietnamese with American citizenship. I cannot say I am American. Black hair, black eyes — how can I say I am American? If I got married to a Vietnamese man and my children were born here, they would still be Vietnamese, but American citizens."

No Tea, Thank You

Setsuko K.

*Setsuko is forty and came to the United States in her twenties. Her hus-
band works for a Japanese firm in this country. Both her children were
born in the United States. The family lives in a New Jersey suburb.*

"I want my children to be proud of Japan and being Japanese, so it is
important that they learn the language and culture. Deep in my heart, I
want to go back to Japan, but my kids want to stay here. If they marry
American people, then I will have to stay here to be near them. I would
prefer them to marry Japanese, but I don't feel they have to. It depends on
the personality of the person. Right now, my parents are in Japan, so I want
to go back. If they die, I won't want to go back. But right now, I would
like to go back.

"The thing I like best about this country is that I don't have to worry
about anything. If I don't want to be a friend, I don't have to. In Japan, I
would have to socialize with everyone. I lived in a small town, so I would
have to socialize with everyone. People are very friendly. I don't know
anything about American society. That is why I can say it is easy to live
here. I don't socialize with the American community, so I don't understand
any of their problems. Most of the time I feel welcome, but sometimes I feel
people are mean. It is the same as in Japan. My friend who lived in the town
moved to another one. They don't say anything to her when she says hello.
In this town they are more friendly.

"I don't think I've changed much, living in the United States, but
everytime I go back, everybody says I have changed. I don't know why
everyone would say that. Here, for instance, I asked you this morning if
you wanted a cup of coffee. You said 'No,' so I did not serve it to you. But
the last time I was in Japan, my mother's friend visited me. I asked her if
she wanted a cup of tea, and she said, 'Oh no,' so I thought she didn't want
it, so did not serve anything. Then my mother came and said, 'Setsuko, you
have to ask more.' So I said, 'Why?' She said, 'You just have to ask more.

And if someone says "no," you better bring her a cup of tea anyway.' Here, if someone says yes, it means yes. If someone says no, it means no. So it is easy to understand. But in the Japanese way, I have to ask more, and I had to serve that cup of tea. Here, I have to say exactly what I want. But in Japan, you can't do that. Like the tea — deep inside, the woman really wanted a cup of tea. But to be polite, she just said no. So you have to really understand what a person wants deep inside. My children are American. They probably wouldn't understand such subtleties.

"I cannot communicate in this country. That is why I feel it is important that my children speak Japanese. So they can talk to me and my family. Speaking English is important so they can communicate with Americans. I speak Japanese with my children. This is important because my parents and my husband's parents are still in Japan, and I hope my children can communicate with them. My oldest son loves Japan, but my daughter doesn't like it as much. My hometown is in the countryside, and the bathroom is in the ground so she is afraid to use it. My younger daughter is more like an American, and the older one is more like a Japanese. They were both born in this country, but they speak Japanese with me. They go to Japanese school once a week. The boy is thirteen, the girl eleven.

"I am a Buddhist. But I don't do anything religious in my home here. When I go back to Japan, I do. I really don't talk about religion with my children. They don't ask me about it or go to church. When they go back to Japan, we have a shrine, and every morning, we serve it tea and water and rice, and they ask me why. But my mother does it everyday. She lights incense and bows.

"I serve mostly Japanese food for dinner. But my kids eat cereal and spaghetti and macaroni. But dinner time is usually Japanese food: sometimes tempura, sometimes fish, miso soup and vegetables.

"March third is Girl's Day in Japan, I have a daughter, so I have a doll for her. May sixth is Boy's Day, and we eat cake on that day. The big holiday is the New Year, and we have a big meal with just my family."

Tensions

Mono Sen

Mono Sen is in his sixties and immigrated from India in 1971.

"I ask my people, 'In the last fifteen years, how many of you have donated to the police association's activities? How many of you get involved with the community centers? None, or very few, right? So get involved, otherwise you are compounding the problem, because the people in the neighborhoods think we feel superior to them, so they don't like that. That impression is created by you (the Indians) — that you are a nation of takers, and not givers. Get involved, into the mainstream, into community service and activities.'

"Our Indian people are a little withdrawn. Unlike the Chinese and Japanese people in America, Indian people are not getting into the mainstream. Until 1982, the Indian people did not get involved in the mainstream. The Indian people are very unique. Many are doctors, engineers, scientists and business people. They don't need favors from the politicians. That is why they keep thinking they don't have to go to the politicians for a job. But at the same time, the melting pot theory has become obsolete. Over the last two years in New York, New Jersey, and Pennsylvania, I have personally handled cases against Indian people, perpetrated by misguided youths. In Philadelphia, two Indian vendors were subjected to physical atrocities and assaults because they were selling hot dogs; the Italian people, or whoever they were, beat these vendors because they were potential competitors. The same things happen in Long Island. You know, Indian family homes were burglarized and broken into. In White Plains, one Indian family — a doctor and his wife — were killed. We have offered twenty-five thousand dollars to catch the killer, but we have not found them. In Jersey City, there is a group called Dotbusters because the Indian women wear dots on their heads, and they tried to assault Indian women. Last month, in East New York, Indian and Pakistani students were physically assaulted by an eighteen-year-old girl.

110

"In October of 1988, an Indian went to Parsippany to sell real estate. He was attacked by a white guy, asking, 'Why are you in my town?' And he replied, 'I am a salesman. I am selling real estate.' So he went to lodge a complaint to the police department, and the police said, 'What brings you here, to our town?' So there is a sense of hostility to the Asian people."

Being Indian in Jersey City

Hardayal Singh

Hardayal Singh is Asian Indian. He is in his mid-fifties and arrived in the United States from India in 1977. He works as a security guard for a medical center. He has also been active in organizing the community. He owns a home in Jersey City where a mysterious group identifying itself as Dotbusters has threatened organized attacks against Indians.

"I think we ethnic people don't know much about the rules of law and order in this country. Because of that, sometimes we have problems and don't know how to take care of them. We had trouble with the local police officers. The mayor, and elected officials helped us, but the low level police officers ignored us. Here, if we complained about some crime about us, they don't care. The lower level police officers were against the Asian Indians.

"One Indian, Mr. Navroz Mody, was beaten unconscious by a group of teenagers in Hoboken. He died. Mr. Mody was a CitiCorp manager in Manhattan. He was only thirty years old. There were four boys arrested in the case, all between the ages of sixteen and eighteen. We wanted them to be tried as adults. I called together our people in the community, and we started the United Indian American Asociation. We arranged five different demonstrations to request that one of the underage boys involved be tried as an adult. They were going to treat the boy as a juvenile. He is sixteen years old. I approached the authorities and asked the governor's office to recommend to the courts that they not treat him as a juvenile, but as an adult. One was six months from eighteen, another was seventeen years old. When we demonstrated, all the media covered it — *New York Times*, CBS, the news stations. And after that, the attorney general's office agreed with us, and they said they would command them to be treated as adults, not as juveniles.

"Since we took this action, things are better. Before, they attacked Indians everyday. They attacked over twenty different families. They broke into houses, Indian shops and stores. They attacked Indian women going shopping. They point their hands at them in the street. They beat up on them. But now it is in control. Now there is less fear when we walk the streets. Before, I received many calls from people in my community every-day. But now it's quiet. Because of this I feel things are better. There is less hostility now. Fifteen thousand Indians lived in this area before. After this last attack, a lot of Indians moved from Jersey City to other towns.

"I believe the people in this country are basically nice people. They treat ethnic people like their own families. If they did not behave, nobody would want to come. There is respect and welcome for ethnic groups. Because of this, our people like to settle in America. My daughter was born in this country, and when we met Michael Dukakis in his election cam-paign, he asked her name, her age, and plans. She said 'I wish to become President of the United States of America.' She said, 'I am born American, but I am proud my parents are Indians.' She's American.

"I am working in the Jersey City Medical Center in the security depart-ment as a security officer during the night shift. I never tried to get another job. When I am free, I do social work. I like to get together with people, and share their problems and happiness."

Marriage by Arrangement: "When we had racial problems with the Dotbusters in Jersey City, I met with some American authorities. One time the Chief of Police said, 'If you teach your young boys to go to the restaurants and bars to make friends — I know you don't allow your girls to go to such places — you can mix with American people, and this will be a good thing. Also tell your young boys to make merry with American girls, not Indians, then they will fight for you, because they will say, 'This is my husband.' When I met with my people and told them this, they said, 'Singh, don't give this advice.' Sometimes for immigration, or the green card, some Indians will marry an American girl. But Indians, they like their own country's girls. It will take time to mix with Americans. Our new generation, after ten, fifteen years, maybe, will do this.

"We are very worried about our religion and culture when it comes to our daughter. In India, things are are totally different from the United States. My daughter has been told many times, she will marry an Indian. We plan to send her back to India next year. She will take all her education there. We wish her to adopt Indian culture. We don't hate American culture, but we like our culture. We will choose a husband for her, but we will give her the freedom to see and talk to him first. This is an old tradition. We teach our children that it is not good to have sexual relations with others when you are not married. In India, no lady can have a child before marriage. No one can have a boyfriend or girlfriend for that. This is illegal. Maybe you are an adult, but it is illegal. I think this is better. Sex is God's gift. No one can control it. Parents teach their children not to get pregnant. But in this country, they cannot control it, because young people have their boyfriends and girlfriends and they just enjoy it. They don't know about their culture or responsibility. There are no thinking fathers, like elders. This is a bad system. Some young girls have many boyfriends. They live one year here and one year there. We don't like these things. Everyone knows that one has sexual relations with the wife but nobody can kiss on the outside. And all the time, we watch our children. Even now, I cannot touch my wife in the presence of my daughter, in the presence of my friends or relatives. When we sleep, we can go to our bedrooms. I can say all Indian children in this country like our own tradition. You never can say, 'I saw one Indian girl with her boyfriend.' You cannot say 'I saw one Indian girl in the beer bar.' You never see an Indian girl smoking, taking beer, or taking wine. Sometimes, highly educated and the richest people, but they enjoy it with their husband; not in public, not in the restaurant, not in the bar.

"Weddings between young people in this country are still arranged. Nobody can trust this through meeting boyfriends or girlfriends. When a young person likes a certain boy or girl, he turns to his parents and says I like this person and it might be arranged that way. I never met my wife before the wedding. Our parents arranged our marriage. In our country when you marry off your daughter, you have to give her a dowry: gifts, gold, money, house, car, motorcycle. This is a tradition. They try to give her a full house. It's still like that today. Parents they try to give their daughters everything for the house. They said, 'If you live with your in-laws, good. If they don't like you, you don't like them, then you can take your separate house, and live with your own stuff.' Sometimes separating means getting a separate room. On the wedding night, they have hundreds of people at the girl's home to celebrate. After that, after the guests leave they say to the groom, this is your room, your wife is inside, go and see her. When he goes in, he will give her a ring. Her face is covered. When he enters, she knows: no one can enter here, except my husband. And he gives her the ring, and presents some gifts to her, and he will open the covered veil, and see the face. That's it. There is very seldom divorce. Most people try to work it out. When a guy gives a problem to his wife, the relatives get together, and tell him not to do this or that. They talk nicely. And if she gives him a hard time, then they talk to her. In our country, there is no such thing as marrying several times. You have only one marriage. If she divorces or he divorces, they can't get a second marriage. Only if the husband or wife is dead can you remarry. You can't have three, four, or five marriages like in this country. We don't like that practice."

Food: "Sometimes I cook; sometimes my wife cooks. We buy our own groceries in Indian shops, and cook at home. Most Indian foods are not ready-made; we cook it ourselves. We cook rice and curry. We make our own bread every day at home. When we are in a hurry, we have American food—ready made food. When we can, we cook. Indians cook at home. That is the tradition. We don't have ready-made food as in the big stores.

We cook two times a day at home. In India, eighty percent of women don't work. They only take care of their husbands and children and home. Husbands earn the money, the man is the boss; he's the head of the family. He has the responsibility to run the house. But in this country both husband and wife work. In this country, all ethnic people come for the money, to make money. They work hard here because of the value of the money. If you send the dollar to your country, there is lot of difference. The incentive to make the American dollar is greater.

"Our daughter likes American food, so we buy it for her. My wife is Hindu, and I am Sikh. We don't eat beef, and we never bring beef home. My daughter knows this, so she doesn't compel us to bring beef home. But when she goes with us to the restaurants, she orders beef, and we don't care. She is American. When she is in school, they give beef to her and she likes it. She asks, 'Can I eat this?' You cannot stop her. The majority of Indians never eat beef. If they eat it, they never tell anybody. If they do eat it, they get it in a restaurant. Nobody brings beef home. The cow is sacred. We worship them. In this country you can get many types of milk for the children. But in our country we don't have milk. It mostly comes from women. We believe if women give their own milk to their child it is helpful and healthy. But if a child's mother is dying, you can give cow's milk. We believe that a women delivers a baby in nine months, and a cow also takes nine months to deliver a baby. Cow milk is like mother's milk. So we believe that if the cow can give milk, butter, yogurt, why do you kill them? Why do you eat them?

"By birth I am Indian. India is a great country. I have the same respect for this country. Legally, if we adopt this country, we should respect this country as we do our country. Still, you cannot ignore your birth country. When I came, my English was very poor. I had problems. I could not work. Now things are better. But because of language, I still feel more comfortable with Indians."

Racial Hatred

Madhu S. Chawla

Madhu is eleven years old and was born in the United States. She is the daughter of Hardayal Singh.

"We don't speak well. They don't like us because of our culture. We get things because we're educated. Some of them are not educated and they would say, 'How come you're educated and we aren't?' They're jealous. But we're really not that educated. My dad went up to tenth grade and my mother went through college. I don't really like it in school when they say, 'Hindu, you ugly Hindu. You're gross. I'm not your friend because you're Hindu.' So I really don't talk to anybody in my class, and I tell my teacher I want to sit in the back row, so she makes me sit in the back of the class. In the front they say, 'Don't touch me. You're disgusting. You eat roaches.' They're serious when they say things like that. They are not kidding around. My school only goes up to the fifth grade. I'm in the fourth grade. There are only about ten to fifteen blacks in the whole building. The rest are Puerto Rican, Filipino and American. There are only four Indians. When I try to go down this block, some of the older black boys put their feet up so that I will trip and fall. It makes my head bleed. Once this girl smacked me really hard, and I smacked her back. They were chasing me, so I had to run to my aunt's house because it was closer than the school.

"I like black people but the only thing is, they don't like us because the Indian people like to dress their own way. Old ladies wear saris. They put this red stuff on their head. They put a dot on their forehead, and that's what they don't like.

"My uncle was doing an interview for an Indian program on a local station, and this man said on TV, 'I don't like Indian people because they own all the stores, but I don't even have one. I wanted to buy this store but an Indian came along and bought it, and the Indians have the stores I want to buy. I cannot own a store, so I don't like Indian people. They are coming to America and taking our stuff and keeping us out of it. I don't even like

116

Madhu S. Chawla, 11 years old

talking on this dirty Hindu microphone.' I don't like it when people say such things. Why do they have to say them?

"What is Asian? I guess I consider myself both Indian and American because if I say I consider myself American, my parents will ask me why I don't like India. I do culture programs, Indian dances, and I get awarded at Indian parties. I like being Indian better. I also speak Indian."

Different by Choice

Sudershan S. Chawla

Sudershan is Hardayal's wife. She was born in India. She is college educated and works as a nurse.

"We wear our Indian dress because of our culture, and because we are proud of it. But there are people who say, 'This is like a curtain.' They embarrass us. 'You wrapping around a curtain?' They don't even know the value. They don't know the culture. They don't know that we want to cover up our bodies, that we don't show our bodies to people, to have them look at us, to give us remarks. In India, we don't use the clothes people in this country use, like bikinis or shorts or clothes that show the body. We cover it up. Pants suits and long skirts aren't bad because you can't see the legs. But if anyone sits and shows her legs, that is not good. It is not right to show a man my legs. We don't like it because we were raised like that. The whole country is like that, not just myself. That's why these people shout their remarks but we don't care. We don't say anything about their dress. My dress is mine, yours is yours. I don't care.

"We don't drink, we don't smoke. One person in a thousand might do it, like film stars. We don't curse like here. Here, every single minute they curse. And we like peace, no fighting, no cursing, no arguments or hitting between husband and wife. We will fight a little inside, but not like here. Today the marriage, tomorrow's the fighting, the next day go to court and get a divorce.

"In our country we stay with our parents until marriage. And they spend the money for our education. We don't work until we finish our education. And we are dependent on our parents for everything. And we don't go outside to boyfriends, and we don't have children before marriage. If a woman has a child before marriage, she is like a prostitute, and the people would hate her and throw her out. Here, if a teenager has a child, the parents seem proud. They say, 'My daughter has a boyfriend. My daughter is pregnant.' They talk openly. We don't talk openly.

Sudershan S. Chawla (mother of Madhu).

that is the difference. Everything like that is secret. But here, nothing is secret."

The Red Dot: "When a girl gets married she gets the red dot. At eighteen or nineteen, she is married off. It is an arranged marriage by her parents. My father gave me a ring for me to give to my husband and he also gave a ring to my husband to give to me. Then the red dot is put on the forehead as a symbol of marriage, to say you're a wife. After the ceremony the woman wears the dot until she becomes a widow. The earrings on the nose are for fashion. The girl, especially after she marries, can decorate herself with jewelry and rings. Five hundred years ago, our culture did not allow a woman to wear makeup or jewelry until she was married. But today, we can decorate ourselves with any color jewelry we like. Even my eleven-year-old daughter can wear jewelry.

"I'm a nurse. My friends have stores, restaurants or motels. We work hard. We cook at home all the time. We don't spend too much money. We don't take the check, cash it, and sit in a restaurant to eat. We bring everything home. We cook and everyone eats together, so we save money. When we save money, then we invest. We have to study to get a good job.

"Some people don't like us, because we come from another country, and they have their own way. They look to us, and want to change themselves, but they can't because they have troubles. They take drugs, or smoke dope, for instance. If I'm smoking, I can't tell my daughter not to smoke. So these problems make it hard for them to make money, and they go to welfare. They steal. We feel something, but we don't get involved. Let them do what they want.

"But the killing, that is no good. If we killed one of them, everyone would come after us. But they killed an Indian, and we had to go to the court and talk to the politicians to get them to listen.

"'Hindu, Hindu, Hindu, Indian girl with the sari,' sometimes blacks call us that, sometimes Spanish, sometimes white. You can't say it is only one particular group. The Filipinos, the Chinese, the Japanese, they are good ones, no trouble.

"If we move to another area you know what they will think: 'These people are scared of us' so they will go scare the others. We don't move. We have to stay here, and we face the people. If we move, they could do the same thing in another area to scare us. So where do we go? That means we go home, that's it. Right? So we don't move."

On Being Asian American

Phil Nash

*Phil is of Japanese Irish English descent. He is in his mid-thirties and was
raised in the United States. He is a lawyer and a teacher.*

"If you really look at it, there is no such thing as Asian American. This
whole notion of an Asian is a European derived concept. And Asian American subsumes sixty different subgroups, different languages, cultures. People eat rice; They eat pilaf. It's really this grab bag of people who are really
about sixty percent of the world's populations. But because of a census
anomaly, we are drawn into a category called Asian/Pacific American. I
think it is a big farce. I think if you talk to any community of people, they
feel differently. For instance, the Korean community will read Korean
language newspapers and consider itself Korean. But the younger kids
growing up here will consider themselves Asian Americans. To be honest
with ourselves, our identities are as Asian-derived people, with sensitivities
to where we are living — in this case, the United States.

"At different points of my life, I've defined myself as Japanese
American, Amerasian, a number of different things. I realize what I call
myself is important, but other people will call me something else anyway.
I would oppose someone calling me Oriental. There is the notion of foreign-
ness, that the Orient is where the sun rises, the Occident is where it sets.
It creates this East versus West dichotomy.

"Asian studies is important. If you look at our skin tones, no one is
really yellow. It is important that Asians in this country study their
heritage. That's why I studied Shintoism and Buddhism and Japanese
culture. I think it was a very important identity for me. Likewise, Asian
American history is important, because no matter what your background,
you're here. You could be Thai, you could be Japanese, or whatever. But
whatever the national differences, when you're here, they say, you're a
chink. They look at you, and you're something, and that's why I think a
lot of immigrants particularly have to unlearn their national pride, their

Phil Nash and grandmother, Ratsu Tajitsu

nationalism. The Koreans justifiably hated the Japanese because of thirty-five years of occupation, but over here, Korean Americans and Japanese Americans will be treated the same — they will be called a chink and they will have to deal with that type of racism. So that's why I think being comfortable with your roots, and also being in touch with the experience in this country are important."

Images of Asian Men and Women: "There are certain expectations about Asian men. At first they were likely to be seen as dull, liking such things as computer programming. But with the rise of AIDS and the yuppie phenomenon, people believe Asian men don't fool around and they bring home the pay check, so Asian men become more desirable. Often Asian women are the worst — they dump on Asian men, rather than help them to be more open. In retrospect, most of the women I dated were Jewish women. And I've noticed this is a real phenomenon. A lot of Jews, because of their marginal status, are attracted to Asians.

My wife is really the first Asian woman with whom I have had a serious emotional relationship. The availability issue is really a very big issue among Asians. For instance, many of my female Asian students grew up in places where there weren't any Asian males, then they went to a big university, saw Asian men and found them attractive. This is a real phenomenon among the Asian community. It used to be growing up in the back of the laundry phenomenon, and now it is growing up in the suburbs phenomenon.

"The image of Asian women has been either that of a super sexy Susie Wong type, or a real passive lotus flower. There is nothing in between. For Asian men, you're either a computer nerd, or Bruce Lee, all brawn, and no brain. A lot of Asian males like myself loved it when Bruce Lee came out, because we would walk through the school yard, and people would go wow, maybe they know kung fu. So you get a little respect. So that notion of Asian men and Asian women, having stereotyped notions of each other, makes it hard to have real relationships. I have never shunned Asians, but I grew up in Maywood, New Jersey, so I never had a chance to meet many. I remember when I was at New York University and was seeing Asian women and men for the first time. People had punk hair — and the things they were into took me aback. I really hadn't thought of Asians to be like anybody else. So I got involved mostly with Chinese Americans, because that was the most concentrated community there was. There was no Japanese American community. There had been after the war, but people disbursed.

"It's interesting, how people looking for a thrill are looking for something different. Black is a little too different, Latin is culturally different, and Asian is close enough, but it's different.

"The notion of Asian is something that I understand, but as a person I see it can also have a real tragic effect. For instance, you're not only Japanese, you're a sneaky Jap, because you bombed Pearl Harbor. It's that sort of thing that goes on. People want to be inclusive as an Asian group, but the residual scars are preventing us from coming together."

Vivian Hom Fentress

Vivian is in her mid-thirties. She is Chinese American born and was raised in the United States.

"Though my heritage is important to me, and we speak Chinese at home, for all intents and purposes, I guess I liked associating with the Caucasian kids. I don't know why. Maybe because I was different when I was with them and was able to feel that I was special. I never wanted to hang out in Chinatown. I don't know why. Maybe I felt that hanging out with Chinese kids in Chinatown would remind me too much of hanging out with nerdy kids and being Chinese.

"When I was young, say second or third grade, I felt really self-conscious because I was Chinese. Even in school when they talked about Marco Polo going to China, I used to flinch. I would think all eyes were on me, because they were talking about being Chinese. And that bothered me for many, many years, until I got older. I saw there were definite benefits in being different. It was special to be different. So then it was okay."

Asian Men: "Unfortunately, when it comes to the image of the Asian male, I think I am prejudiced, because sometimes I see an Asian guy who doesn't fit into the perceived American stereotype. You know, he would be well built, articulate, with a sense of humor, and fairly good looking. Then for a second, I find myself thinking, 'He's Chinese. How did he get to be that way?' This is a horrible, horrible thing to think, but these are truths, and I still think them from time to time.

"Maybe part of this is because I grew up in the suburbs. You know, all the people you see in school, the popular guys per se, none of them are Oriental. And I guess anytime you did see someone who was Asian, you'd see them in Chinatown, at weddings, where you're surrounded by family, probably acting a certain way, acting Chinese, just because you're all together. And so maybe that's how that stereotype just keeps going on, and on, and on."

Asian Women: "There is the other side of the prejudice because I don't think an Asian woman is any different from a Caucasian woman. I don't see why an Asian woman can't be attractive, can't be articulate, can't be successful. I don't think twice about it. I think, sure, it can happen. But for the Asian male, given the same qualities and attributes, I question how they got to be that way — how they got to be so together. I just wonder how they broke from the old nerdy mold, and became just normal, average guys."

Sam Sue

Sam Sue is a Chinese American in his mid-thirties. He was born and raised in Mississippi.

"The self image of the Asian male is not being there at all. We're either presented as Fu Manchus, or made to feel we don't count. I guess my sense of this goes back to my days in Mississippi when I was dating. I was made to feel that way because you don't feel you meet the physical attributes and white women just didn't seem interested in relating to you in the sense of wanting to date you. Even among Chinese college age women at the time, a lot of them felt they had to date white men because they thought it was a step up from dating other Asians.

"Today I don't think marrying a white woman is a step up, although at one time, I guess when I was a teenager, this might have been true, especially since there weren't any Asian girls around to date. You were fixed with this notion of what was beautiful, and what was not. So I didn't really think Asian girls were attractive. An Asian woman would be my sister. My cousins might have been good looking, but you really didn't think of doing anything because they were your cousins.

"Today, I feel I get along better with Asians than non–Asians. I date mostly Asian girls. It's nothing political. Also there is a certain amount of resentment given my past, my experiences, my class.

"For instance, I went to college in Oberlin. This was my first big experience outside of a fifty-mile radius of Clarksville, Mississippi where I was born and raised. The largest city I had been to up till then was Memphis. So I show up and meet these rich professors' kids, and you feel inferior towards them and you resent all the privileges they've had, so there was a class thing, too. I never felt I was limited to working in the sciences or going to medical school. In fact, I felt I could do anything. As for stereotypes when I was growing up, my parents always told me, 'Oh, you're Chinese, and better than everyone else.' or 'You're better than the Japanese, and the Japanese think they're better than anyone else, etc.'

"There is the perception that Asians aren't aggressive or vocal. I didn't want to get in the habit of thinking too much of the stereotype and letting it get in the way. So in college, I talked a lot because I didn't want to give people the impression that I was a quiet Asian."

Will Hao

He is in his mid-thirties and is Hawaiian Japanese. Will was born and raised in Hawaii and is an actor.

"I've only seen pictures of *Fu Manchu*. I never saw the movie. It's just not my cup of tea, I guess. But I have seen pictures of the different actors that played him. It seemed kind of fun to me. I don't know what the fellow did to make him offensive as a stereotype. So I don't find that figure objectionable. I mean, why take it all so seriously?

"A stereotype is what the society at that time portrays as the stereotype. Ten years from now, the stereotypes will be different. There is not one Fu Manchu that is the same. The name of the characters is the same. But if you look at it, they all are different. It's like the Hunchback of Notre Dame. Twenty years ago it was different, twenty years from now, it will be something else. It's what society makes it. There will always be stereotypes. If you think of characters, there will always be the man who makes the rice; there will always be the guy who works the fields, and there will always be the guy who works in the big office. Then I guess you will have some people crying that we don't have enough of our people working in the office. So I don't know. I don't consider myself an 'Asian' male — just a male. Once you start putting labels on yourself, you start limiting yourself, and giving yourself pressure. Maybe that's why they make fun of Japanese guys when they look stiff. It's all this pressure. And I know a lot of Asian guys who are regular guys and they have no problems. It has everything to do with where you are in your life, and what you're doing. I had problems with some of the Asian actors in the company. They go around with their chest up in the air. I don't know what it is with Asian American men. Some of the ones I see at the theatre are so macho. I don't know what sense of fear propels that to happen. I think it's kind of strange that they have to be so macho. And it's not just them. I mean, I go to the Korean market here, and the young son is working, and he's really macho. One stereotype of an Asian female is the very soft-spoken woman. You don't get to see that too much anymore. Everyone's out trying to assert themselves, doing things. They even have female wrestlers. I turned on the television one night and saw Japanese women wrestlers. I just started laughing hysterically. If anything is going to break a stereotype, that will do it. It was great. I was just wondering what their parents were thinking."

On Appearance: "Sometimes the way Asians look at me is really strange. They're all trying to figure me out. In New York, I would get on the subway, and they would all look, but they couldn't figure me out. Some would say Filipino, and a lot of Koreans would say Japanese. Some Chinese think I'm Chinese. But for the most part they think I'm Asian Caribbean. A lot of Puerto Rican guys stop me in the street and start spouting off in Spanish, and I can't understand them. I had this experience. This one guy told me something, and I said, 'I don't speak Spanish.' And he said, 'Why are you embarrassed to be Puerto Rican?' I said, 'I'm not Puerto Rican. I'm from Hawaii.' And he just kept screaming at me. So I showed him my ID from Hawaii. He wouldn't even look at it. He said, 'Listen, you should never, ever be ashamed to say you are Puerto Rican.' And he walked away from me. I thought about it for a week. I was in awe of the situation. I can tell Chinese, Japanese, Filipino, Korean, and now Southeast Asian people. I can tell by the tone of the voice — not the accent — just tone. There's something inside me, and I can just tell because I grew up in Hawaii. Our neighbors were Chinese, and we had Japanese and Portuguese living on the same block. In Hawaii, we have jokes about every nationality. It's just for fun. I can tell a book-book (Filipino) from a Pake (Chinese). There are many words for Japanese people, but the one I like best is rice eyes (chuckles). The Koreans were Yobos. We grew up with our parents saying these things (laughs). It was all done in joke format. I mean, when you say it one laughs, but the other person you're talking about laughs, too. They call Hawaiians, Glalas, or hulks. So it's funny. So you can't take this stuff very seriously."

Cao O

Cao is a Chinese from Vietnam who is in his mid-thirties. He immigrated to the United States in his teens.

"No matter how many years I am here, even till the time I die, I will always speak English with an accent. That is a fact that I cannot deny. That is a fact that I cannot escape. And people will never see me as an American because the conventional wisdom is that if you are American, you should speak with no accent.

"To this day, I still don't know who I am. I am Chinese, born in Vietnam. Now I am an American citizen. But what does that mean? There is no place that I feel is home. In Vietnam, it was my birth place, but I never felt comfortable there, because we were treated as foreigners. It is my place of origin but not a home I feel close to. When we were growing up, we were taught to believe that China was our home. That's where your ancestors are, so one day you will go back to China. We heard that kind of talk. Then I ask myself, 'Do I know enough about China?' I don't. I've never been to China. The only association I have with China is the fact that my grandmother is still there. Also we have a house there. So I can't see China as my home either, because I don't know the place. So now is America my home? It is in the sense that I live here, and am a citizen. But that doesn't mean much because people still see me as a foreigner. So in terms of identity, no place is home. I can't talk about a hometown when people ask where I am from. So psychologically, I am sort of nowhere. Culturally I am Chinese, so that is pretty much ingrained. But when you talk about Chinese, there are so many types of Chinese. There are cultural differences between Chinese from Hong Kong, Chinese from mainland China, Chinese from Taiwan, and Chinese who are from America. When I was a kid, I used to hear stories from my relatives that people from Hong Kong looked down at us because they thought we were not civilized. Sometimes, the Chinese from Vietnam would travel to Hong Kong to do business, and those in Hong Kong would say, 'Who are these people?' Hong Kong is a much more developed society compared to the Chinese society in Vietnam. Meanwhile, the Vietnamese Chinese would say, 'Gee, the Hong Kong people — you can never trust them, they never tell you the truth. They're so arrogant.' Once in a while you even hear people say, 'Don't get married to a Hong Kong girl.' You hear things like that. But when I came to the U.S., I met some Hong Kong people. They are okay.

"Then you have the Asian Americans with their identity. That was quite new to me. I had trouble understanding that in the beginning. Just the way of seeing who you are — you are American, yet you have a partial Asian identity. Asians and Asian Americans don't always get along for cultural reasons, or for ideological reasons. Socially, it's hard to mix the groups together. The music they like is different. The things they like to do are different. Asians from Hong Kong and Vietnam are also different. I think Asians from America are more aggressive compared to Asians. I also think Asian Americans are less formal. So socially, it doesn't work out. It takes a lot of understanding from both sides.

"Asian Americans dress the American way. Whereas Asian, regardless of how long they've been here, are basically Asian in look and dress. I don't know how to describe it, but there is some subtle difference, and I can tell. There is a difference in the way they comb their hair, their gestures and the types of clothes they wear. When I was in college, I had trouble getting accepted by Asian Americans. I also had trouble getting accepted by Chinese from Hong Kong. At New York University, I knew a group of Chinese students from Hong Kong. It was not that they wouldn't accept me, but there was a barrier. Sometimes when I talked with them, they just weren't interested in what I was talking about. Since most of them came from Hong Kong, there was a common bond, and I became an outsider. So yes, we were all in one group as Chinese students. But there was a more inside group, and I was a bit more on the outside.

"But in another sense, being in this country makes those cultural differences less important. For instance, when two Chinese students see each other in a strange place, automatically you felt association — being closer than to someone from another ethnic background. I've seen that happen in many instances where I've been at a meeting or class, and you look around and see a Chinese. You sort of gravitate to him, or he would come to you.

"I can generally tell the difference between a Japanese and a Chinese. It's most intuitive rather than intellectual. It is just like the difference between Chinese and Vietnamese. Vietnamese have a slightly darker complexion. The younger ones tended to have longer hair. I think generally the

Koreans have smaller eyes. They have high chins. There is something that I can't pinpoint."

Image in the U.S.: "I suppose if you compared the Asian to the average American male, Asians would not seem as aggressive. And it may be that we are seen as weak. But I don't necessarily see being less aggressive as something bad. I think it's a matter of confidence. I think if you have confidence then you don't want to subject yourself to stereotypes. So I don't think about comparing myself to the average American. I know I cannot be one because of my background. I think each person from overseas always brings along his own baggage. And although sometimes you wish you could be like the average American, it's not realistic. I don't pretend I will become one, because I know I would never be treated as one. Also, in terms of your appearance or behavior, it's nothing you can change drastically. I think the key thing is values. Believe in who you are instead of trying to become someone you can never become. After a while, I don't care much about image anymore. I just want to be comfortable with myself. Image is relative."

Tony Hom

Tony is a twenty-five-year-old Chinese American who was born and raised in the United States.

"The stereotype of an Asian is of someone who is quiet, studious, and who plays the violin. (Actually I saw the violin bit in a news report one time, and thought it was funny, so I use it all the time.) The main thing is that they believe education is the way to break out of the sweat shop, restaurants or laundry business.

"I wouldn't say there is a brotherhood of Asians. You might have Chinese getting together, or Koreans, or Japanese, but not a brotherhood of Asians, so to speak. In school, for instance, there were cliques of Koreans who had just come from Korea. I had a definite sense that they were trying to feel me out, to see if I was Korean. As soon as they found out I wasn't, they left me alone. In my freshman year, there was a guy on my floor who was involved with the Asian American club, so I tried it for a while. But it didn't work, because I wasn't raised in Chinatown, and I had not had the upbringing where all my friends and peers were Chinese, so the goals they were striving for just didn't interest me whatsoever. As for the stereotype, it may be that that's the type most people come into contact

with most, either in school or at work. It's sort of like if you see ten people who are different in the same way, you're going to pick up on that
stereotype. I am sure there are blacks and whites who are just as intelligent. But if there are more Asians like that, then the stereotype will
stick."

Victor Merina

Victor is a forty-year-old Filipino American journalist.

"In the Filipino community, I think there is certainly that feeling that
we don't want to have a specific ethnic identity. We sort of just want to
blend in. We've grown up speaking the language in a country in which
America has long had a presence. So what you do is find yourself in the
middle if you want to keep your Filipino consciousness in a sense. And yet
you do find many Filipinos who just want to come over here and blend
quickly into the culture.

"I've had people come up to me and ask me if I am Samoan or Eskimo,
or even Tongan (a Pacific Islander group). When I was at UCLA during the
height of recruiting on campus, I was walking up Bruin Walk. They had
tables for all these different organizations. When I was going to class one
time, I was approached by the Chicano Students Association. I laughed it
off at the time, and said, 'I'm not Chicano.' And so the next group would
come by, the American Indians. There was a separate Japanese caucus that
approached me, too. It happens all the time. People want to know what
I am, and few get it right on the first guess. When I was first hired by the
LA Times, a veteran reporter came up to me and said, 'I think it's really
great of the *Times* to begin hiring Chicanos. I think it is really outstanding.'
and I said, 'Well, I'm not Chicano.' And he said, 'Well, what are you?' and
I said, 'Filipino.' And he said, 'Well, those too.' People I've worked with
expect me to talk to the various groups like I'm supposed to understand all
the ethnic groups just because I'm not white.

"My wife is of German Irish background. And we have four children
who have even more of that blend. So when they get to school, people come
up to them and say, 'What are you?' They ask if they are Indian or Eskimo.
And so they've had to deal with that and explain that they are Filipino. And
people act as if they're from another planet.

"I see myself as an Asian American, who is Filipino. And I would have
to emphasize the Filipino because that seems to be a group that is slighted

so much. Often, other Asians don't even consider Filipinos to be Asian. I think there is a lot of this in the Asian community. Let's take the media. Because of the lack of visible presence of Filipinos, you have a lot of people who automatically think of the great successes among Asians — primarily those who are on the air — as non-Filipinos. So since there isn't that visible presence, I don't think many people associate Asians with Filipinos. So when I talk to school groups, I have students coming up to me saying, 'I didn't know there were Filipinos in the media.' To add to the confusion, a lot of us have Spanish surnames, so I can see if you're looking at my byline, you might not consider me a Filipino.

"It's not only in journalism. I think Filipinos in this country have an invisible presence in films and in books. In part that's because there are a lot of Filipinos who just wanted to blend into the mainstream and go about their business and become real Americans, and not feel there was a need to band together, or to kick up a fuss, or to be visible. You can, as a Filipino, move into the mainstream quicker because inherent in the culture is the language. English is widely spoken in the Philippines. So you don't have that as a problem. Then there is a real affinity to American culture. Even during the revolution, things were so American there. In Manila, when the whole city was nervous, you could hear Chuck Norris movies playing, or as I walked down the street, I heard the American top forty blasting away in the streets. Many of the demonstrators wore UCLA college shirts. There are about a dozen daily newspapers. And all but two or three are in English. So English is the hybrid culture. And the presence of the bases all lend themselves to that. So I just think that when Filipinos come here, they work hard and integrate themselves quickly into the society.

"When the whole Marcos and Aquino struggle started, a lot of people acted as if they just discovered the Filipino community. So when I told my editors that in California, this was one of the largest single Asian American groups, they were stunned. They would ask how it got to be so big, or what happened. It is partly our fault for not being more visible. There has been this running debate in Los Angeles about establishing a community, like Chinatown, J-Town, or Koreatown. I would hear in the community, 'We don't have a Manilatown.'"

How Asians See Filipinos: "There is a secondary status, in so far as how other Asian countries see the Philippines. Other Asian countries view Filipinos the same way as some Americans, in taking the Philippines for granted. One time I was joking around with a Caucasian friend, talking about politics. And he said, 'You poor Filipinos. You take it from both sides. You're not thought to be quite the elite of the Asian mainstream, and you're certainly not considered bona fide Americans.' I think there is something to that, in a way. When people talk about Asian Americans, they will talk about the tigers — the economic powers; the countries that are really strong, like Japan, China, South Korea, and Hong Kong. The Philippines is not in the big tier. And I hear jokes about the way the Philippines is run. There are jokes about Marcos, and how they have a former housewife running the country. And people don't quite accept the legitimacy and the authority of someone like Corey Aquino. I think some of that transfers down in America to Asian Americans."

Carolyn Ayon Lee

Carolyn is in her mid-thirties. She is a third generation Korean American who was born and raised in Hawaii.

"Everybody likes Asian American women. They're cute and feminine. But there are also negative stereotypes of Asian women. The typical one is like, Madame Butterfly — about a military officer in Japan who picks up this woman and they have this kid and he abandons her, and she's so faithful, and waits for him to come back. That is traditional.

"American men fighting in the Vietnam War pick up bar girls, or American soldiers stationed in Korea pick up bar girls — I don't like that. The Asian women they meet are in that profession because they don't have other advantages like an education or a good family. So American men meeting Asian women overseas in this sort of environment are not meeting very well educated women. So they form an impression of Asian women as sexually available, which I don't like at all. But in general in the American culture, if you're a professional Asian woman, clearly you're not from that class, and you're extremely acceptable. In fact, I think it has become fashionable for white men to marry Asian women. Chinese American women married to white men are really pervasive. You don't really see the reverse as much — Chinese men married to white women.

"So basically it is fun to be an Asian American woman, while for Asian men, it is much more difficult. In general, Asian men are seen as the enemy. We have all these Vietnam movies, and they are called 'gooks,' or 'Japs,' and they are usually men — the enemy. There are some very harmful stereotypes of Asian men — like laundrymen or men with pigtails, so I think it is very hard to be an Asian male. I don't think you can be assertive. If you are, I think you won't get very far because you will be seen as a pugnacious person."

Charles Ryu

Charles is a thirty-year-old Korean American minister who immigrated from Korea to the United States at age seventeen.

"In 1983, I was at a fraternity party which my roommate went to. He was Germanic American — beautiful, blond, handsome. I was the only non-blond, non-blue eyed person there. When I walked in the party froze for a second. Then the party resumed as if nothing happened. I didn't exist. It was incredible this could happen in Boston. Because my friend was a well-built guy, all the girls were after him (chuckles). My friend tried to make me feel comfortable, and stayed with me. Girls would come up but they stopped just in front of him. So about twelve minutes into the party, I just pushed my way in, and said, 'Hey, I'm Charles' (chuckles), and they didn't know what to do. It's that kind of thing that still exists.

"I like to consider myself as a Korean American. That's what I'm struggling with now. I might change. I have some difficulty calling myself Asian American. It's a helpful identity, but nobody talks about having a European American identity. We say Caucasian. So, to lump together Asian Americans or Hispanic Americans is part of racist talk. It is meant to define us. I hate the term Oriental. Oriental meant Middle East for the longest time, and unless Westerners are willing to be called Occidental people, we shouldn't use the term. Asian is a good term. But I don't know that Asian people have a collective identity, as defined by Westerners. So I don't know that I can call myself Asian American. But I do know what the Korean identity is, and what American identity is, so I would like to be called Korean American."

Dating and Marriage: "I've dated all kinds of people. Chances are, Korean Americans, especially transgenerational Koreans, will tend more to cling to their own kind, than others. I'm good at music, so I tend to go out with white girls or black girls in the conservatory. But it's more than music, and this core of me has a lot to do with my transplantation experience. And unless a person understands that part and excepts both the wounds and the glory of it, I would not feel at home. So in that sense, the tendency is towards dating Asian Americans, or more specifically, Korean Americans. But that is not the only right thing to do. My sister married a Caucasian man. They met in Japanese class. If that cultural gap is bridgeable, that is fine. The Korean community looks upon such marriages with a great deal of difficulty. The Koreans have been a homogenous people for five thousand years, so they have yet to learn to accept a foreign element or to understand a intercultural marriage. Generally speaking, there is a resistance to an interracial marriage. There is a stigma against those who marry non–Korean, even among those who marry other Asian groups. There is a stigma with children born of mixed marriages. People might say those children are Korean, but not really 'Korean.'"

Henry Moritsugu

Henry is a Japanese Canadian born in Canada. He is in his mid-fifties.

"I think interracial marriage is fine. There is a lot of it in my immediate family. My older brother has married Caucasians. And many of my nieces and nephews mave married Caucasians. It's inevitable. It's probably a progressive step. It doesn't matter to me. I can't say my parents felt the same way; it mattered to them. My brother is actually married the third time — to the third Caucasian wife."

Minorities Within

Cao O

Cao O is in his mid-thirties. He is a Chinese from Vietnam.

"I remember one year, some kid took a plastic bag, filled it with shit, and threw it in our home. The animosity in Vietnam against the Chinese was quite obvious, and not at all subtle.

"My family in Vietnam were somewhere between poverty and middle class. I had to help out with my grandfather's business. At the time, my grandfather's store was downstairs, and we lived over the store. My father used to manage my maternal grandfather's soy sauce business. At one time, it was a big booming business, but then things got bad. Later on my dad had to retire because there were problems with the business. He didn't do much after that. He just stayed home or went out with friends. So we were basically staying with my grandfather's family. So my immediate family was poor, but we were able to enjoy the support of my grandfather, so we wouldn't have to be on the street.

"In the old days, the intention of the Chinese was to go to Vietnam, make some money, and go back home. And then they realized later on they couldn't go back home, so they stayed, but had their own community. You did business with the Vietnamese, but culturally and socially, you didn't mix. Interracial marriage would be discouraged. I think the worst thing to the Chinese would be to bring home a Vietnamese wife. Also, a lot of Chinese didn't try to assimilate. Take my family for instance, we looked down at the Vietnamese. My grandfather used to say that the Vietnamese were dirty. He gave them a nickname — dead dog. On one hand you had the Vietnamese resenting the Chinese for the domination and control, and then you had the Chinese who looked down on the Vietnamese. When we were there, we were treated as foreigners, although we were Vietnamese citizens. People would see us as foreigners, and once in a while you would hear remarks like, 'Go back home.' Sometimes kids would take stones and throw them into your home. Historically, there was animosity between the

135

Chinese and Vietnamese. It is a kind of love-hate relationship. By that I mean, on one hand, the cultures between the two are very close. Vietnamese are strongly influenced by Confucianism. Confucius was honored as the greatest teacher by the Vietnamese. In terms of values, they are the same as Chinese. Sometimes you can't even distinguish. They celebrate similar things like the lunar New Year. In food, there is commonality. As a whole, Vietnamese respect Chinese for the culture and the literature. In the old days, the Vietnamese wrote in Chinese characters but then the language was Romanized after the French took over. But still in the older generation, if you talk to a Vietnamese who is about seventy years old, he would be proud of the fact that he could write in Chinese. So that is the love relationship. The hate part is that I guess no one wants to be colonized by anyone. So the fact that, historically, the Chinese dominated Vietnam for so long makes them resent the Chinese. The Vietnamese are very proud people. Sometimes they are too proud — especially the North Vietnamese. So they hated Chinese. Also the Chinese in Vietnam dominated the economy, such as the rice trading. Vietnam used to be a rice producing country before the war. So you had Vietnamese coolies working, and then you had the Chinese middleman. There was very tight control of the rice trading both in terms of exports and internal distribution. So that became a threat.

"In this, the United States is different because the Chinese and Vietnamese are all immigrants, so the issues are not the same. Also they face the same survival issues and they get along better. Also I think once you've stepped out of your own environment, you can see it much better. Now you're in a strange land, and you go through the same experiences. You don't see the other person as the enemy anymore; you see him as being from the same country, the same identity, the same affiliation. You feel closer. But the Chinese from Vietnam and the Vietnamese did have trouble breaking into businesses in Chinatown. It was difficult to get accepted. Now you do see some stores run by those from Vietnam. But that has been only in the last four years. Initially we were not that well received by the Chinese community here because there was some lack of understanding and some jealousy because we came as refugees and were entitled to certain benefits that immigrants didn't get.

"Ten years ago, Vietnamese or Chinese from Southeast Asia would go to the social service agencies in Chinatown, but you could see the gap, because most of the staff were Chinese from Hong Kong so they had no understanding for what the people went through. There were barriers. The service was not as good. For instance, one Chinese who came from Vietnam was involved in a program helping refugees. She had a tough time there. It's not that the people in the agency didn't like her, or tried to get rid of her, or were nasty to her. They just didn't consider her projects high priority, and would make subtle remarks."

Lang Ngan

Lang Ngan is a third generation ethnic Chinese who was born and raised in Vietnam. She is in her mid-forties.

"It is difficult to tell a Vietnamese from a Chinese if they don't speak because there has been a lot of intermarriage. I think I am at least twenty-five percent Vietnamese because my mother's mother is a Vietnamese. Only my mother could speak Chinese. The rest of her side of the family speaks Vietnamese. I feel more Chinese than I do Vietnamese because we were discriminated against in Vietnam. I think many Chinese were the economic leaders in Vietnam, and the Vietnamese didn't like it. They say the Chinese were holding and controlling the economy. As you can see, wherever the Chinese go, they are interested in business first.

"My grandparents migrated from China to Vietnam, and my father was born in Vietnam too. In Vietnam, our family is middle class. My father was an accountant, and we had houses for rent. In the family of seven children, I am the oldest.

"I think about five or ten percent of the people in Vietnam were Chinese. But were were not allowed to go to the public schools in Vietnam because we weren't fluent in Vietnamese because we spoke Chinese at home. In the community, they tried to isolate us. We weren't welcome to join any Vietnamese organizations, so the Chinese had their own community, like Chinese all over the world. They try to clutter in one place, live together, and help each other. That was the way it was in Vietnam. Many of the Chinese lived in Cholon. That is the Chinatown in one part of Vietnam. My grandmother had been in Vietnam for sixty years, but she could not speak any Vietnamese because she stayed only in Cholon. But I do speak Vietnamese. Still, I have the feeling of discrimination. There is still resentment because, at one time, China colonized Vietnam for a thousand years. And because of that, the Vietnamese feel we should not be there. We are foreigners, yet we do so well. So they think the Chinese exploit their people. Also the Chinese are not interested in politics, only in making money. Where we lived before in Vietnam, the people gave us a hard time. The children would harass us for no reason. When you walked by their houses, they sometimes threw stones and made us embarrassed. This didn't happen in Saigon. It is a city and more civilized. But in this place we lived, in Cholon, because the Chinese were very strong in the community, the Vietnamese felt we shouldn't be there. I hear the Vietnamese all say that the Chinese have a very good brain in business. Many say they learned how to do business from a Chinese friend. The new government in Vietnam tried to get rid of the Chinese because they knew those holding the economic power were mainly Chinese. In 1979, there was a wave of refugees they allowed to leave — the boat people. At that time, they gave priority to the Chinese because they felt the Chinese were controlling the economy, and they wanted to get them out of the country.

"But now without the Chinese, they are not able to do better. And I just read an article a few weeks ago, that now, they welcome the Chinese back, and allow them to join discussions about how to develop the country again. They try to get the Chinese (from Vietnam) back on party committees.

"But the feelings haven't changed, even in this country. Even though on the surface you can't tell, deep down, you can't change people's minds. For instance a Chinese will not open completely to a Vietnamese, or a Vietnamese to a Chinese. My sister wanted to join the Vietnamese Students Association at MIT because she came from Vietnam and felt she could share experiences with the others. But she said she felt isolated because the students felt that since she didn't speak Vietnamese she shouldn't call herself a Vietnamese and join their club. So she ended up socializing with mostly Americans. She felt this happened because she was ethnic Chinese. That sort of problem exists between Cambodians and Vietnamese also. They don't mingle because the two countries have been fighting one another off and on, and there have been problems between the countries for centuries."

Alicia Diem

Alicia is a forty-year-old who was born and raised in Vietnam. Alicia is a pseudonym used at her request.

"I have a lot of Chinese friends. Chinese people like me because I look Chinese. But historically, we don't like Chinese people because they wanted to take over Vietnam. They want to control Vietnam; they want to cross out Vietnam on the map. So in our minds, Vietnamese people don't like Chinese people.

"When I was growing up, the Chinese had the money and they had the power. So they controlled the economy. They ran the businesses, so they had money. You have money, you have power. You have everything, even political power. And they stayed separate. They do not mingle with the Vietnamese. A Vietnamese married to a Chinese was not accepted. The Chinese looked down on the Vietnamese. I had a friend, for instance, who fell in love with a Chinese man. And the Chinese man wanted to marry my Vietnamese girlfriend. But his family forced him not to do it. It was not allowed. It was not always this way, but very often it was.

"In 1979, the Vietnamese government wanted only the Chinese to leave. The communists felt they could not control the Chinese there. There were a lot of Chinese in Vietnam. And before the communists, the Chinese controlled the economy. They have money, and they have power. They were like the Jews in New York. And the Chinese people in South Vietnam were the same like that. After the communists took over, there were a lot of clashes. They wanted to throw the Chinese out. It was hard for a Vietnamese person to leave, and so those Vietnamese who wanted to leave said they were Chinese just so that they could leave Vietnam easier. And the Vietnamese government did not allow the people to leave to go to the United States. If they wanted to go to Canada or France, that was easy. But it was not easy to go to the United States."

FAMILY

The Power of Duty

Rose Eng

Rose is eighty-two years old and immigrated to the United States from China in 1929. She speaks little English and could be more detailed speaking Chinese. The interview was conducted in Toishanese (a Chinese dialect).

"When I was thirteen, my father returned to China, and after six months, took my mother back to the United States with him. She spent five years here, looking for a husband for me. Finally, she found him and arranged for me to come to this country. I never opposed my parents. I just obeyed what they as!.ed of me. I didn't question whether it was right or wrong. I knew they went to a lot of effort to find someone for me to marry and spent a lot of money to bring me here, so I was grateful and didn't go against them. I arrived in Boston in 1929. I was eighteen. I lived with my parents for two months, and then was married. I had never met my husband before. By 1947, the Japanese were defeated, war was over, and my husband, who had not seen his mother for over forty years, said he wanted to go back to China to visit her. So he was back there for a little over a year, and probably he wasn't used to the water, because he died there. So after eighteen years of marriage, I was alone. He never returned. Here I was, by myself, running the laundry. I was looking for a way to earn enough to eat. I got ten cents for a clean shirt. Things were even better during the war, I got fifteen cents a shirt. It was tough, especially being a woman, running the store all alone. By 1956, I couldn't do it anymore. I left, and came to New York. So I was in the laundry business for twenty-seven years, and then worked in the sewing factory for another twenty years.

"I have no children. When my husband went back to China, he took a second wife, and she had a daughter by him. As he didn't have a son, the family adopted one. So I would send money back — several hundred dollars a year — to support these two children until they were full grown. To that end, I feel as though I have fulfilled my obligation to him and his family.

"As a seamstress, I can't say life has been good or bad. I did it to eat.

As long as I could make a few dollars every week to pay for the rent and food, I survived. These days, you can make a few hundred dollars a week if you are young and fast. But when I was working, I would be lucky to bring home thirty or forty dollars a week. I couldn't read or write English, so there wasn't much I could do or try to accomplish. My main concern was finding something to do to pass my days, and to support myself.

"As for marriage, I never wanted to marry again. And there wasn't an opportunity for me to think much about it. I was already old when I came to New York to work. So my heart wasn't into getting married again. My 'fake' daughter got married, and her sister-in-law brought her to San Francisco. When she got there, she knew that I was alone so she came to visit me in New York. She stayed on, saying it would be easier to get work here than in San Francisco. So she is sewing in a factory here. So my daughter doesn't live far from me now, and on the weekends, she comes to visit. She also has three daughters. The oldest granddaughter even stays with me because she says I live closer to her school. So now it is like having a family again. Even though the daughter is not my own, I feel I have someone close to me whom I can discuss things with if anything should happen.

"My life (fate) was not a good one. I was never able to have children. Still, it is good that I have a family again after so many years.

"Things are very simple now. I go to the senior citizen's club, chat with my friends, spend the morning, and eat lunch. Then I go home. I stopped working at seventy. That was twelve years ago. With a small pension and social security, I get about four hundred dollars a month. I have enough to live on and to eat. That is all. Even if I wanted more in life, there is no more. Sometimes I might have a few dollars left over, sometimes not. If I had to give a gift that month, then it wouldn't be enough. But my heart doesn't think of big things. I am content just having food, clothing, and a place to live. Talking about my past makes me feel sad. I have had a very lonely life.

"I don't know words [meaning she can't read or write], so I am afraid to go to vote. I didn't go to school in this country, and in China, I couldn't afford to go to school. When I first came over, I did want to go to school, but my father said to work in the laundry, so that is what I did. What little English I picked up was in dealing with customers in the laundry. Once I came to New York and got a job in the sewing factory, I never got to use much English again. All my friends are Chinese.

"I became a citizen in 1961. When I want to, I travel. I've visited China twice, and even went to Taiwan. But I would never think of going back to live. I still believe that this is the best country to live in. I saw enough and know enough about China. I came when I was eighteen, and that is old enough to understand many things.

"My heart is content now. As long as I have enough to eat and live and don't have to go begging in the streets, I am content."

Permanent Sojourner
Ng Hing

Ng Hing is an eighty-year-old, first generation Chinese American. The interview was conducted in Toishanese (a dialect of Chinese).

"I took a ship from China and landed in Ellis Island in 1934. I stayed on the Island nearly two months before they allowed me to enter New York. From there I went straight to Syracuse where my cousin had a laundry. I was twenty-five and married. I didn't see my wife again until 1970. I had two daughters and one son. My son died, and my two daughters are in Hong Kong.*

"The laundry business was seven days a week. We opened at eight and closed at six. Sunday was the only light day. I would work only half a day, ironing shirts. The rest of the time, I washed and ironed every day. My cousin and I lived in an apartment not far away from the laundry. It was a nice place with running water and heat. There was nothing else to do but work.

"I never thought about going to school or trying to better myself when I got to this country. As soon as I came, I had to go to work and make money to support my children and wife in China. I barely speak English, even today. I just picked up enough to deal with customers. I finally had to close the laundry after thirty-five years because there wasn't enough business. The clothes are mostly machine washed today, or they are dry cleaned. I came to New York to look for work, but I wasn't able to get anything else so I just retired. My wife is constantly ill these days. I guess she isn't used to the water in this country. I've been trying to get

*The Chinese Exclusion Act of 1882 was the first of a series of acts that suspended Chinese immigration to the United States. This made it essentially impossible for most Chinese to bring over their families. It wasn't until 1943 that Congress repealed the act, allowing Chinese to be naturalized and giving China a quota of 105 immigrants to come to the United States per year. Until that time Chinese were not entitled to become naturalized citizens.

more medical assistance for us. It is just myself and her in this country right now. My son died a few years ago. But we still have each other. I am glad for that, even though she is not well, and I have to take care of her."

Men without Women

Victor Merina

Victor Merina is in his mid-thirties. He is a first generation Filipino American. He talks about the tough time his uncle had in the 1930s.

"For decades, many Filipinos would send money back to the Philippines. Even my parents did that for the longest time. My dad always sent a portion of his paycheck to the village, to the people. As a routine, I would have to take it to the mail. So what would happen is that in the twenties and thirties, there were all these Filipino men working as laborers on the farms and in the canneries. There were also people in the Philippines acting as brokers. They would recruit from the Philippines, and shiploads would come. Some came to California, and others to Hawaii.

"When I was in elementary school in Los Angeles, I had an uncle who was very traditional. He had to pick me up from school one day. I was in grade school. I had volunteered to help the teacher dust the erasers and clean the blackboards at the end of class. So when he arrived, I had just finished doing the erasers and was cleaning the boards. He saw me from the doorway, and turned to the teacher, and said 'What is he doing? He's cleaning up! Why is he cleaning up? He's a student here.' My uncle was absolutely irate. He said, 'He's a student. He's here to learn so he doesn't have to do those things. That's why he goes to school. To avoid things like that. And you make him do these things? Why? So that Filipinos are the ones to clean for you?' And the teacher was speechless. His anger was so intense. He just grabbed me by the hand and said, 'We're going home.' He turned to me and said, 'Don't you ever clean up for these people again. You're here to learn.' And he took me out of there. I remember really crying. I felt I was doing this great thing, and my teacher was stunned at his reaction. So when I went home, I told my parents what happened, and for the first time, they told me his history, how he'd come to this country years ago, went through really terrible times. And my father said he was one of the most adamant in the family that the next generation of Filipinos should not be in the fields.

"My uncle (he wasn't a real uncle, he just came from the same village) was part of the earliest migration of Filipinos to this country. He came to work in the fields by himself, in the days when single Filipino males were allowed in this country to work as laborers in the fields and canneries. He grew to be very skeptical about integration for Filipinos because he saw a lot of discrimination. He was in Stockton when there were no Filipinos allowed in hotels. There were anti-miscegenation laws then, where no Filipino men could be with white women, and things like that. This was in the thirties. What happened in the twenties and thirties was that many Filipinos came over to work as farm laborers or in canneries.* A lot of the men thought they could make money, and be able to bring family members over and resettle here. And there were many others who felt they could make enough to retire in the Philippines. For the most part, many just stayed, without doing either one. It was tough, financially. In order to find work, they often had to migrate from place to place. There wasn't as much money as they thought they could make. In my uncle's case, he said he was determined to make something of his life here. And what happens is the years go by, and the loved ones they had back home have their own lives. My uncle stayed here to make his stake, and he was caught in that era, because there were no women to pursue families with. So men of his era were caught. They had left behind their lives. Everyone had gone on and done other things, and they were here, with no way of integrating into this society. So my uncle never got married."

---

*The first large wave of Filipino immigration took place between 1907–1934. They were recruited as cheap labor by agents of the Hawaiian Sugar Planter's Association. By the 1920s, the Filipinos formed the largest ethnic group working in Hawaiian fields. From there, some Filipinos moved on to California following the failure of two major strikes on Hawaiian plantations in 1920 and 1924.

By 1930, there were 30,470 Filipinos in California. Whether in Hawaii or on the West Coast, the men were viewed as social outcasts. Filipino men outnumbered Filipino women by fourteen to one. Few were married; most left their families behind. As such, Filipinos sought the companionship of white women. This led to several anti–Filipino riots in California.

A Los Angeles Superior Court Judge handed down a ruling in 1930 classifying the Filipinos as members of the Mongolian race. This invalidated Filipino mixed marriages in California. It wasn't until 1948 that the State Supreme Court struck down California's legal ban on interracial marriage as unconstitutional.

By 1934, the Tydings McDuffie Act was passed, limiting to fifty per year, the number of Filipinos coming to America as immigrants. Filipinos were not allowed to become naturalized citizens until 1946.

Growing Old

C. Ng

C. Ng is an eighty-year-old Chinese American who speaks very little English. The interview was conducted in Toishanese (a dialect of Chinese).

"These days, in this country, you see Chinese in their seventies and eighties in senior citizen's clubs. That's because they don't come until much later in life, and then they stay in this country once they retire. But in the old days, the men who came to this country worked until they were in their fifties then returned to China to retire and prepare to die. Things are different today because many people have their sons and daughter here. So they grow old in this country.

"I consider myself very fortunate, much more so than in my past. It is not that I live in luxury, but here I can eat. Food is abundant. Where I live is good, even compared to my days in the village. I mean, in China, we were considered the landed class — we had money. I was persecuted by the communists for being a landowner in 1950–51. My family owned three houses in the village, and they were all confiscated. At the time, three of my children were still living with me, so they gave us five rice bowls and pushed me, my wife and children into the streets. We were sent to a broken-down house which leaked all the time. We strung leaves on bamboo poles so that the water wouldn't fall on the children's heads. That's how we lived for two years. The harsh bitterness of life at that moment was so oppressive, I can't begin to describe it. Here I was a boy of reading [term for an educated man which connotes a certain amount of privilege, education, wealth and lifestyle], and sort of weak. I never imagined that life meant going through such hardships. By 1954, they were treating those with overseas connections a little better. The government took the money my daughter, who was in the United States, sent to us. They said it was to compensate for past oppression committed by landowners. The money was turned over to the commune and the party and they asked her to send more. It got so that she finally had to write and say that she was barely able to survive in the United States. She pleaded with them not to be so demanding. They even gave me back my property, and allowed me to go to Canton. From there, I applied to leave to Hong Kong as an overseas Chinese. But they wouldn't let me take my family out. They just let me leave. They wanted to keep my family behind, so that I would send back money. Gradually, the rest of my family petitioned to leave, and by the 1960s we were all in Hong Kong. From there, I came to the United States in 1962. I was fifty-three years old. My first job was as a dishwasher in a Chinese restaurant. I got the job through my friend. I stayed at that job two and a half years. Then I did some odd jobs in the kitchen. At that time it wasn't hard to get a job in a Chinese restaurant. In the eleven years I worked, I worked for four different places. I was making an average of two hundred and eighty dollars a month. It was hard work. After I retired, I got my benefits. On occasion I would find a job on weekends, washing dishes. I found it hard to pass the day without working.

"The only other thing Chinese were doing in those days was laundry. My cousin said he would buy a laundry for me, but I said I didn't want to sit in a laundry all day by myself. It is a very lonely thing to do. And what if something happened to me? Who would take care of the store? So my daughter helped me find work in a restaurant.

"It was really just to do something, because I never really got used to working in a kitchen. I had no thoughts of coming to the United States as a child. In fact, I didn't come to this country until I was over fifty. In the village in Toi Shan, when I was growing up, all I did was be a boy of reading. After I grew up, I went to Canton (which is the big city for us), and opened an electronics business until the Japanese invaded China. At that point, to escape the Japanese, I returned to my village to live. There was absolutely nothing to do in the village. There were no jobs as you think of jobs. People didn't have any other way to live, outside of working the land.

"My father went to Europe when I was young, and returned in 1949, during Liberation. In those days, people would go away for many years, then go back to China for a year or two then leave again, to earn money. After the communists took over, there was still nothing to do, to make a living. I think back to those days now and can tell you that life wasn't worth anything. It was better to be an ant in those days than to be a human being. Even today, it is hard to live in the villages.

"I like living in the United States. The living conditions — where you live, how you live — are far better in this country. The worst thing is if you don't want to work. If you want to work, you can even take two jobs. Because I was persecuted under the communists, I don't care how hard a job is, I will do it, and be grateful to have it. An average person who is straight and hardworking will definitely do well in this country. The only people who don't have money are those who gamble, drink, are lazy, or are afraid of hard work.

"In my heart, I deeply hate the communists. But over the last ten years, looking from the outside, I guess I am proud of what they have been able to do, to lift their stature around the world.

"I have a son who came to this country when he was eleven. In those days, we had to buy the false papers for him from one of my distant uncles. My father had gone to Europe, but he wasn't allowed to bring any of his family over, so it was a dead end so to speak. At the time we realized that, as hard as it was, it was still possible to come to this country. So we bought the papers, and chose the live road. It was really hard for my son. He stayed with some distant relatives to help raise their children while he went to school. It was really tough. He eventually married a Filipino woman. He was the only one. The rest of my children married Chinese. My daughter — the one who brought me over — came to this country after she got married. I eventually brought the rest of my family over. Three of my children live in Connecticut, the rest in Los Angeles. They all own their own houses, and have their own restaurants, except for my youngest son who is an accountant. My wife passed away a few years ago, when I was seventy-five. And my children told me they wouldn't be able to take care of me, so they asked me to take another wife. My friends introduced me to someone in her sixties, who had lost her husband. We married. She still works in a senior citizen's home. I have twenty grandchildren and eight great grandchildren. I seldom see them. They mostly call me by phone. My youngest son comes home every year during Easter to walk the mountain of his mother. (The Easter season coincides with Tomb Sweeping, an annual occasion to visit the graves of ancestors.) We don't celebrate Chinese New Year anymore. There is just no way we can get together as a family.

"I visited China last year, because I still have two stores in Canton that I had to re-register deeds for. A friend told me only yesterday, 'Ng, the stores in Canton are now worth a lot of money. My store, I rented it for two hundred dollars a month before, now I get five hundred dollars. Your stores are worth at least double the rent you're asking.' I charge three hundred and fifty dollars a month, but I haven't thought of raising the rents.

"I still send money back to some relatives, but mostly to maids of my family. The past two years, I have collected a good amount of rent money — about nine thousand dollars. So after taxes, maintenance, and other fees, the remainder goes to the old servants of the family. I also send money back to tend my ancestors' graves.

"I spend most of my days at a senior citizen's center, where I play mahjong, Chinese checkers, and watch Chinese programs on videotape. My first wife, when she was alive, loved to play mah-jong. Every weekend, we would set up two tables. It would start in the morning, we would go for a dim sum breakfast and play to the late evening hours.

"I live just outside of Chinatown on Madison Street. I've lived there ever since I came to the United States. I fixed it up really nice. All my friends tell me I have one of the nicest apartments in Chinatown. But I'm constantly in fear of being robbed. They come in and take everything. I've been robbed four times already. One time, it was really scary. My daughter, who was visiting me from Los Angeles, was taking a shower in the kitchen. (The tub is in the kitchen.) The window in the living room was open. I was in the bedroom. Halfway through her shower, there was a knock on the door. I told her that I would answer it after she showered because there was no way I could get to it without going through the kitchen. At that point, I heard a thud. I ran to the living room, and someone was already climbing out the window with her handbag.

"Today, I'm not as concerned. I fixed it up – there are now bars on my window, and I have special police locks on the door. Now, after six PM I don't go out – not even to special functions. I only go if I am invited to a banquet or something."

Life as a Senior

Katie Lee

Katie is a seventy-four-year-old Chinese American who speaks fluent English. She was born in Australia.

"I don't know China — not enough to say I like it or hate it, because I didn't live in China during the political changes. Besides, I like living in this country. I feel a part of it. I vote. I keep up with the news and the politics. I feel very much a part of this country because I am a citizen. I will always see myself as a Chinese, though.

"Early in the day, I go to the senior citizen's club to play mah-jong. And in the afternoon, I go home and watch soap operas on TV. At four o'clock I get ready for my supper, and then take a bath, watch the news, then a movie on TV. I am free now. I do what I want, as long as my income is okay. I have no responsibilities at this point in my life, so it is a good time for me. The only thing that is not good is that I am old. That is not good.

"I still live in Brooklyn. That's where I raised my family. I never considered myself a part of Chinatown. Until I retired, I would go to work, then go home. I never associated with those Chinese people. It is only now, as I am older, that I joined a senior citizen's center, that I spend more time with the Chinese. For the most part, I don't really know them by name. I don't talk to them much because there is nothing to say. All the old people talk Chinese, so I talk Cantonese to them. The same is true with my relatives. But my children are different. My daughter speaks a little Chinese, but my son can't speak any. He speaks only English, and he hardly understands Chinese. He's a technician in a hospital. My daughter's a high school teacher.

"Two years ago, I went to Australia. And last year, I went to China. I still have friends and relatives in both places. I like to travel, as long as my health is okay. But I don't send any money to China. I figure they can support themselves. Only when I visit do I bring them gifts. My father was

150

a citizen of Australia, though I don't know how he got there. I'm not sure if he was born there. My mother went there from China. I was born in Australia. I don't know a thing about my grandparents. My father died when I was seven, so my mother, brothers and sister left Australia, and went to mainland China, to Canton to live. My family had a house there. I finished high school and went back to Australia in 1940. The war with the Japanese was on in China, so we left. I worked in a Chinese restaurant there, and I met this Chinese American soldier because he always went to eat there. So we fell in love, and I married him and came to the United States in 1946. I had two children, was a housewife for a while, then I went out to work again. I made hamburgers, sandwiches, malts, that kind of thing, in a restaurant in Chinatown. The place is closed now. It was a hangout for teenagers in Chinatown called Lonnie's Coffee Shop. I worked there quite a while, and retired when they closed.

"I wouldn't consider moving to China to live right now, because both my children are here. And also, I don't like communism. But if I didn't have any children, I might consider going back because they could send me my social security, and it would be enough for me to live on very comfortably."

Food and Mah-jong

Tony Hom

Tony is a twenty-five-year-old Chinese American who was born and raised in the United States.

"The main social activity for my family was mah-jong, cigarettes and Chinese food every weekend. That was the social focus of my family. And while the adults played, we kids just ran off having a good time. Every weekend, they would have friends over by noon, set up the tables, and play until late evening. And the kids would play in another room, so it was great. Otherwise, growing up in Harlem, my folks were always afraid to let us out.

"My grandfather is a chef and food always seemed to be a central part of the family. There seemed to be great honor in being able to be a good cook. It didn't really come into play until college. You can impress a lot of girls when you can cook. I strived to be better at that because there wasn't that much competition around me. Maybe it's part of my ego. But I don't think being able to cook is unmanly. My father cooked, his father cooked, my maternal grandfather cooked. It was just a natural part of growing up. Food is *the* main gathering point around the table. Mother would spend the entire day preparing, with my grandfather helping. It brought them together. All the time it would be a chicken, fish, beef, and vegetable dish. We were just inundated with food. We got together for the one big meal per day, which was dinner time. My mom cooks just about anything and everything – shark's fin soup, bird's nest, quail, pheasants, abalone, conch, and oysters. The area they grew up in, in Canton, seemed to have a big fish bounty so there was a plethora of food types. I'm sure if she didn't grow up in that part of China, there wouldn't be that emphasis on seafood, just because the availability was not there."

Education: "There was always pressure to do well in school. It didn't matter if we studied four hours, or forty. We had to maintain the grades or there would be corporal punishment. So there was incentive to do well.

152

And college — it was always understood that I would have to go. So I think my parents are happy and proud that their son had a college education — something more than they had, or their group of friends had."

On Grandparents and Respect: "It would just seem natural that you would take care of the elders once they reached that point in life. My grandparents were always close by. When we lived in an apartment, they were always a few floors up. Now, my parents have a two family house, and my grandparents live next door. So this was always pointed out to me. Maybe they are fearful that one day we would become too Americanized and not take care of them. You always hear them talking about how the 'lo-fans' (referring to Caucasians) don't take care of the elders, while the Chinese community prides itself on how it takes care of its old family members. I was very happy and fortunate to be able to grow up with my grandparents. We shared many things like how they grew up. There were stories about how my grandfather hunted with his brother and caught fish. But they were so poor they didn't have oil to cook the fish in, things like that. They were in the position of authority and respect. If I got a 'no' answer from my parents, I could always fudge it and get a 'yes' from my grandparents.

"Right now, thank God, my parents are in a position where they can take care of themselves. I even talked this over with my wife before we got married. I know I would always take care of them regardless, and I was hoping that my wife would, too. And fortunately enough she stated that we would take care of my parents when the need arises."

Obligation

Cao O

Cao O is a Chinese from Vietnam who is in his mid-thirties.

"My uncle in Canada is supporting my grandmother right now, so we let him do that. Once in a while, my mom would talk about the need to support my grandmother or the relatives at home. But I try to stay out of the issue, not denying the fact, but not making commitments. We are told that we have a home in China. My grandmother is still there. I have never visited China. I grew up in Vietnam. Actually we don't talk much about ancestors, but we talk about family obligation. For example, my grandmother is about eighty years old. Someone has been taking care of her for half of her life. So once in a while, my mom would remind me and the other siblings that we have an obligation to that person who has been serving my grandmother. Meaning, when my grandmother dies, we should support that person by sending money over there, because that person spent her whole life, more or less, serving my grandmother. So the least we can do is to support her. Now that person is kind of old too. Because she never worked outside, she is not entitled to the government's retirement benefits. Therefore it is our obligation. It's hard enough, talking about whether we should be supporting grandmother, herself. We don't talk about tending the family graves. I don't really know where they are in China. We also have some in Vietnam."

Bossa

Valerie Corpus

Valerie is in her mid-twenties. She was born and raised in the Philippines and immigrated to the United States in 1979.

"Family is very important to Filipinos. Whenever we're together, we speak Tagalog. In America, family just means mother, father, brother, and sister; that's it. But with me, family means my mother's sisters, brothers, cousins, aunts, uncles, my father's side, and their relatives. It's a lot bigger. When I say I have family in California, it doesn't mean only my brother or sister. I have cousins there. Even my aunt's (uncle's wife) cousin, or aunt's sister, is treated as family.

"My grandmother was very strict when I was growing up. I couldn't go out with my friends unless I had a maid along. We prayed the rosary every night, mass and confession once a month. My grandmother is Spanish, my father part Chinese, my mother part Spanish. We celebrate Catholic holidays. Eighty-five percent of the Filipinos in the Philippines are Catholic.

"We were middle class. All my friends in school had house help. Very often, the students would have their maids in school with them. When I was a kid, my ya-ya (a nanny) would wait outside while I was in school the whole day. At lunchtime, she would give me my food, then she would wait for me until I went home when school is out. That's still done today with children, until the fourth grade at least. Labor is cheap there. People from the provinces don't have any jobs. They go to the city. They can't find work so they end up as maids.

"When I was in high school my grandmother would ask, 'Who are you going out with, what time are you going to be home, and I want the number.' Usually my friend's mother would have to speak with my grandmother about me going out with my friends otherwise I wouldn't be able to go out. I can't say that all Filipino families are this way, but my family is pretty typical even today.

155

"Most of my friends and classmates came from homes just as strict as mine. My grandmother (she's still in the Philippines) ran everything. That is true in many Filipino families. My grandmother is Bossa (female boss). That's what my grandfather calls her. My grandmother handled the finances and the house. She took care of pretty much everything, so my grandfather could do whatever he wanted. My grandfather is pretty laid back. They have seven children and seventeen grandchildren, and four great grandchildren. My grandmother is now eighty-six, and doesn't do as much anymore. She just had a pacemaker put in. My aunt told me once that when my grandparents are out together, my grandmother walks all the way in the front, and my grandfather lags behind. Whatever she says, goes. I think it is typical in Filipino families that the woman is strong, because with my aunts and uncles, you can see who is holding the family together.

"Interracial marriages are not a problem. My sister's boyfriend is Jewish. One of my aunts has a Greek husband. That's no problem. It's never been discussed in my family that I have to marry a Filipino boy as long as I get married."

Company Is Family
Hideo K.

Hideo is Japanese and in his forties. He has been in the United States for twenty-one years. He is the general manager of the service and quality control department of a Japanese electronics firm. He lives in a suburb in New Jersey with his wife and two children, both of whom were born in the United States. Japanese is the language spoken at home.

"My family comes first, but without company, there is no family. A lot of Japanese employees feel that way. I feel very close to my company. Traditionally, there has been a long history of serving the samurai. Everyone works for the boss in the area. Once you leave the family, you don't have a job. Japanese history says you must work for one company. But these days, it's slowly changing. For younger people, it is different. But for those over thirty-five, most would still tend to stay with one company. I think it is easy to stick with one company. Americans don't feel the same way. They like to have different experiences, to work for different places, to move up. In Japanese companies, once you step out, you could end up falling, or going up; there is a risk. Once you make this decision, it is very, very important.

"If a Japanese has had two or three jobs previously, the new boss might think this applicant is not loyal to the company. Typically, in my generation we work only in one company. You stay with the same company because of the benefits. There is the accumulation of vacation. In the U.S., it is ten days plus holiday. In Japan, many companies give up to forty-five to fifty days. Interestingly enough, many people don't take it, and let it build over the years. So once you give up the company, you don't have the vacation accumulated anymore. Also, positions change every three to five years. You can be moved to do other types of work within the company, so you get to know everyone in the company. It is unlike the United States, where once you're hired for a certain job, that is the only job you do. But in Japan, you have to study accounting, engineering. You go to many

157

places to communicate with your workers. Everybody knows everybody. There are almost three thousand people in my company, but most of us are the same age, so I know everyone. Every year, there is a changing of duties. You can say, I don't want to do this job anymore; I want to do something else. If the company thinks you can be of value in that area, then they will switch you. But sometimes it is the other way around. If you don't do a good job, but you don't want to move, but your boss thinks this is not good, he will move you. You may not like it, but you must obey. At that point, you have to decide whether you want to leave the company or not. No one is fired in Japan unless you steal something, or do something bad. Usually, if you are not good for the company, you will get a job that is not important. Retirement at our company is at age fifty-eight. If they don't need you, no one will say you must leave or retire. Instead, they won't give you any job — just a desk. You have no responsibility, but you must come to work. If you are of a strong mind, you might stay. But if you have pride and feel you can do more work, you leave. Your chance of getting work when you are in the fifties is very slim. Japanese companies have retirement benefits. Usually the benefits are for months of pay to thank you for your long service of thirty years.

"You have to think very carefully before you take a job. I have a unique position in the company. Usually a company sends you — they choose you to go to the U.S. But I have permanent residency here, so I don't worry about it too much. Of course, if my boss doesn't think I can do a good job, he can offer me a job back in Japan. Usually Japanese come over on a work visa. It used to be Japanese companies sent specialists here for three to five years. Now it is for five to eight years, because it takes a while to get used to the language. Banks still only send people for three years.

"I am the only person who ever left my company and was rehired. It is very, very unusual. They took me back because they needed someone in the U.S. Usually they won't even talk to you. They first approached me to ask me to help them look for a site, then I helped them look. Then they said if you want to come back, come work with us. I was very surprised. But at that time, they only hired me as an American worker. After three years, they said we want to hire you back. As a Japanese employee, there is a major difference in pay and in benefits. For instance, they pay for the Japanese education of my children. They will help pay the mortgage on my house, they will pay living expenses, and for trips to Japan. This is not done because of my position, but because I am treated as a worker to the U.S. from Japan, who may return to Japan one day. I am happy about that. I feel I belong to a company again. It is important to me.

"When I was still employed as an American employee, I felt some distance from my coworkers. The feeling was that I had worked here before, but was not really back as one of them. But once I became a 'Japanese' employee again, the feeling was that I'm in the same boat with them. So now I feel more camaraderie and identity with my Japanese coworkers. We usually have many, many visitors from Japan, so we would have to go out to dinner. If you're employed as an American, you feel as though you don't belong there, and they may not invite you for the dinner. So it's not like you're truly in the family. Once you get back as a 'Japanese' employee, you feel more like a part of the family. I guess this is because I am Japanese. We have two Americans that are officials of the company, and they are viewed as just as important as Japanese employees. Once you're into the family, you don't have to think about certain things. Before, I would have to think about whether I should go with them to dinner. Sometimes I ended up not going because I wasn't sure. Now I am automatically included, and I don't have to think twice about it.

"Japanese companies are unlike American companies in that it is primarily a man's world. Inside an American company, there are no men, no women – only workers. But in Japan, it's still a man's business world. It's changing little by little; some important positions are going to women. But for the most part, it's still a man's world.

"I like what I'm doing. I find it challenging. We have many people in Japan, doing what I do, so when I go back to Japan, I am one of them. I am nothing special. But here, because of my language, I can fill a special need, and I'm more important to my company. I'm still talking broken English, but I still feel that my English makes me valuable to the company.

"I work nine to seven everyday. Others might work till midnight, but I leave at seven. There is always a sense that things have to be done today, that it can't wait till tomorrow, because there are only seven of us in this country for the company. The pressure is very high. Business has to make profit. Without profit, the business would not exist. We have seventy people working. So we have to have new models introduced every six months. In order to have profit, we have to have a smooth flow of products. So it is a very, very tight schedule. We must create products.

"My business is as an engineer, and it is easier for me to work with people I know in Japan. I know how the department heads communicated and think. So it would be easier for me to communicate if I know the people there. Usually, I go back to Japan to take care of business for a week, then the next week I see family. I do this maybe a few times a year.

"In our U.S. office, there are only a few departments, engineering which I take care of – accounting, credit, sales, administration, and warehouse. So there isn't much chance to move around this company in the U.S. In the U.S., we follow the U.S. system, and we don't move people around.

"The company actually tried to start an American subsidiary here twice. The first time was in 1965, but they closed the business in 1972 because of economic reasons. Then the company returned to the U.S. in 1980. Between those years, I left the company and worked for Sanyo.

"In 1968 when the company first sent me, we had a joint project with General Electric in Utica, New York. Unfortunately, or fortunately, we had a big problem with the project, and the company sent me to the U.S. But as you know, twenty years ago, the airfare from Tokyo was about two thousand dollars. At that time my salary in Japan was fifty dollars a month. So two thousand dollars airfare was big money. It was cheaper to have me stay here. So after the GE job, they told me to stay and work at the subsidiary. I was told to come and stay for three years. When I came to the U.S., my salary was increased to five hundred dollars a month. That was a ten-fold increase. But most Americans were making seven hundred dollars a month. We couldn't afford to live in a private house. We stayed in a small apartment. Today with the change in the yen and the economic circumstances, it is the other way around. I am sure Japanese businessmen get better pay than their American counterparts. So living in this country is better now than in the past.

"When the company closed its U.S. plants in 1973, I went back to Japan. But I saw no hope to return to the U.S. within the next few years, so I left and worked for another large trading company. They had just started an electronics plant in the U.S. I got married, and came to the U.S. the second time. When that company folded, I went to work for Sanyo.

"When I was young I left, but now I wouldn't consider leaving. When you are young, there are more opportunities to think about such a thing. Once you reach a certain age, your job is secure, you've worked a long time for an employer, gotten good pay. So I have no intention of changing jobs now.

"I have lots of video coming in from Japanese TV for my children. It is important for them to keep up with the language. Ten or fifteen years ago, it was hard. But now with the video, it is much easier. If we give up everything and go back to Japan, I want my children to understand Japanese. Someday I feel I will go back. The children think they have Oriental faces, and when they go back to Japan, they don't want strangers to think they don't speak Japanese. It would be very embarrassing.

"I might stay here for another ten years, and then maybe go back to Japan. I miss it a lot. I go back every year. My family goes back every three years. The company sends them for vacation. They usually go back for two months.

"I play golf in my leisure time. Most businessmen coming from Japan like to play golf. It costs about two hundred U.S. dollars to play in Japan, and you have to reserve the spot three months ahead of time. I like the space here."

RELIGION AND RITES
WITHIN FAMILY

Koreans and Church
Charles Ryu

Charles is a thirty-year-old Korean American who immigrated from Korea at seventeen. He attended Yale Divinity School and is assigned to the Korean Methodist Church and Institute in New York City.

"As a minister for first generation Koreans, I tell people they should be ready for their death, in the sense that unless they die and are buried here, Koreans cannot claim the land. I think that is very Asian. Where your ancestors are buried is your home. And if the first generation who have been here twenty years are still in the mode of 'making it' when they reach their sixties and seventies, the second generation and 1.5 generation will be forever lost. If the first generation says I will make my home here — this is where I will live, where I will be buried, and I will let my children inherit the land and be responsible citizens of the U.S. and of the world with Korean heritage — that would be wonderful. So in a way, I sort of push that, here and there.

"In America, whatever the reason, the church has become a major and central anchoring institution for Korean immigrant society. Whereas no other institution supported the Korean immigrants, the church played the role of anything and everything — from social service, to education, to learning the Korean language; a place to gather, to meet other people, for social gratification, you name it. The way we think of church is more than in a religious connotation, as a place to go and pray, have worship service, to learn of God and comfort. Your identity is tied so closely to the church you go to. I think almost seventy to eighty percent of Korean Americans belong to church. And it becomes social evangelism. If those who had never considered themselves to be Christian want to be Korean, they go to church. They just go there for social reasons. You are acclimated into the gospel, and you say, I want to be baptized. Your life revolves around the church. It could also become a ghetto in the sense of a Chinatown or a Korea-town. But at the same time, it can be a place, if done properly, where the bruised identity can be healed and affirmed, because living in American society as a minority is a very difficult thing. You are nobody out there, but when you come to church, you are a somebody. The role of the black church in the civil rights era was the same thing.

"Probably American churches have become specifically religious. I have my love life, my civic life, my professional life, and I have this church, religious life. But the Korean churches provide a new community of some sort that permeates the social matrix. It is such a solid, close knit community, because everyone feels in a sense alienated outside, so there is this centripetal force. At the same time, most who come are well established or potentially well established.

"A lot of people who belong to the English language service (which I am a part of), come here and say this is the only place they feel is home. I mean, they are executives in big corporations, or they might work at *Time* magazine or Morgan Stanley. And they do very well, yet feel America is like a wilderness. They come here and feel affirmed. They say, 'I don't have to prove anything.' When I am with Koreans, I have to prove I am Korean. When I am with others, I feel I have to prove I am American. You gather all these English speaking Koreans in one place, in the religious context of God loves you as you are, and the sense of community, and the whole being is affirmed. I see that need, and civic organizations don't provide that. They may take care of one or two needs, whereas church can provide holistic needs."

Religion and Korea: "There have been so many dissertations written on why Koreans are so into church and religion, but no one seems to know why.

"Korean culture has been a very religious culture from the beginning. It is fraught with religious symbolism. Koreans tend to use foreign religions to express their religiosity. First Buddhism was introduced to Korea. It ultimately became a state religion. Buddhist religious language became the medium for Korean religiosity. Then Confucianism came, and then Christianity. And somehow Christianity made sense to Korean people because it is a very powerful or attractive religion. Even now, after one century, over twenty-five percent of the Korean population claim to be of the Christian religion. So whether you belong to an organized religion or not, Koreans always saw their lives in somewhat religious terms. Christianity is a universal religion, but Christians are still very racist, sexist, and parochial — including Koreans. So this open brotherhood and sisterhood is more of an ideal to be reached than the reality.

"American white missionaries who went to Korea are of fundamentalist sorts. They somehow confused the kingdom of God with American culture. To become Christian meant destroying Korean culture, which is part of the painful history of Korean Christians. So from early on, the way we understood the Korean culture matrix was always in terms of Western Christianity. So I am struggling very hard today to understand what it means to be a Korean-Christian, or a Korean American-Christian.

"For instance, when they [missionaries] came to Korea, every family had a little shrine to their ancestors. The missionaries asked them to destroy it, so my grandparents destroyed it. But my family kept that remembrance part, and made it into a Christian memorial service, which is very interesting. We still have the memorial service in L.A. (where my parents are). We still remember in Korean. The annual ceremonies for our grandparents are a blending of Christianity and Confucianism which is very similar to the veneration of saints in Catholic Christianity. The stories and oral histories of our families we share are still very much a part of our lives. The first week of January is when people gather to remember my father's father — where he was born, where he was educated. Three or four years ago, my father started making maps in English so that the second generation, now being born, can understand. But in terms of understanding our ancestors, that's very Confucianistic. We learned that from Confucianism. Confucianism was the state religion for five centuries."

Family Gathering

Sue Jean Lee Suettinger

Sue Jean is a forty-one-year-old Chinese American. She was born in Canton, China and immigrated to the United States at age four.

"My family is traditional in attitudes about how we were raised. We have a respect for our elders, and a very strong sense of identity in terms of heritage. We were encouraged to learn more and be sensitive to our history, where we came from, our people.

"Whenever I visit my mother during a Chinese holiday and she has the special food and settings out to honor our ancestors, I always light some incense, kowtow several times and kneel before pictures of my ancestors. In my parents' living room, my dad has pictures of my grandparents and great grandparents. It's set up against the wall, and sometimes oranges and flowers are placed there on special occasions. My parents, who are both in their seventies, still journey twice a year from New Jersey to Washington D.C., to pay respect to my grandparents at the grave. It's become a way for my family to get together. We would bring a chicken — special ordered because it must have a head and feet — roast pork, and a slice of pork fat and some sweet cakes to the cemetery. Then there are oranges and apples. First we trim the grass around the grave markers, clean them off with water, then we place flowers and the food, and light candles and incense by the graves, offer them the food and then pour three tea cups of Johnny Walker Red on the ground. The food and whiskey is symbolic; it is our way of offering them a special meal each year to honor and remember them, so they won't go hungry. Then we burn paper money, lots of it — gold-sheeted, and even fake bills, so they will have money to spend. Then there are color sheets of paper which symbolize clothing. We burn that too. It's all done in a metal container. And we bring along a cassette of Chinese music which we play, so that my grandparents can enjoy the music while they are eating. We do this every year, and it is a part of what my family feels is our obligation to our ancestors."

Ancestors

Chin Cai Ping

Chin Cai Ping is in her mid-twenties. She immigrated to the United States from the People's Republic of China in 1984. The interview was conducted in Toishanese (a dialect of Cantonese).

"We try to keep the same traditions at home today as we did in China. On Chinese New Year and holidays, we light incense and bow to our ancestors. We moved our family altar here from China. We still send money back to the village to have people tend the graves for us, but here, we also pray to our ancestors. For the ancestors, I make a chicken, prepare a large slice of pork, a whole fish, and sauté all sorts of vegetabes, rice noodles, Chinese seaweed, and soup, and little pastries. I place all that in front of the altar with three wine glasses and a plate full of oranges, stacked like a tree. The altar would have the names of my husband's ancestors going back several generations. Then we would light incense and bow.

"If we feel that one of the ancestors is especially influential to us in spirit, we would have a picture of that person. For instance, we have a picture of my husband's godfather. It is framed, and sort of set on the side. If we have any difficulties or we feel we need some comfort, we might light some incense by his picture and pray to him. You have to keep the direct ancestors of the family as the main part of the altar and any other relations, such as the godfather, separate, on the side.

"In China today, New Year's is celebrated much more than it was in the past. That's because things are more liberated. When I was growing up, about fifteen years ago, we were not allowed to worship our ancestors, and we were told to dismantle our altars at home. So if we bowed to the ancestors, my mother would tell us to stand guard at the door to make sure there weren't any red guards or patrols around. The cadres of local people would just come in the house at any time and inspect it. So my mother would make us stand guard at the door, and she would quickly light the incense, set up the table and altar and bow. And then she would quickly remove everything so there would be no trace. But today, it is different. New Year's is celebrated in a much more liberated fashion."

Cao O

Cao O is in his thirties. He is a Chinese from Vietnam.

"On New Year's in Vietnam my mother liked to light some incense, and do the whole ceremony, but it is not done in this country, because it is something I do not want to see at home. There are two aspects of it. One is burning incense to the deities, during the New Year and other special occasions. Then it is done also to commemorate the birth date or death of the ancestors. Each elder who dies should have his name on a family altar so that you can burn incense in front of it. My father's side has his set of ancestors, and my mother has a different set. You're not allowed to mix family altars together. In this country, my mother has never asked me if she could set up a family altar, but I have always given her some message that that is something I would not allow. Basically they are staying at my place, and they have to respect me in terms of who I am, and what I believe. I don't believe in that type of stuff anymore. Even though I was brought up in that tradition, I see a lot of it as superstition. My mom knows that, so she will not insist on having incense. But she would do things quietly. On New Year's, she would buy some oranges or tangerines and put them on the table by an open window, and get a pot of tea and pour it into three cups, and then she would kneel down and pray through the open window. To me, that's fine, as long as she doesn't have any permanent artifacts at home such as altars. So I think she respects my values."

Tony Hom

Tony is a twenty-five-year-old Chinese American who was born and raised in the United States.

"We don't have any religion that my parents maintain. At least not in the typical American Anglo idea of religion, and a God. Everything seems to be more along the Chinese tradition. I feel there are a lot of superstitious traditions that are carried over from generation to generation. For instance, my parents have always told me, you can't wash you hair on a holiday. Maybe it's because you wash it after a funeral — evidently to cleanse yourself of the death. So if you wash your hair on a holiday or a birthday, it symbolizes mourning, and you can't mourn on a holiday. That was the main thing I couldn't understand or couldn't uphold all together. You can't mention death at all. That is a big taboo. There is a hangup about death, so you shouldn't bring it up.

"When I was growing up they seemed to worship a dead relative on certain holidays. Prior to Chinese New Year for instance, they would burn this paper. It looks like a wad of napkins (actually it is fake money), and they would light incense. But before my mom did that, she put out three Chinese spoons and poured wine into three cups. Then she would lay out rice that was a few days old. There were always settings for three people. but I never had any idea who they were for. I thought they were toasting three deceased family members from way back when. But they never told me. Very recently, I found out the three settings aren't for any particular dead relative. Three is a lucky number, and so it is customary to set three places when going through the ritual of honoring ancestors. The table was laid out to symbolically invite the spirits to eat. So that shattered that lifelong thought (chuckles)."

Advance Purchase

Wong Chun Yau

Wong Chun Yau is a seventy-year-old Chinese American who immigrated to the United States in 1979.

"I told my daughter and sons that I don't want them to have a big feast for family and friends following my burial. In this country, there's no need to do that. It also costs too much money. They have this deal for senior citizens, where a local Chinese funeral parlor is selling sites for five hundred dollars a grave. So my daughter said she would buy one for me. That's considered cheap, considering that piece of land will be yours for thousands of years. I haven't seen it yet, but they plan to have an excursion for seniors on Tomb Sweeping Day in April, where for ten dollars, they will drive you there to look at the site and also provide dim sum (pastries) for lunch. Of course, you can't pick the site. They just give it to you by numbers. The first one there gets the first site, and so on. They bought this big plot of land, so that seniors can buy the spots individually. They probably won't make much money from it. The idea is, if you're not ready to use the plot yet, they will take your five hundred dollars and put it in the bank to collect interest, and to fix up the place. So the money from seniors eventually will be used for seniors. And if I don't like the plot? Well I guess I can always donate it to someone else who doesn't have the money and buy myself another plot. Taking care of this is a very natural thing to do. Look at it this way. It saves the young people the need of running around, looking for a plot, and spending money. So you eliminate some headaches for the next generation. So a lot of people do this."

One God

Alicia Diem

Alicia is forty years old and immigrated from Vietnam in 1984. Alicia is a pseudonym used at her request.

"My family's religion is Buddhism. My mom would always go to temple to pray. In Vietnam, when I wanted to leave, I would go to the temple and pray all the time. 'Help me,' I would pray.

"Now sometimes when I have trouble I just pray to God. I think God can help me. God is one God—Catholic, Christian, Buddhist. It is all God. There is one God, only one. I have been to churches a few times in my life. I have been to a Catholic church once or twice in my life and to a Christian church a few times. I have been to temples maybe twenty times in my life. I just want to go to church because I want to feel good. I want to rest, and not to think too much. But I believe in God. God is for everyone, not just for Christians, or Moslems, or Buddhists."

Immigration Theology

Wontae Chu

Wontae Chu is the head minister of the Korean Methodist Church and Institute in New York City. He arrived in United States from Korea in 1972.

"In my sermons, I talk about immigration theology. We would liken our experiences to what happened to Abraham and the wandering tribes. It is a way to incorporate our alien status in this country, to justify our existence and why we are here. It can be justified by religious faith and many Bible characters who were uprooted from their homeland. They had direction, so we try to apply that.

"We regard our church as an exodus community, constantly moving. We have four hundred members. It is the oldest church in the East Coast. It was founded in 1921. It has a special role to play. As the firstborn church, we think we have a mission to lead and help our community. Last year, we had some internal problems, so unfortunately, the church split. Part of the membership went to Passaic Korean Church in New Jersey. Before the split we had more than six hundred members. The split was not theological. What happened was there was a rift between old-timers and newcomers. Some had been in this country more than thirty years so they are quite Americanized. So I think last year's problem brought out the differences. We are not very sad about it; we take it as a matter of course. It is a very shameful affair. The pastor, my predecessor, moved with that group. That's why I came here. He had been here thirteen years. We are still communicating, though. There are some differences between both groups, such as lifestyle. Americanized lifestyle has somewhat of a controlled style. Korean is not. They tend to be emotional, and aggressive. The Americanized people don't want to take unnecessary risks. But the newcomers are more aggressive in taking risks. The issue was of church relocation. We didn't choose a spot, but we did do fund raising. We had more than a million dollars raised, and because of that, there were differences. The old-timers wanted to stay in this building, but the newcomers were more adventuresome, and they wanted to find a new place. The old-timers felt the amount was not enough; that more fund raising was needed.

"We are at the point of studying relocation and looking for a good place to move. This place is too small. We are borrowing a church next door and we are paying one thousand five hundred dollars a month just to use the church for a few hours on Sunday for services and some classes. It is very expensive. So we want to have our own place. We do have a small meeting place but it is only for one hundred and fifty people. The church was the exposed rift, but there were other tensions. The newcomers thought they were less privileged, and the old-timers more privileged. They felt that the people who have been here for a long time were better off. So it wasn't an age thing or a language thing. It was more of an economic thing. We are still analyzing what was our fault. We'd like to call it growing pains."

III. Reflections on Interracial Marriage

Thirty-eight states had antimiscegenation laws at some point, though not all those states prohibited Asian mixed marriages.

1922: Congress passes the Cable Act, stripping a female of her citizenship if she married an alien ineligible for U.S. citizenship. (At the time, no Asian was entitled to become a naturalized citizen.) Should she end the marriage, a Caucasian woman's citizenship would be reinstated. But if an Asian woman divorced, she would not regain her citizenship, as Asians were not at that time eligible to be naturalized citizens.

By the end of World War II, 31 states still had laws against mixed marriages, among them, Virginia, Maryland, California, Washington, Missouri, Alabama, and Georgia.

1948: The State Supreme Court declares California's legal ban on interracial marriage unconstitutional.

1967: *Loving v. Virginia*: The U.S. Supreme Court ruling bans antimiscegenation laws as unconstitutional.

Twenty-five Years
Jim and Kate Mishra

Jim and Kate met while Jim was a graduate student in a Midwestern university in the 1960s. Kate was born and raised on a farm north of Albany, N.Y., and Jim is from India. He is Hindu. They have two children and own a home in a suburban town. The living room is done in early American. There is little sense of an Asian presence in the furnishings. Kate is a university administrator. Jim holds two master's degrees and was between jobs at the time of this interview. Their names have been changed at the request of both.

KATE: "I don't consider my marriage to Jim an interracial one, rather, it's intercultural. I don't consider Asian Indians to be of a different race, so I want to set that straight up front. Jim's skin may be a little different from mine, but he's not a different race. If I married a black individual, it would be interracial. This is not interracial. We're from different cultures. Jim was brought up in India, and I consider him to be of Caucasian stock."

JIM: "I do feel that there is resentment because I married an American woman, although it hasn't been shown. If I go to a fund-raiser and I run into a group of people, their spontaneity becomes subdued, like they don't know what to expect from me. They sense I am different. It would be easier for them to handle it if Kate were married to some blond-haired man."

KATE: "If anyone asks me about an interracial marriage, I will make it very clear that Jim's world is Caucasian. In this country, interracial marriage often means marriage of a black and a Caucasian person. I would consider many of the Asians to be of the Caucasian race. There is the Caucasian race and the Negroid race. I'm not an anthropologist, so I'm not sure of the precise classification of people. But I do know certainly, in my learning about Indians, that many, many centuries ago, we were really dealing with Caucasians and many tribes that came into India. In some parts of India, those groups of people were not invaded by tribes, so they are Caucasian. We're not different races. We're different cultural groups. I'm emphatic about that.

175

"My family's major concern when they found out that I was marrying Jim was that we would move to another part of the world. I think to the best of their ability, they welcomed Jim. These were people with extremely limited backgrounds. They didn't travel. They married and lived their lives in this one area and they were marvelously open insofar as welcoming a son-in-law from Asia into the family. They did a super job. I hope I could be so open if my sons brought home an Asian woman. I would hope that I could be as accepting as my family was towards Jim.

"I was brought up in the fifties when one tended to marry right out of college. You worked for one or two years, then you established a family, stayed at home and did lovely volunteer work. That's not how my life panned out. I found I needed to assume an economic role and wasn't prepared for it mentally. Once I got into it, I was okay. So the fact that I married an Asian who has some limitations in the marketplace has affected me. We worked really hard. Jim has had a lot of trouble economically in getting integrated into this society. He has yet to find his niche. I have found mine. He hasn't been happy with his positions, and it's been difficult for the whole family because of this. This is a sophisticated town, so I don't know if Jim's problems are because of his surname, his credentials, or because of age discrimination. When you get up in your fifties, employers may look at you a certain way, regardless of what background you have. I taught throughout our marriage, and for the last few years, I have been an administrator in the college. We have lived in this town for twenty-four years. Last spring I was elected as a member of the township council which was a wonderful honor. It brought together a lot of effort that both of us have put in this town. I got the most votes out of anyone running for town council. When I first ran for office a year ago, it was not a good time for our relationship. He was extremely depressed about it. He felt I had taken on a public personality, and he was sharing me with the whole world. Despite that, he does attend functions with me occasionally, and he knows a lot of people in this town.

"In terms of work and leisure, we had to adapt because we had very different views. I grew up on a farm, and I'm very ambitious in terms of my work, and that old Protestant ethic is very strong in me. I'm terribly hard working and I want us to move ahead, economically, and for my own situation, professionally. And I think Jim's family was a bit more aristocratic and saw life in an easier vein than I did. In that sense, Jim in his culture, would have been more content, more relaxed. Life was easier there, I'm sure.

"One of the cultural differences was certainly in bringing up the children. I think one of the hardest things was this male-oriented thing about the father having absolute say in raising the child. One time we were visiting Jim's family in India, and my oldest son, who is very active, ran someplace to play which I thought was fine. I didn't see any danger in it. I remember my father-in-law turning to me and asking, 'Why do you not take my permission to go there?' It never occurred to me he should. I felt this type of autocratic childrearing just didn't work.

"The companionship I observe in American males — such as doing boy scout projects or playing baseball with kids — the companionship of the father sharing didn't come easily. Jim remembered the children were brought to their father at dinner time when they were nice and clean and well disciplined, and that's what he was seeing them as, and not in the democratic American family setting. There are some things you accept in life. I know Jim would never take them to go play baseball or watch football with them because that is not his background. But there are things he will do, like we have a wonderful hill in the back, and in the winter he will take them sledding. He had trouble doing things with his sons on a casual basis. There wasn't any sharing.

"This was difficult for the time standpoint for me because at one point I went back for my doctorate. Even though he would sometimes help out with things, I don't think he was happy with some of the things I was doing in terms of my goals. It was difficult to teach, to go for a doctorate, to raise a family, and to have a husband who's not talkative or supportive. Once in a while he would do the dinner dishes when I put the kids to bed, and I would be deeply appreciative. So sometimes it worked out, and many times it didn't.

"The male has a very important role in the Asian culture because he is the major wage earner. But when you have two major wage earners in the family, the woman can't be a major wage earner and at the same time be the provider and child nurturer without help. The woman needs help and with the Asian man this is much harder. It's worked itself out, only because the kids have grownup. I don't think I could look back. You should look ahead. This is the time in my life that is the best. Those early years of childrearing are behind me. It was rough. My sons don't speak any Indian, and they were raised in American fashion — in Christian fashion. We had Jim's blessing on this. He felt if in Rome, you should do as the Romans.

"We travelled back to India twice. His father was marvelous, his mother was so dear and sweet, but you know this woman was married when she was sixteen or seventeen. I don't know whether they accepted me or not. They were polite. They hide their feelings. It was hard to know.

"Jim has some very good Indian friends and they may invite us to their homes. But they're not always comfortable with me. The pattern of entertainment is always interesting. And I am getting better at accepting this. There would come a time at the dinner party that the women would go in one room, the men in another. Often times, I would just stay with Jim. I find, frankly speaking, that the men are interested in politics whereas the women tended to talk about food and their children, so I found I could relate to the men better than to the women. And what is interesting is that after several drinks, the topic would turn to what's wrong with this country. And being the native born American there, I let no opportunity pass where I would argue for this country. Several times I found myself taking on these men, and I found myself enjoying it. And I know exactly what their concerns are — the treatment of the elderly, materialism. I could argue either side, of course. With them I always argue pro–American. But now I guess I no longer am as ready to jump into the issues as before when I was younger.

"I feel I'm one of the luckiest people around here. As a woman, I have two lovely children who are almost on their own. I'm terribly fulfilled in many ways. Jim is a very dear husband. I've had absolutely no sense of discrimination because of the marriage. In a college community, there is a lot of acceptance of different cultures. We meet a lot of people. I've never sensed any discrimination."

JIM: "I was at this very traditional gathering at Christmas time. All the old money of the town was there. It was 99.9 percent white. The first time I walked in, the waiter looked hard at me and then at my invitation. Of the three hundred people there, I had the darkest complexion. There was a reaction all over the room before they got acclimated to me. It's that kind of resentment. There is still this understated resentment because I married an American girl. Now they test me to see how I can handle myself now that my wife is a town council woman. They want to see how I will handle getting a job. I am between jobs now. People know me around town as Kate's husband.

"Indians have a patriarchal society. Men dominate. It's almost the same as Japan where the woman walks behind you. The husband is revered. But in this country, I have changed. You get used to things here and forget the expectations of younger days. It doesn't bother me much anymore.

"Marrying an American woman has also made it more difficult for me to mingle in Indian society here. Americans really don't care that much. They feel as long as you are happy, you can choose your own partner. But I sense a difference for Indians. As an example: I would be at the bottom of an Indian guest list because they don't know whether Kate would want to come. So they decide maybe they shouldn't invite Jim and Kate. These are the subtleties. At Indian parties they also take their frustrations out on Kate. Many are doctors, engineers, PhDs, who feel they should be doing even better in this country, so they attack her personally and she fights back. She is used to it. After a few drinks, you tend to be freer, and everybody has some frustrations, either job or business. And she gives as good as she gets."

On Life: "Sometimes because of your color, you don't feel you fit in, especially, in a very white or WASP society. I still feel my roots are in India. But more and more this has become my homeland. My life changed so gradually that it changed without my knowing it. I've become more Americanized by living in this country. You start losing track of feelings for the other half of your life — the brothers or sisters. In India, the brothers or sisters are very close. If a brother comes here, you have to take care of them. Here, the longer you stay, the less feelings you have for them. I do wish I had more family ties in this country. I think American society is very closed. There is no warmth. Indian society is family oriented, and society is much more open. Here, suppose you live in this neighborhood for ten years, you would still be saying, 'Hi, hello,' to your neighbor. But in India, you would have your neighbors over at least once a month.

"Twenty-five years ago, I wouldn't think of living here. Once we tried to move to India. We stayed for two months, but things didn't work out. Nobody would hire Kate in India, even though she had a master's degree. 'How come you hire other Americans,' I asked? They said these were experts sent by places like Ford Foundation. Indian companies wouldn't hire an American. I had a job but she did not, so we packed up and came back to this country. I know I've changed. People like us lose a lot of tenderness by living here. We become very rigid. This society is mostly work and your nucleus family. There is no extended family here. So these are the changes. I'm not sure how I've changed, I just know I have — every aspect of me. I don't think I would have changed as much as if I had married an Indian woman. I probably would have more Indian friends.

"I don't think I was ever accepted by one of her sisters. There is coldness in her behavior. The mother didn't say very much about this marriage either. I was born Hindu. But Christmas time, I go to a Christian church with my family. We decided since my sons were born here, they would be Christians. If we were in India, they would be raised as Hindu. We really didn't push our sons to learn the language, though I do wish they could speak Bengali. I don't particularly want them to go to India to live. I know they would be totally lost. But I would like them to visit.

"If I had to do it over again, I probably would have gotten a doctorate and tried very hard to be in Indian society in India. Living in India would have made me a different person today. You pay hard for what you get here. In India, the help in cooking, running the house, would have been easier. Indian society is much warmer. My lifestyle would have been different if I had stayed in India, gotten my PhD, with or without marrying Kate. If you have a good position there, life is less hard. But that is my fantasy. I think my greatest disappointment in life so far is my financial stability at this point. At my age and with my education I should be vice president of a company, but I'm not.

"I think being Indian in this country has held me back economically. If I were a European or an Englishman, I would have a better job. You don't have to be very smart to know this. It's just being foreign — that you don't look or talk like the other ninety percent — and because of that, there is a fear. I suspect this. I've never confronted it. It's difficult. When you go for a job interview on a one to one basis, it is hard to prove. But this is my feeling. I don't think this feeling will go away in my generation. My sons have white fair skin, no accent, and they tend to look more white, so maybe the feeling will disappear in their generation.

"I did not like my wife running for office. In fact, the woman's independence was the greatest thing I had to adjust to. An extreme difference between Indian and American women is their openness. I was amazed that Kate would even shake hands with a stranger. And as for kissing, that would never happen publicly in India."

Looking Back: "The hardest part was raising the children. Now that part is over, and we've grown together in the process of raising the children. We are at a different stage of our lives now. The hardest part of our adjustments is behind us. The beginning, raising children, making a living, that was the toughest.

"There were always differences but you felt that you could work them out. I didn't anticipate all the changes that I would have to make. I think it is best not to think of the changes and cultures. It can't be described. I think I changed more than her because we live here. If we lived in India, I think I would see more change on her side. The issue of divorce was discussed but our children kept us together. We were scared to death about what would happen to them. They were our responsibility. Now they are almost grown. We are growing old, and we are growing old together. All these years we have been together, raised the children, now we have thirty-five percent of our life left, and we have spent much of our life together, and that keeps us going. It's a nice stage for us now.

"Twenty-five years of experience says maybe it would have been better if she had married someone American and I had married someone Indian, because looking back, the adjustments have been so great and the changes so major."

Biting the Bullet

Vivian Hom Fentress

Vivian is in her thirties. She is a Chinese American who was born and raised in the United States. She was told from childhood that she must marry Chinese. She didn't. She has been married to Mark Fentress for three years.

"I met Mark when I was nineteen and in college. In high school, I had never been allowed to go on a date because my parents believed I was too young to consider that sort of thing. So they assumed that when the time was right I would meet the correct Asian guy, and that would be it. But that's not how it worked out. There was never consent from my parents to date at a particular age. The feeling was that when you graduate college and your studies are over, you could concentrate on finding a guy to marry. My parents saw dating as a waste of time, or as an activity that took time away from school work or led you to evil. So it wasn't one of those things that was condoned.

"After the first couple of years with Mark, it was apparent things were becoming more and more serious. Still at that time my parents assumed I was going through a rebellious stage. They accused me of not wanting to date Asians and not giving anyone else a chance. So they, like other families, started setting up blind dates for me with their friends' sons. I hadn't met them at all. Just because they were Asian, they fit the bill. These were the people they wanted me to meet. I found it pretty offensive that character didn't mean anything as long as they came from an Asian family. Some of the people they sent to meet me did not have the type of person-ality that I wanted the guy I dated to have. And yet it was a disappointment to them when we didn't hit if off. I went on a couple of dates just to satisfy my parents. I had to please them and to prove I wasn't doing it to rebel. But I guess it was a formality because I knew I was just going through the motions, anyway.

"One guy was truly a typical stereotype. He was a really skinny guy with stringy hair and no conversational skills at all. I mean it was to the point where I took one look at him, and I thought of the closest restaurant that we could go to, so we could spend the least amount of time together. I wanted to go there, eat, and go to the movies, so we wouldn't have to talk or anything. Then we could come back home. That was certainly a one-time experience. But there were some others who were truly nice people. I didn't use them and I never led them on. Letting them pay for me was a definite no-no because that would have meant I was obligated to them. So it was stuff like that.

"It was a rough period because that offended Mark too. He knew that I was seeing these people, just to see them. He couldn't have been happy about it although he didn't express an opinion one way or the other. Mark was the only serious relationship I had, and the times I went out with Asians, I was set up by my parents. The first guy I brought home was Mark. And that went fine for the first two visits but by the third visit, they caught on. After the commotion was raised that we were seeing each other, they came up with threats of cutting off my school, and stuff like that. At that time I was nineteen years old, and I was not ready to throw everything all away for that. So we had to go underground. So from that point on, to make our lives easier, we pretended that Mark did not exist. I mean, I had to tell very elaborate stories about where I was going, who I was seeing, and what I was doing for years and years and years. That restored calm at home and allowed me to continue our relationship until I had to face it and decide if we were going to get married or not. You always had to cover your tracks. The name could never come up. You had to remember to substitute the correct name for the whole period that you were going out with this person. Phone calls were also very difficult. You had to coordinate times when you were calling because a phone call received by a parent would most likely not come through to me. I guess for that whole period of time my parents thought I wasn't dating anyone. Never once did I slip. I didn't feel guilty about the deception because I felt I was being denied my right to have a relationship with someone I cared a lot about. I was denied spending time with him on holidays. I was denied basic things like going to a show, seeing friends, things you'd like to talk about and share, but couldn't because you had to pretend that you didn't do any of these things. I think there is a definite generation gap between my parents and myself, because my parents weren't brought up in the United States. Here we are going through the teenager and young adult stage, and you expect to be able to date and hang around with guys, but from their standpoint, it was taboo. You couldn't do it."

On Breaking the News: "Breaking the news to my parents was hell. Seven years had passed due to the fact that all along I knew about the expectation that I should marry a Chinese, and if I didn't, I'd bring disgrace.

So knowing that expectation for years and years and the disappointment it would bring, I dreaded the reaction. I knew what the reaction was going to be. It was going to be hysterics. That stopped me from committing for all those years. I mean there was really no reason why we had to wait that long. But the simple fear of breaking the news to them stopped us quite a number of times. But it was coming to the point where it was becoming ridiculous. We were just dragging and dragging. He wanted a commitment and to settle down and have a traditional life together. He wanted to be recognized as a person and someone who is part of my life, rather than as someone hiding in the background. He never really pushed it or made it difficult for me. I knew I would have to get on with it. We couldn't go on that way forever.

"My mother's reaction was exactly as I imagined it. She had a period of crying and screaming, followed by periods of total silence. She didn't talk to me for a period of two to three months. She just pretended I wasn't there. And in the meantime, she would be crying and crying and warning other family members against going to my wedding and stuff like that. Probably the realization that I was going to go through with it, no matter what, changed that. I guess she decided she would rather be a part of it than not to be.

"I think in the end, I had to come to the realization that I would have to give up my family for Mark, before I could break the news. Those things as I saw it went hand in hand because I knew the potential was there. I knew that the hysterical reaction would bring about threats of being disowned. Once I made that choice it allowed me to break the news. My dad had a pretty calm reaction. He just wanted to make sure I knew the difficulties an interracial marriage would entail. He wanted me to understand that children produced from such marriages wouldn't be as accepted as other kids because their parents are different, and that kids would make fun of them in school. He was also afraid because of the stereotype that Americans are quick to divorce. But aside from that, he just assumed that I knew what I was doing."

The Wedding: "Aside from all the hysterics surrounding it, a lot of times I thought it was theatrical in nature. I thought the hysterics were intended to make me see my ways and change my mind. After a while, it made me angry because I thought it was too much. They were trying to play out everyone's emotions for something that was going to happen. You wanted to be wished well and if they can't participate in it, you want to be able to do it yourself peacefully. It was a very important time in my life, and I resented not being able to be joyous about it at home. I still felt I had to keep it quiet because I didn't want to look too happy. And another thing is that the news wasn't spread to aunts and uncles as I know it would have been if I were marrying an Asian guy. I think it was a month or two later that they got around to telling them because they had to tell them. I mean, I heard some of the conversations. And after the first couple, when I heard the wavering in the voice when they were telling them, I thought they were making excuses. There was the implication that I was not a good girl because I didn't listen when they said I must marry Chinese. I mean, I know that is a ridiculous thing to say but that was the gist of most of the conversations.

"I think everything was forgiven months before the wedding.

"I guess the only ritual before the wedding is sort of a shower for all the family to come over. Mark's family had to give my parents money to buy food and wedding cakes. I can't even remember what the cakes symbolize. I don't think I even know. It's just something you do for the bride, but I can't remember why. If I have a daughter, I am not going to insist on wedding cakes for her. It was a nice touch. I'm glad we did it. I didn't oppose it but I didn't push for it. It was just something that was important for my mom and I was glad to be a part of it.

"On the wedding day, you'd hope for some calm, but it wasn't. There were lots of people around cooking lunch for everyone before we left for the church. I guess that is a standard part of the pre-wedding activity. The wedding wasn't quite what I had in mind because of the priest we ended up getting. We had an Oriental priest from Chinatown. He had a very, very heavy accent. I could hardly understand most of what he was saying. It wasn't as solemn an affair as I had envisioned it would be. Aside from that, it was a perfectly happy day."

Differences: "The obvious differences between Mark and myself come from family practices. Many Chinese families have a very supportive mom and dad who try and do everything for the children. And the children are not to disappoint them or go against them. So if you live your life that way it makes you a different person. That made me different from Mark.

"Perceived respect equated to obedience and not making waves, not doing anything out of the ordinary that would draw attention to your family. Once we bridged the gap, and they accepted the fact that we were getting married, they treated Mark as family. And now I truly believe they have accepted him. I'm sure there are still some times when they wish he was Chinese like their other friend's spouses, but I don't think they begrudge the fact that he is not Chinese anymore. I guess once I got married they finally saw me as an adult. I was twenty-seven, and until you're married, they don't feel that you are an adult and can stand on your own.

"I am proud to be Chinese today. I think in terms of the heritage and the family unit, it is a definite plus, compared to how I see a lot of my friends' families, and their lack of commitment to each other. I would say my family is very, very, close. It is almost to a point where it is considered unhealthy to spend so much time, and do so much together. The fact that I go to my mother's house so often may seem unusual to Americans. I mean if my parents had it their way, we would be eating dinner there every weekend. I mean, they don't see why you need time alone at home. They think we should just be there with them all the time. I know we do a lot more that what Mark deems is normal time spent with the family. I don't know. I feel it's right. It's a good balance, so we do what we feel is right.

"I consider myself a Chinese who is very Americanized. I don't cook Chinese food at home but for a silly reason. You get all the grease all over the kitchen. I know, it's a shame. But maybe one day I will get a wok, and go outside and cook."

Chinese Wedding

Mark Fentress

Mark is in his thirties. He grew up in Syosset, Long Island, New York. He is married to Vivian Hom.

"I dated Vivian eight and a half years before we got married. I guess I knew after a year of going together I wanted to marry her. I had never dated any Asian girls before. Syosset was just one of those towns where there weren't any. I did have one good Chinese friend, a girl who lived in my town. But that was only a friendship. Her father owned the local Polynesian restaurant. Before Vivian, I had dated Caucasians. Vivian and I went to school together. I was being set up for a blind date with one of Vivian's sorority sisters. But when I saw the girl I was being set up with I decided I wanted nothing to do with her, and I ended up dancing with Vivian and kept dancing with her all night long, just to avoid the other girl. As it turned out, we went to the other girl's wedding this past summer.

"I first met Vivian's parents while she was still living at school. I lived close enough to school so that I could live at home. And we dated at school for a couple of months. Then the summer came and Vivian had a party at her home. I went to the party and was very welcomed in the house, because I was one of her friends from the party. And then a week or so later, I came and took her to the movies. The parents knew that I was the same person showing up twice. I don't think I got to strike three before I wasn't welcome in the house. I represented the ultimate threat. I was not Chinese, and I could be taking their daughter out of the possibility of meeting some nice young Chinese guy. At that point I simply wasn't welcome anymore. It didn't take long. We don't all look alike, apparently. We continued seeing each other, but it was your basic lying and deceiving for an awful lot of years. She would say she was going to visit friends in Long Island, and it would have to be Suzy this, or Kathy that, and the fact of the matter is, she would be visiting my parents' house. This was not even to spend the weekend; it was simply to go out. Even if they knew 'who she was going

186

to see,' it would never be brought up. I think that was their way of dealing with the situation. If I became the persona non grata, hopefully I would go away, drift into obscurity. And I didn't.

"In terms of timing for our marriage, the numbers of years we waited, and how we got married, I wouldn't change a thing, because it wasn't my choice to make.

"My parents are very warm, open people. They would accept probably anything. They immediately understood who Vivian was as a person as soon as they met her. And as a result, they liked her immediately. They didn't care if she was Chinese, Swedish, or a giraffe. She was simply this terriffic person. Part of that is probably because my dad is about as Waspish as he can get. You can trace his family back to the signing of the Declaration of Independence, while on the other hand, my mom is the immigrant in the family. She was born in Dublin, Ireland. My dad is Protestant, my mom is Catholic. My mother's parents both passed away when she was very young, so she came to this country to live with her aunt and uncle. Her aunt is an old fashioned Irish woman of the classic kind. I mean she came off the boat and worked as a cook for a wealthy family, and her husband was a butcher. She had her way of doing things, and every bit the closed society that you might associate with the Chinese or Oriental family. My father was not welcomed. My Aunt Katie literally attempted to throw my dad down a flight of stairs the first time that she realized that he had 'romantic inclinations' towards her little niece. At the same time, my dad didn't know if his parents were going to show up for the wedding. At that point in their lives, they were as Waspish as they could be. They lived from the South to the Midwest. He was a.) marrying someone who was an immigrant, and b.) marrying someone of a different faith. That was just completely out of the question. So my dad was literally shocked to see his parents show up for the wedding.

"People mellowed. Happily, while his parents were alive, it turned into a very loving relationship between everyone. So my family has a history of bucking the system. So I had nothing to lose in my relationship with Vivian. I mean, if it worked out I got a wonderful girl. But if things didn't work out, I still had my family, and we took the shot. With Vivian on the other hand, there was a decided choice that had to be made. She had to decide if I was the person she wanted and if I was worth the possibility of losing her parents. Her mother is very strong headed, and she was very verbal in her threats. The situation worked out so that by not talking about it, or not paying any attention it, everything remained status quo. I mean, we saw each other, her parents left her alone, and her parents probably kept themselves comfortable with the idea that so long as my name wasn't mentioned, I didn't exist. And if I didn't exist, then things are okay. We let all of this turbulence ride for a very long time without bringing it to a head.

I wanted to push something to happen a long time ago, but like I said before, I had nothing to lose. Vivian did, and it was her choice and her decision. I simply had to wait until she was comfortable with it."

Breaking the News: "Finally the decision to get married was sprung on Vivian's mother after we had dated for over eight years. Lily, Viv's mother took the rational choice. She wanted to know the specific date that we were getting married because that was the day she was going to be in Hong Kong. She was going to boycott the hemisphere. She wanted nothing to do with us. I was living in New Jersey, and Vivian was living at home. And I was most definitely not welcome in the house. Vivian was home, night after night, taking the verbal thrashing, and whatever abuse could come her way. Her mother tried to talk her out of it. But she was resolute. Lily's parents lived next door, and what worked for us, was they were in our corner. Vivian's grandmother, who doesn't speak any English, was my best ally. So Viv's grandparents' comments were 'your mother will get over it. She's just old fashioned.'

"We proceeded to buy a house and set up a wedding all on our own because we were paying for it. Her parents didn't want anything to do with it so we set the whole thing up. Fortunately her mother wasn't as tough as she thought she was, or she had counselling from some good people, and they talked her into the idea that it was better to have a lo-fan (term for white person) son-in-law, than to have no daughter. At that point, I was suddenly welcome in the house. I was suddenly worth talking to. And more importantly, I had to set up a wedding in Chinatown in no time at all. And we did. We literally set up two complete weddings in four months. What happened was, we first set things up for a wedding in Sparta, New Jersey, where our house is. We had the church and the caterers set up. You name it, we were all set to go in Sparta. We instantly scrapped that when her parents decided they would accept this thing, but it had to be done in the Chinese way. Which meant we had to find a church that was accessible to all the family and friends, etc. and we had to find a place to have a banquet in Chinatown. We cancelled the wedding in Sparta to do it in Chinatown. Was it worthwhile? Yes. Every minute, tension, headache, every penny — it was all worth it, because it made the right people happy. It comforted those that needed to be comforted. I would get married anywhere. It doesn't have any particular significance to me whether I am married in a church or whether I am married under a beautiful tree on top of a hill, or whether I am married at a toll booth at the Lincoln Tunnel. I believe in God and He would have shown up, no matter where we did it.

"But a wedding to Vivian's parents isn't a wedding unless there is a banquet in Chinatown. You want to talk about Chinese reasoning or thought? Maybe that's hard to understand for a lot of people, but that's extremely important. It's where all their friends have their banquets and weddings and stuff, so that's where you have got to go. There is all sorts of pride and posturing from having a big, elaborate fancy wedding, so they got to do that. And I had a great time."

The Wedding: "I'm a kid of the suburbs, so to have something as important as my wedding in New York City, in a place as crowded and cramped as Chinatown, was kind of a shock. Weddings for kids who go to Syosset High School usually take place in either North Shore Synagogue or St. Edward's Catholic Church. Both of them are along tree-lined streets with big parking lots and big sidewalks, and steps for people to usher themselves in and usher themselves out. They don't get married in places where there are ducks drying in the window across the street.

"It was a culture shock to most of our Caucasian friends and my side of the family. The church was on Mott Street and there was shopping and traffic on the outside of the church. The back end of the church was literally wide open so that passers-by would walk into the church to see what was going on.

"Here we were, in front of the altar, and strangers were walking in and discussing how you look from the back of the church. People finally felt compelled to shut the doors to keep people from the street out. But being the good people from Chinatown, the passers-by just looked in from the side door. They were utterly dauntless. I guess that must have something to do with the Chinese culture. A wedding is not something that belongs to somebody. It is something that is shared by everyone. They felt they had as much right to be there as the so-called invited guests.

"Instead of going to a large catering hall and sitting around with a cocktail hour and a little ensemble playing elevator music to you, we started things off by having the wedding cake first, and Chinese dumplings and things like that served to people in the basement of the church right after the ceremony. There were people talking loud — very loud. There were lots of people talking very loud. It was almost deafening at times. That's the way Chinese people talk. Then the lo-fans got into the act, and started screaming at the top of their lungs too. Everybody ends up hoarse, except for the Chinese, cause they're used to speaking that loud.

"We then proceeded to move from the basement of the church, three blocks up Mott Street to the restaurant. It was all set up for us. We took up most of it. The bride and groom and the families of each sat on a raised platform with dragons and lions and these great big red and gold statues behind us, with lights on them. There were approximately three hundred people. Friends are invited. Friends that you haven't the slightest idea who they are. They were people Vivian's family knew, people her mom worked with, relatives. If the Homs were invited to a wedding of the Engs, you can be sure that at an Eng wedding, all the Homs would be invited. So as a result, it certainly was not an intimate little gathering. But nonetheless, it's very important to them. Of the guests, I probably knew close to half of them. Everybody sat below us. Once again, the family is the important unit. In other weddings I would go to, the bridal party would be at the head table, the dais. But at a Chinese wedding, the families were set up at each of the front tables.

"There was a twelve-course meal of things that certainly nobody ever pulled out of a white container. There was shark's fin soup, sea cucumbers, jellyfish, abalone, chicken, fish, steak, vegetables, rice, and the sweet bean drink at the end, which is my favorite. My best man at the wedding, and my best friend, was extremely gullible. We had him convinced the entire evening that anything and everything that was brought over was the entrails of some sea beast. And he didn't eat a thing the entire night. At which point, because everything is served family style – the food comes on a dish, which is served onto the plate – all the rest of the people at his table split up his portion, and they ate it. He, I believe, was the only person who went home hungry that night. It was a whole lot of fun. There were lots and lots of people walking around toasting to our health and happiness. I had no idea who they were at the time, but they were ever so sincere. So I raised a glass along with them.

"Alcohol seems to have a minor role at a Chinese wedding. At an American wedding chances are the people, whether they are consciously trying to or not, would just keep drinking so they feel woozy or sick by the time it's over. But I had a great time toasting everybody with two parts tea and one part cola. It's terrible for your teeth, but it doesn't give you a headache. [The bride and groom, along with the parents, would go to each table to toast the guests. The idea is to drink alcohol, but very often, it's a non-alcoholic mixture, disguised to look like straight scotch or brandy.]

"My wedding was the best day of my life. I had more fun. I was tremendously elated at calling Vivian my wife and seeing people having a really good time."

On Being Accepted: "As a person, I am pretty malleable. If a person needs or wants something, I pretty much just get up and do it. And that is something that is received extremely well around here. I think it would have made a difference if they perceived me to be lazy or whatever. It certainly wouldn't have helped my cause. But an equal part of enthusiasm and common courtesy goes an awful long way. They anxiously show me off as their son-in-law to anyone who will look.

"There are times when it is pretty lonely at the dinner table. When I eat with Vivian's family, especially on holidays, everyone is talking away and I do not speak the language. But at the same time through association, there are a lot of times when I know what's going on, and I understand what is going on without knowing the language. For me, I've learned to listen to eye contact, body movements, secondary languages if you will, and you can tell what's going on. There's another thing that happens. Because they're living in this country, there are many times when a Chinese word just doesn't fit the bill. So they throw in the English word along with the Chinese phrase. So all they have to do is throw me a tidbit, and I can generally scramble along, and maybe I can't catch the nuances but I have an idea where things are going. I remember the first few times I did it. People would be asking questions in Chinese and I'd answer in English — not specifically asking me anything, but I'd throw in my two cents, and it would be in English. And it just shut the room up, they didn't know what to think (chuckles).

"Chinatown seems to be very important to the family. For instance, Viv's mom commutes into the city every day from New Jersey. At eight thirty in the evening she's still not back from work in Chinatown. She's there not because she makes a Rockefeller type salary, by sewing in Chinatown, it's just that it's very important for her to be with a roomful of women who listen to the kind of music she listens to, and they all talk and gab in her own language, and that creates its own peer pressures, norms and mores.

"Vivian has a very strong sense of family, and so do I. But in truth, her family is much larger than mine. My family is confined to my parents, my two sisters, one sister's husband, and aunts and uncles as a distant peripheral, whereas Vivian's family just goes on and on and on. And that's just great. The way her parents live for instance is in a two family house with the grandparents next door. I don't know if something like that could ever work in my family. There's sort of a different sense of family."

On How Other People See Them: "I have never felt uncomfortable around here [New Jersey, New York area] about 'being who we are.' Are people aware of it? Yeah. In our neighborhood there are two retired couples. It's not discrimination, or anything like that, but they're trying to be neighborly. One of the guys came around one day, and he had just gotten something from Time-Life books on China. 'Oh,' he said, 'this is great, and you will learn a lot.' He was convinced Vivian was going to open this book and recognize everybody in the pictures. I can't say it is distressing. It's just old people who came from closed nooks and crannies of neighborhoods. We are unique. There is no question about it. They don't refer to us as the little girl with dark hair and the big chubby guy. Undoubtedly it's Mark and the Chinese girl or something along those lines.

"I only once found myself all but enraged over somebody's comments. And that was when Vivian and I went on a cruise for a belated honeymoon, of all places to Alaska. And one of the people on the ship was a retired air force, navy or marine guy. I forget which. And he was one of these people who walked around with a silver star lapel emblem on his jacket. He probably also has it tattooed on him somewhere. He could have been the greatest American since George Washington or whatever. But his rage was distinctly with the Japanese — with cause. He was a flyer during the war, and they shot his plane out from under him. Supposedly it was an observation plane, and they kept shooting him as he floated down on his parachute. I think I could harbor a little hate myself under those circumstances. I probably would never drive a Toyota. Nonetheless, his comments were a yellow this, slant-eyed this, that and the other, constantly. He didn't say it to our face, but we would be standing close enough so that we could hear him. Whether he thought Vivian was Japanese or Chinese, I don't know. It got to the point where I avoided him at all costs. He was about a seventy-year-old man. I literally could not stay in the same room with him because I would have hurt him. I had enough. That was the only time I encountered blatant slurs against Orientals. And it bothered me. It annoyed me greatly.

"If someone is harboring an inner hate, that upsets me. And if people are two-faced about it, that upsets me. I play rugby with a great bunch of guys. They are really friendly and supportive of each other. There happens to be two guys on the team who are black; both exceptional athletes. One of them is just the smoothest character — real confident, bubbly. He sells insurance. I guess that says a lot. He is just the nicest guy you'd want to meet. On the field, everyone will cheer for him because he's a really hard player. It's one of those games where you find yourself in a situation where you need someone big to help you, and he'd be there for you. I was in a car with a group of people going to tournament. And I had no sooner closed the door to the car after talking to him, than they referred to him as an 'uppity nigger.' Within moments, I just wanted out of the car. I didn't want to see these people whom I thought were my friends. They probably say things about me in light of my marriage to Vivian. I wouldn't be surprised. It seems as though maybe I've stepped across some mythical line but I haven't done the unthinkable. I think those people can accept the idea of Orientals easier than they can accept the idea of a white and a black person, for whatever reason, even though there is probably more commonality between white people and blacks than there is between whites and Orientals. So those people who would make cracks like 'uppity nigger' would be the same people who would find some way of talking about Orientals and non–Orientals being together. It's a shame but that still exists, and it doesn't seem to be going away too quickly."

Kids: "When we have kids, I would hope they be raised as 'Chinese-Americans.' I think there is a gift of language that Vivian speaks, that I can't. I think it is terribly important that if we do this soon enough, that my kids are not only going to know their grandparents, but they will meet their great grandparents. And I think it is really important that they can be able to talk to all of them. This way, I can have somebody else to ask, 'What'd they say?' It's only been in the last year or so, that we missed out on the chance to have not only great grandparents, but great, great grandparents. Vivian's great grandmother passed away in China. That's a line that we haven't been able to get together on my side of the family. And it's such an exceptional opportunity for someone to have that, that it would be foolish for someone to say, no you're in America, you're going to be raised as an American, so you learn to drink beer, drive pickups, and go to Columbia or something like that. It's ridiculous. I want them to know both sides of the culture."

On Marrying Out: "I have never thought of the idea of marrying up or down without sarcasm. It doesn't fit in my values to say you're marrying up or down. Would I be marrying down if I were marrying someone from an extremely wealthy Oriental family? Would that be marrying down?

"Fortunately, I don't think you get any particular social status out of biologically pairing yourself. I would think Vivian married up not because she married white, but because she married me. And I would feel the same about marrying Vivian. If I could walk through the streets of Chinatown, and say, 'You, the girl with the slant eyes, come to the great white father,' and she came to me, would that be moving up or down? I'd be stuck with someone with no self-esteem and she'd be stuck with a lout."

So He's Not a Jewish Doctor

Jody Sandler Hom

Jody is twenty-three years old and has been married to Tony Hom for a year. She was raised in Woodmere, Long Island.

"I remember thinking when we were first dating that I would never marry him. I was brought up to believe that I was going to marry a Jewish doctor, and that was it. A lawyer would do, but a doctor was the ideal goal, and preferably someone from the five towns I was living in. You were always brought up to believe you would marry somebody Jewish. It wasn't preached to you. It was just in the air. Like you knew after high school, you would go to college. And I knew someday I would marry someone Jewish and I never questioned it. It never bothered me, and I never thought that anything different would happen.

"I met Tony at the college drinking bar. I was with my friend Roberta, and Roberta was very good friends with Tony. Tony was there that night, and we just hit it off from the beginning. I guess my thoughts when I first met him was that he smiled too much, and I thought he was really funny, had a good sense of humor, and enjoyed making fun of people. That is a favorite pastime of mine too. So we had a pretty good time that night, and he got me pretty drunk. I was a goodie-two-shoes when I met him. It was kind of like a first for me.

"Tony and I just spent so much time together. Everything was in such close proximity. It was almost like living together when you go to school together. I'm not sure at which point things got serious. I remember when we first started dating he would hide from me. He was the president of his fraternity at the time, and there was a lot of pressures on him to be with his friends. And I was taking him away from that. So he would hide from me when he saw me because then he would have to spend the evening with me. He told me this afterwards.

"After the first semester, things got a little more serious, but I still didn't contemplate marriage. I was seventeen years old. It wasn't something you

thought about at that time. We used to talk about it, in the beginning, as
a very hypothetical thing. We used to say maybe in five years, but five
years at that time was an eternity. When you're seventeen, one year is like
an eternity. We didn't think about it so much as things started to happen.
We took on the role of husband and wife a long time before we were
engaged, even the monetary aspects. Our money was together, and we did
things with it together.

"When I first started seeing Tony I had a feeling my parents wouldn't
be too happy about it, and I couldn't understand why they felt that way.
I called my parents and told them. First I said, 'He's not Jewish.' My father
said, 'Oh.' Then I said, 'He's also Chinese.' My father said, 'Well, in that
case, I don't think you should see him anymore.' So it was a day or two
later I told him I wasn't seeing him anymore. And of course I was still going
to see him. My parents were never very protective of me. If I went out, they
never asked for me to call them when I got there. They never asked me what
friends I went out with, despite the fact that they were living only twenty
minutes away. They never came to visit unannounced, except for once. We
got past that one. But they never really bothered me, so it was very easy
to get away with what I was doing. Soon afterwards, they moved to
Florida, so it was even easier. My father's best friends, and his sister, knew
about Tony. They were scared for us. They thought my father would react
violently. He has a horrible temper. But he shocked everybody. I remember
how he found out. Tony had a fraternity brother named Hy David. And
one time my father went into a store where Hy David was working, and
when Hy was writing up the receipt, he saw the name and said, 'I know
your daughter, Jody. She's dating a fraternity brother of mine.' My dad
said, 'Oh really? Who?' and Hy said, 'His name is Tony Hom.' So my father
went back to Florida and didn't say anything. Then he called me the next
day and asked me what I was doing the next night. He came up and we went
to a Japanese restaurant of all places. There were about six strangers at the
table, and my father said, 'How's Tony?' I choked on my shrimp tempura.
I just spilled my guts in front of these strangers. They just sat there the
whole time, listening to me. But I didn't care, I was so nervous. My father
was very cool about it. He didn't react or get angry. And he has a horrible
temper. He has destroyed dining room chairs. He never directed it at us
physically, but he would break everything around him. It was very scary.
My parents had a real hard time when they got married. They eloped. He
didn't want that to happen to me. And he didn't want what happened to
my mother and her parents to happen between us. So my father wanted to
take me and Tony out to dinner. It was one or two nights later. I never saw
Tony so nervous. He was shaking so much. We went to this place that was
pretty informal. My father spent the whole time eating and staring at Tony
at the same time. After that, my father said he thought Tony was adorable

and that's what he went home and told my mother. And from there on in, everything was just fine.

"My father pushed us to get married, actually engaged, a lot faster. Especially since I was graduating college and wanted to stay in New York. Tony and I were going to be moving in together. My father didn't want us to be living together if Tony's intentions weren't clear. So he kind of pushed us to get engaged a lot faster, and I think Tony felt pressured into it. But that's why we agreed to such a long engagement. I was twenty when I got engaged. Tony was twenty-three. We were really young and not ready to marry yet. My parents kept telling us how we were going to meet so many hardships aside from being married. They discussed all the prejudice we were going to encounter. We just wanted to be sure it was a relationship that would last. It was really tough in the beginning. I have encountered a great deal of prejudice. When I was first dating, it was bothering me a lot. I lost almost all my high school friends as a result of it. In Woodmere, Long Island, where I grew up, it's 99.9 percent Jewish. There's one black family, one Italian family, and one Irish family. Everybody else is Jewish.

"I don't want to stereotype Jewish people as whole. I have met a lot of Jewish people, after high school, and after getting away from the five towns, who I have gotten along with. But the five towns where I grew up is a very 'keep up with the Jones' type of place. It is a difficult place to grow up and a very difficult place to live. It is also a very difficult place to go back to, if you're not with that Jewish doctor.

"After a few years, I kind of adopted a 'mightier than thou' attitude where I felt above anybody who directed a prejudiced remark against me. It just didn't bother me anymore. I felt superior to those people. It probably exists now. But now I feel hardened. No, that is too harsh a word. I just ignore it and it really doesn't bother me. It's kind of like 'sticks and stones can break your bones but names can never harm you.' So there are no difficulties other than the ones that are self-imposed. In fact, I think the Jewish remarks bother me a lot more. As long as no one burns a cross on my front lawn, I don't care what the rest of the world is doing. I'm not the type of person who needs to have everybody accept me. I have my friends and family, and that's all that matters. It took a while for me to grow to accept that and believe that.

"The prejudice in the five towns was cruel. First of all, I was losing all my friends. These were people who wouldn't even be friendly with those who weren't Jewish. I mean the parents wouldn't allow a non–Jewish person into the house. Sometimes it was that severe.

"The Jews that I grew up with looked down on anyone who wasn't Jewish. When I first met Tony, I used to tell him that when you go into someone's house and you're not Jewish, there is a certain feeling there. It's very difficult to explain, but you feel like you don't belong. And Tony got

Jody and Tony Hom at wedding banquet.

really mad. He said, 'I can't believe you feel that, because nothing is there.' I don't feel that way anymore. But I do remember feeling that way. It was the way I was brought up. And you're also brought up to believe that everybody hates Jews, and everybody's out to get the Jews. They believe World War II should never be forgotten. They act like no one else has ever been persecuted. I mean, I don't like to minimize what happened, but enough already. It's such a very, very strange way to grow up. But I think they bring prejudice onto themselves. I hate to think I'm prejudiced against Jews, because when somebody says something to me like, 'You don't look like a Jew,' I get very defensive and very angry. So I don't know if it is fair for me to get angry if I'm saying the same thing.

"But my friends just wouldn't associate with me. They didn't want to have anything to do with me. I was very, very close to my friends. I think I was closer with them, then they were with me. That's the way I felt after everything happened. I used to not be able to look through old scrapbooks without crying. I guess time heals all wounds. Tony didn't feel comfortable there either. You could feel all the stares.

"If you weren't wearing the right jeans or you didn't have the right sneakers and you didn't go to the right place on vacations, you just weren't accepted. When I first met Tony, I thought everyone in the world had a gardener. And when Tony told me he had to go home on Saturday to help his father mow the lawn, I was shocked. The fact that I was so narrow-minded was because of where I grew up. I didn't know how to put in a light bulb, because I didn't know you screwed it in. I never had to do it. My mother always had a maid. In my neighborhood, if there was a black woman on the street, she was a housekeeper going home. And if there was a black person in a car at night, the police would stop him. Jewish people in the neighborhood I grew up in had a superior attitude, and that will not leave them. I think the best thing that happened to me was leaving to go to school, and getting away from those people, and actually being an out-sider, looking in, and seeing what I could have been and what I was. I lived my life in high school controlled by things like, if you didn't spend fifty or sixty dollars on a pair of jeans, then they weren't worth wearing. I just hope and pray this type of thing won't happen to my children.

"Up to the day I got married, my parents' best friends were trying to convince me not to get married. They said it would be a very difficult life for me. But it is only difficult if you let it affect you. People would say things to me like, 'Oh well, at least he's Chinese and not black.' That used to really hurt. Then my Aunt Cookie, who is my favorite aunt and who I like a lot, asked my mother, 'Why is Jody marrying him? She could do so much bet-ter.' And I said to my mother, 'I am so shocked Aunt Cookie said something like that. What do you mean by better? Tony treats me like a queen. He's a great listener, he's my best friend,' and I just went on and on about his good points. So what does she mean by better? There is no better. And if the fact that he is Chinese and not Jewish is what she means by better, then she has a lot to learn.

"The reasons why I married Tony becomes so apparent to me when I listen to the women at work bitching and griping about their husbands. Tony and I were talking the other night about what I perceive as divvying our household duties, and I said, sixty-forty. He does sixty percent of the work, and I do forty percent of it. And all these women at work say, my husband never does this or that. Tony and I go food shopping together. We have a great time. I love going food shopping. These women are all moan-ing and groaning about how all their husbands do is sit on the couch and watch TV and drink beer while they're lugging in all the big bags. And all their husbands can say is, 'Did 'cha buy any lunch meat?' I just don't think I will have to go through anything like that because Tony and I enjoy doing all these things together. That makes him very special. He's very different in many respects. I don't think there are too many others like him.

"During the time my parents didn't know about Tony, I tried to con-vince myself that I hated my parents, so that it would be easier for me if they rejected me and my relationship because I knew regardless of what happened with them I was going to go through with what I wanted. This was my life. I think that was pretty tough. It was such a heavy relief when my parents did accept it. I didn't know what to do with my emotions. That was a very hard thing to sort through. Another very hard thing was dealing with Tony's mother. I can't even remember it being that way, but I do remember the instances when she was pretty mean. Every time I would call Tony she would hang up on me. I would say 'Is Tony there?' and she'd say, 'No,' and hang up. And then Tony would get really mad and yell at her. 'When someone calls me,' he said to her, 'you come and get me.'

"But there was a big fear there that his family wouldn't accept me. The first time his grandmother ever met me, she told Tony I was ragged looking. Now I couldn't figure out if that was acceptance or not. Was that an insult or not?

"I didn't hear most of the insults. Tony didn't want to hurt my feelings. He just needed someone to talk to when things upset him. When Tony's sister, Vivian, and Mark got married, Tony's mother locked herself in the bathroom and threatened to drink Clorox. She didn't do anything that drastic with us, but I wasn't included in any of his family functions. When Vivian got married, I couldn't go to her wedding, which I understand completely now, but then I was very hurt. Vivian went through so much that when the time came that her mother finally accepted it, she didn't want anything to ruin it. And I certainly would have put a damper on things.

"Then Tony was very close to his family and he always liked to go back on the weekends and help. And his parents put a lot of pressure on him to come back as well because they wanted to see him. That's something I wasn't used to because my parents are not like that. My parents are kind of like the way I am. They are very to themselves. I always went to camp every summer so that my parents could travel and be together. And my parents used to go on vacations a lot alone. They weren't as involved with us as Tony's parents were. So Tony used to leave on weekends when we were living together and he would go home to his parents, and I would sit in the apartment and watch TV all weekend. He was back in his home and I couldn't be there. That was kind of hard. But by the Christmas before we got married, things started getting better. But all of that was hard in the beginning. You don't marry into your husband's family. You don't marry into your wife's family. But family support, if it is not there, does put a strain on your relationship. And I was very much afraid I would resent Tony because he would have caused me to lose my family. I worked pretty hard at convincing myself that it didn't matter. I tried to convince myself that I hated my parents, which was very far from the truth."

Family: "I love Tony's family. I think they're wonderful. I feel closer to Tony's parents than I do to mine. I value Tony's parents' values more than I do my own family's. My parents are very selfish. Tony's parents are not. My parents are very geared towards spending time alone together and away from the children. I know my parents love us, but they had children because that's what you do when you get married. Tony's parents live for their children. They devote themselves completely to their children. Their children come first; they come second. With my parents, they come first, then their children. That's the major reason why Tony and I chose to remain up north, as opposed to moving down south to be with my family. I would much rather my children grow up with Tony's parents than with my parents. I don't want to deprive my children of my parents. I think my parents would make wonderful grandparents, but I want them to grow up the same way Tony did. I think Tony had a happier childhood than I did. And I want that for them. Maybe I perceive it that way because I don't know what's going on, not being able to speak Chinese while everyone speaks Chinese in Tony's family. I never know when people are fighting. Chinese people talk so loud all the time. You never know when they're angry, or happy, because it all sounds the same. My family is always fighting. When my father comes up here, we spend a lot of time with his sister. She has a daughter and a son. And my father and her son are usually on the verge of killing each other. And we go to restaurants, and people stare at us because my father is constantly yelling at his nephew.

"There are times when I don't realize I am saying things that are offensive to Tony's family. For instance, I have this expression, 'could you die,' and I have a tendency to say that, and you're not supposed to talk about death. So that doesn't go over very well. And one time I said, 'Let's go to the mall. I have to get out of the house.' I said that once, and I made Tony's mother cry. I never said it again. I never realized how seriously my words could be taken when I didn't really mean anything against them. And I certainly didn't want to get away from them. I just wanted some fresh air and a change of scenery. So I learned these things pretty quickly.

"Sometimes I do feel like I am a daughter in Tony's family, but other times they still treat me like a guest. When I eat dinner at Tony's grandmother's house and I wash the dishes, the grandmother pushes me away. She tells Tony I shouldn't be washing dishes because I am a guest.

"I feel very close to Tony's mother now. I feel as though I can trust her, and that she's someone I can go to if I needed anybody. I never had a very close relationship with my mother. My mother was always very distant from me. And Tony's mother is more motherly towards me than my mother was. When I am sick, she would cater to me, whereas my mother would always say, 'I'm going out. Take care of yourself.' Compared to my own mother, I would say Tony's mother treats me like a daughter."

On the Name: "Most of the dealings I have with strangers is at work on the phone. They usually think I'm saying 'H-a-h-n,' or 'H-a-r-n,' or even

'H-o-n.' Even one of the supervisors walked by my office the other day and he saw my plate outside. I guess he never noticed it. And he said, 'Hom? I always thought it was H-a-h-n.' So he's another one. Nobody ever asks me what is it. Maybe it's not an Asian sounding name, or maybe they just don't care."

Children: "When we first got married, I thought I wanted to raise my children in the Jewish faith. I don't think I would ever feel comfortable raising them in the Christian faith. But I think the children need to believe in God. It gives them a sense of security that nothing else can. But I don't believe in religion. I think religion tears people apart. I want them to feel as though they belong to something. So I probably will bring them up as Jewish in name, and carry on the three high holy days — Yom Kippur, Rosh Hashanah, and Passover, in the same way that I was brought up with it as a family holiday. When we were very young we went to temple. By the time we were eight, we stopped. It was ridiculous. Everything was in Hebrew. We didn't understand what was going on. All we did was fidget, and my parents couldn't take it anymore. So we didn't go. I don't see any purpose in dragging my children to temple. But I think it is important for them to belong to something, and to carry it on as a family tradition. I'll teach them what it stands for, but I'm not going to go gung ho on religion. When I grew up, we celebrated Santa Claus. We didn't celebrate Christmas. I didn't know that Christmas was the celebration of the birth of Christ until I was old enough to also understand the difference in religions. A lot of Christians would disagree with me because that's not supposed to be the purpose of Christmas, but I think Santa Claus is such a fantastic childhood fantasy. It's a shame to deprive a child of that. I never celebrated the Easter Bunny, but I think that's terrific too. And the more family holidays you can have, I think the better. But I think more than anything, we're going to bring them up as Chinese American. I really enjoy the Chinese New Year celebration, and his family takes it so seriously that I think that's going to be the primary focus.

"I worry about whether my children would be accepted in a temple. From what I have been exposed to, Jewish people are not very accepting. I don't think I would have my children bar mitzvahed, and I don't think I'll ever bring them to temple except for a funeral or wedding. That's not the place where I'm going to teach them about religion."

On Chinese Food: "My parents used to take us for Chinese food every Sunday night, and that was what I thought Chinese food was — Chinese American food, Chinese food for lo-fan. I thought Chinese food was egg rolls, spare ribs and soup. So it took me a long time to get used to the food in Chinatown. The first time Tony and I went to Chinatown for dim sum (Chinese pastries), I really got nauseous from it. I don't know if it was too heavy or what. But gradually I developed a tolerance for it, and eventually

I started to like it. But the food that his grandmother cooks, sometimes I like it and will eat it, like chicken or beef. But there are certain things that look like they are still alive, or certain parts of the body that I don't care much to see much less to eat like fish head or chicken feet, missing two fingers. Even shark's fin soup, I can't keep down. I can't eat slimy, jellyfish or things like that. The Chinese style of cooking I like, but there are certain foods I will never be able to accept. Like at our wedding banquet, they served this stringy, filmy looking thing. I think it was jellyfish. A lot of my friends knew this food probably cost a fortune, but couldn't bring themselves to eat it."

On Asian Males: "I think before I met Tony, I always thought Asian women were very beautiful, and I didn't think Asian men were very good looking. The majority of the ones I saw were extremely skinny. The two times I went to Chinatown before I met Tony, the men wore these big, thick black glasses. I never really paid much attention. The first time I met Tony I thought he was very good looking. Since I met Tony, I think that there are just as many good, and not good looking Asians as there are good and not good looking Caucasians. The stereotype is that you think all Asians are computer geniuses and they all get straight A's in school. So there are stereotypes, but I don't think there are any negative ones against Asians."

It All Worked Out

Tony Hom

Tony is twenty-five years old and is married to Jody Sandler Hom. He was born and raised in the United States. He is Chinese American.

"As a child growing up, I thought one day I would be married, but it was odd, in the sense there was a conflict. I knew my parents wanted it to be someone from their particular village in Canton where they had grown up. But for myself having been exposed to media where they don't play up to Orientals and the main sex symbols are Caucasian, I thought I would marry Caucasian when the time came.

"I am a risk manager for a Fortune 100 company. That means I'm in charge of the insurable risks and assets of the entire corporation in the U.S., Mexico and Canada. My company is basically self-insured. I monitor losses and renewals. I like my job, particularly at this point in my life. I don't think anyone ever chooses insurance; it seems insurance goes to them. I don't think I was ever cognizant of getting in. I never grew up thinking, I wanted to get into insurance, although I am happy with my position. If I weren't doing this, I guess I would really want to be a chef; from buying to handling the foods. I don't know if I would like to do that for a living, cooking hundreds of meals in one hundred degree heat. In the past I wanted to be a ball player, but I guess that is every little kid's dream. Then I had some interest in stocks and becoming a broker. After I graduated with a BA, I thought of going for the MBA, but I just didn't know where to take it from there. So I tried a lot of entry level jobs, and one of the first that came up was in insurance. And from there on in, it is just a natural flow of things. There is the stereotype of Asians being more studious and hard working, so I think that helps me at my job. As first impressions go, if you're going to pick ten John Smoes, and one happens to be Asian, people tend to have stereotypes and the Asian stereotype of being studious and hard working helps. So being an Asian works in my favor at least in the New York area.

203

"I feel like I'm a Chinese American. I feel mostly American. If there was a war between China and the U.S., by all means, I would side with the Americans. There would be no questions or doubts. That is where my loyalty is.

"The stereotype of a Chinese male is of a guy with glasses and a bowl haircut. He is a science student and gets good grades. As far as fitting into that mold, I don't think I do. I think I am more mainstream, though I carry strong ties to my heritage and bring that out in my work, with my friends. I think what allowed me to escape that mold was not being raised in Chinatown. Actually, I was raised in Harlem. And because Harlem was a rough area, my parents sent me to Catholic school, so the education I received there helped me to break out of the mold. It just wasn't a homogenous society in which all I saw was Chinese people, day in, and day out.

"I don't really associate with other Asians, or for that matter, Chinese. It's not that I don't like them. It's just that I don't come in much contact with them. If I saw a Chinese I wouldn't say, 'Hey, fellow Oriental come bond with me.' I wouldn't make a conscious effort to go and introduce myself if I saw one. In the same way, I wouldn't go and introduce myself to a black or a white. Unless I had something in common with a person, I wouldn't associate with them. It doesn't matter what they are to me. I've only dated one Asian girl in my life, and that was for a short stint. Again, there weren't very many Asian girls where I was growing up, and they didn't band to-gether. So in the group of friends I had there weren't too many Asians.

"I guess when I was growing up, my idea of a dream girl was the center-fold of a *Playboy* magazine. That, or any attractive celebrity you would see on television was the dream girl, not the average Jane Smith who was your neighbor on the block. It would be those you see in the limelight, those you would see thrust upon you. Therefore, I didn't think of a dream girl being Asian, at least when I was younger. Maybe when I got older, I did. But when I was older, any female would have applied and been ap-plicable."

Dating: "I always got pressure from my parents to date Chinese girls. They even pushed it up to the very end before I got married. It would be, 'We have a friend who has a daughter studying science in some university somewhere. Why don't you go out and date her?' Actually, my parents didn't really have a concept of dating. For them, it would be one date, and up to the altar for the wedding. So the main thrust was, one day you will date an Asian and marry her. Not several—but just one girl, then you would marry her. I would characterize my mom as old fashioned. My dad worked in an engineering setting out of the mainstream Chinese commu-nity, so he has more exposure. But I think he is old fashioned as well.

"I went out with Jody for four years before we got married. My parents knew I was dating. And I guess children always think their parents are blind, or know nothing. But they seemed to have known all along. There were the little things like the same girl calling all the time for a few years, or that she was the only one I ever brought home. So they had an idea. They knew I wasn't asexual all together. They tried to discourage me. I mean, it wasn't like they had seventeen children — it was just me and my sister. And so they did notice a pattern going on there with Jody. Their idea was that eventually it would blow over, and it would be done without them interjecting their thoughts. They mentioned sternly a few times that they wanted me to marry someone who was Chinese. But I didn't pay much attention to that."

The Wedding: "I actually broke it to my father first. I figured he would be less upset with the situation than my mother would be. It was a long engagement of two years, and I had to figure out a good way to tell them. So when I finally did tell Dad, he said, 'Just wait a little longer. Don't tell your mother just yet. You know she will get upset, so why get her upset for a year, when she can be upset for four, maybe five months.' Fine, I was a coward, but it sounded good to me. Then one day in passing he had mentioned it to her. And that is how she found out, by the way of my father.

"We had set the date before telling my parents. We kind of gambled that it would work out. I knew it was just a matter of getting enough courage. My sister broke the gap. She was the first one to go. Without a doubt she had it twenty times harder than I did, maybe even thirty or forty times. So by that time, it really wasn't as much conflict as I had expected. My mom was angry and upset in the beginning. Primarily she felt that she would lose face in front of her friends. She's still in that close-knit society. I think Chinese people are prejudiced towards any other outside group, even down to the point where only those from the Canton region are acceptable — the real Chinese. Those from the North really don't count because they're 'backwards, and barbaric,' etc., etc. So for twenty some odd years my mother and her friends would gather around and talk about so and so whose child is such a disgrace, she married out of the Cantonese community etc. Now the shoe was on her foot, and I think she was upset from that standpoint. She was worried about how she would fall out and be dishonored. My grandparents were always supportive, even from the beginning. They felt it was fine if that was what I wanted. They were more concerned with how my mother — their daughter — was going to treat this. They were one step removed in the hierarchy of ruling my life. Just as they have control over my mother, and my mother over me, they would not step over that. She's pulled out of it completely, thank goodness. In the beginning, the first few months, I knew she was accepting, but I didn't know if she totally accepted the entire situation. But now clearly, I have no doubts in my mind.

"Originally we had planned our wedding in Long Island. Neither one of our families were very religious. I couldn't really get married in a church, because I hadn't gone to church in years. By the same token, she couldn't get married in a temple, so we chose this place out in Long Island — a place that catered to weddings — and there was a rabbi who performed the services. It was really an innocuous service. It wasn't the most religious of ceremonies. As there was a rabbi there, it made her family very, very happy. Religion never played much of a part in my family, so it wasn't really much of a compromise. A rabbi was fine. But my mother said we couldn't break with tradition. We had to have a Chinese banquet. All along we were saying no. So the final compromise was we would have the ceremony on Sunday, and the next day, on Monday, we would have the banquet. There was no Chinese minister there, just a toastmaster mentioning the marriage, and the introduction of the families."

Jódy's Family: "They knew about the wedding all along. They were great from the very beginning, while I, because I perceived my family's prejudice, expected other people to be prejudiced. I think the main problem with my parents or the Chinese old-fashioned side, is they think less of other groups, so in turn, they think other groups think less of them, so they have this perception that other people would think differently of them. Growing up, I had that feeling all along. It was in the back of my mind, the question of how accepting another family would be. But from the very beginning, her entire family was just great. I was very happy there was one supportive side. They were there from the time I proposed through the planning — the band, the flowers, to picking the hall. Even going back to her grandparents I thought there might be some problems because of the older mentality. But they too were very accepting from the very first day. There was never any aloofness or discrimination from them."

Comparing Families: "The thing that surprised me most about Jody's family is the lack of family support. My family goes out of its way to help each other. My parents are very, very giving. They never went anywhere their whole lives. Their dream was always to save the money, send the kids away to college, do better for the children. And the children, in turn, will take care of them in their older years. Whereas, in Jody's side of the family, it seems to be everybody for themselves. The parents seem to indulge themselves and don't take care of the kids the way I was taken care of or the way I perceive we would take care of our kids. And that would seem the odd thing. They are more self-centered, more materialistic. Possibly it is because of the environment they grew up in, in Long Island. It seems to be a very materialistic environment. That was the odd thing I saw in Jody's family which I didn't expect.

"I'm sure that Jody in her wildest dreams, would never have pictured herself as eating fish and rice with my eighty-year-old grandparents. But while I'm away on a business trip, that's what she does. We grew up with totally different lifestyles. I don't see us as having cultural differences. It's more like family differences. Like my parents live next door to my grandparents, and we really are one family."

Never Rebecca
of Sunnybrook Farm

Betty Ann Bruno

Betty Ann is in her mid-fifties. She was born in Hawaii. Her mother is Chinese Hawaiian and her father is Irish Dutch.

"I grew up with a lot of crises in the making, which all came to a head when I was in my twenties. I wanted to be blond and blue-eyed. I did not want to look Hawaiian. I didn't know what it meant to be Chinese, because I didn't have any Chinese friends growing up, or know any Chinese people.

"Whenever the idea of being Chinese came up, it was rejected or denied. For a long time, I thought I was just Dutch, Irish, and Hawaiian. Somehow the Chinese came in when I was an adult.

"When I was three, we moved from Hawaii to Texas. My mother lasted only three months in Texas. The racism was very bad there. We couldn't even sit on the same side of the rope in the theatre when we went to the movies. My mother, my brother and I had to sit on one side, in the segregated part, and my father who is Dutch Irish sat on the other side of the rope. My mother said, 'I'm not living in this place.' My mother is Hawaiian Chinese. We were in my father's hometown, Wichita Falls, in the panhandle of Texas. So after three months in Texas, the compromise location between Hawaii and Texas was Hollywood. My father went into business there. My mother raised me basically on American culture. We were not Chinese at all. We didn't speak any Chinese. I was never told I was Chinese. There was a suspicion that there was some Chinese back there, but my mother never acknowledged that. My father was third generation American, and the Chinese side of the family goes back four generations. As far as I know, my Chinese grandfather came to Hawaii as a peddler. My mother's side of the family still has very strong ties to being Chinese. She had one brother who was sent back to China to be raised by Chinese relatives. And her brothers and sisters who grew up with her real

Betty Ann Bruno, age 6.

parents, and not her grandparents, those brothers and sisters speak
Chinese, and have a very definite Chinese identity. For those people,
Chinese was the dominant identity. It was just for my mother, who was
raised by her Hawaiian grandmother, that the Hawaiian part was the
stronger identity. I think the Chinese part was denied because part of that
can be traced back to feelings of possible rejection my mother had toward
her father. Her parents had given her to her grandparents to be raised. She
didn't know who her parents were until she was a teenager. At first, she

thought her real parents were an aunt and uncle. So I think there were feelings of abandonment. In a sense it was tied to the race issue. You know that Honolulu and the Hawaiian Islands are very racist. And in Hawaii in those days the best thing to be was Haole (Caucasian). If you had to have mixed blood, then the next best thing to be was Haole and Hawaiian, or Happa Haole (half Hawaiian). Then in kind of descending order, (taking it from Hawaiian and something else) Hawaiian and Chinese, Hawaiian and Japanese, and at the bottom of the whole thing was Hawaiian Filipino. From the point of view of Hawaiians, those were the positive and negative blood mixtures. This was in the thirties. And I think that attitude went on into the forties. The first time I went back to the Islands was when I was in high school. And of course my family was totally mixed up. I mean they were Hawaiians with Haole, Chinese, Japanese, Filipinos, everything. And people spent a lot of time talking about who was better than the other cousins. So my Chinese heritage at that point in my life was a negative thing to me.

"In college, when Chinese guys would come up and ask me to dance, I would just shrink. I had been taught that the direction I had to go towards to be successful was in the direction of the Haoles — the Caucasians. I look very ethnic. I have brown skin, brown eyes and brown hair. And it was a terrible thing to look that way at the time, especially since I looked ethnic but didn't know anything about my Chinese part or very much about the Hawaiian part. I grew up in a relatively small town. We were really the only Asian Pacific people there. So I had no context in which to put my Chinese ancestry. But I knew life would be sweeter somehow if I had blond hair and blue eyes. At least that was what I thought. And I think ethnic minorities in the thirties, forties and fifties all felt the same way. I mean, the melting pot in America was a place where brown-skinned people should disappear and become as white as possible. And blacks should be lighter too. I mean you talk about the light-skinned blacks. Everybody wanted light skin and to fade into the majority.

"There were a few times when I was growing up that I experienced racism. I don't remember the racism in Texas that my mother felt. But I remember when I was ten or eleven. One summer my mother dropped my brother and me off at the swimming pool in the little valley in Hemet, California, where we lived, and there was a new coach there, and she wasn't going to let us swim. She thought we were children of immigrant farm workers. And the braceros [laborers] weren't allowed to swim in the high school swimming pool. So my mother had to go down and do battle. And again, that was because we had brown skin.

"I went to Washington, D.C. after college, and couldn't get an apartment. This was in the fifties. I was not allowed to rent a particular apartment. It was never said. The landlord was very cordial over the phone. The apartment was available. And when I appeared, the apartment was suddenly not available anymore.

"On the flip side, there were people who were attracted to me and interested in me, because of the way I looked. I remember one time, when I was twenty-two, working in Washington, D.C. I was in a building which had military people in the next wing. There were about twenty-five guys in the army and navy working in that wing. We all ate together in the same company cafeteria. They sent a delegate over to me one day, and he said that he had been picked to find out what my ethnic background was, what my 'nationality' was; I think that's how we said it in those days. I was crushed. It turned out they were all interested in who this cute chick was in the next wing, and they wanted to know what I was. I took it as an insult. They had a pool. Everybody kicked in a dollar. I bet she's Thai, I bet she's Spanish, I bet she's Indonesian . . . whatever. And instead of taking that as flattery, it just made me so nervous.

"I think I'm 'Island'-looking, which means both Hawaiian and Asian. And I have that Island aura because people see it in me. Even though I didn't grow up there, I apparently carry it around. Being Hawaiian means to have the Aloha spirit. The Aloha spirit means to want to give, to be able to give, to be free to give, without expectation of getting something in return. It's living without laying trips on other people. It's trying to be positive about things, enjoying beauty, enjoying nature. It's being calm and kind, I guess. That's what I strive to be. I'm not always that way, but that's what I like to be. I'm not as sure about what being Chinese means to me. I think of being Chinese as being very smart, and being very rooted in some solid tradition and history. When I was going through my identity crisis in my twenties, I used to ask myself, 'What are you, Betty Ann?' And I always described myself as an intelligent, not bad-looking young woman. I kind of left the ethnic part out.

"The other fifty percent of me, my father's Caucasian side, doesn't mean a whole lot to me. I grew up in white society. So that is my background. I don't have any accents except a California accent. If you think of identity as food or dance or customs, I grew up on a small farm in a small town. But I don't identify with the Irish or the Dutch. Those were my father's nationalities. I don't identify with Texas. That's where he grew up. I think basically that if you're part Hawaiian, you identify with being Hawaiian. My children, who are one-eighth Hawaiian, feel Hawaiian. It's because that part is the strongest to me. People who are part Hawaiian identify as Hawaiian. And I don't know why that is so. I think maybe it's just a magic place to be from. Everybody wants to go there. It's paradise. It's where everybody is wonderful. It's where life is abundant, without effort. It's where nature smiles on you, where happiness is. It's the end of the rainbow. And there are all those wonderful associations with being Hawaiian.

"When I was growing up, I never had to go out of my way to tell people I went to school with that I was part Hawaiian or Chinese. It was a small town, and most everybody knew everybody else. There were only thirty-three hundred people in the town. I wore bobby socks, had the long sloppy joe sweaters, and learned to drive when I was fifteen. I played ditch, and chicken, and ate at the drive-in, and did everything that everybody else did. I always had a lot of friends. My first serious boyfriend was when I was a senior in high school. And he was a Mormon. His parents made him break up with me because they didn't like the fact that I was Hawaiian, that I was brown-skinned. That was the first real direct racial thing in my private life. The same thing happened in college. I went with a guy from Idaho for three years and we were going to become engaged. When his parents heard about it they said, 'No, she's from a different race. You may not marry her or you will be disinherited.' I never dated an Asian man. There weren't any when I was in high school, and when I was in college, I didn't want to because I didn't want to be Asian at that point. I didn't want to be thought of as an Asian. I still wanted to be 'Rebecca of Sunnybrook Farm.'

"My father was a businessman so everybody knew us. I never had any problems growing up in a small town. When you are a minority of one, you're not really a threat to anyone. There wasn't any prejudice. We were the only ones in town who were like us. There was a reservation of American Indians, and there were prejudices directed towards them and there were Mexican farm workers and there were special prejudices against them. But we were a family of a local successful merchant who made some contributions to the town. My brother and I were outstanding students, we did plays, entered speech contests, and essentially were like everyone else.

"The only time I had problems because I looked different was when I went to college. This was a new community, and people wanted to know what I was, and where I was from. I had difficulty with that because I never had to answer those questions before. In college (I went to Stanford), a couple of things happened. There was a group of Haoles who came from Punahoe (*the* private high school in Honolulu where a lot of people graduate and then go to Stanford). They all knew how to play the ukelele and dance the hula. They knew kitchen variety Hawaiian, could speak pidgin, and were from the Islands. I was from this little hick town in Southern California, didn't have an Island background, but I looked this way. And everybody would say 'Oh, you're from the Islands? Do you know so and so?' I didn't. I developed feelings of inadequacy. I felt totally out of it. People who didn't know that I was from the Islands would ask me about my national background. And I tell them that I grew up in Southern California. I would never say I was Chinese, or Hawaiian, or Dutch or Irish. Part of it was that I felt inadequate. I didn't know what it meant to be Chinese or

Betty Ann Bruno, today.

Hawaiian. So I was very defensive about that. And the other part of that was there were still remnants of wanting to be blond haired and blue-eyed. I was actually in this horrible position of being prejudiced against myself.

"A big part of thinking white was beautiful came from the outside. All the images were white. Everything you got in the newspapers was about whites. We didn't get a television set until I was a senior in high school, so I can't say much about that. Images on the radio were all white. There white voices. Everyone was white except the assistants to the super heros — the Tontos, the Robins, and the Katos. They had the accents, and they were the second class super heros. So there was the message that if you were brown or a minority that you were somehow not as good.

"I used to wish I was born looking different than what I was. I mean, why couldn't I look like Rebecca of Sunnybrook Farm? That's really who I wanted to be. But I wasn't. So when I was in my twenties I said 'Okay. You look the way you look. What does this mean?' I decided to take hold of my ethnic destiny. I forced myself to learn more about the Chinese. I began to get some Chinese friends. I even went to a Hawaiian night club to meet a Hawaiian dance teacher because I love to dance. I told myself I was going to learn how to hula. And I met a woman whom I adopted as my Hawaiian mother, and we are still very close friends. I danced with her for twenty years.

"Eventually I even went to China. I went to China with my mother, and it was a wonderful trip because she had not until that time dealt with her Chinese ancestry either. If I had made that trip when I was younger, I feel my whole life would have been changed because I feel very strongly now that pull of China and things Chinese. It is a very proud ancestry. I wish I knew more personally about it.

"The food has always been there. I love all the Island food, and I eat it all. When I was growing up, that was my mother's ethnic identity. We always had poi, a staple made from the root of the taro plant, and it serves the same purpose of rice or bread or potatoes. Poi was always very special. Even during World War II when poi was hard to get, I remember bags of poi coming out on the train, and we would go down and pick up the poi. The poi was there, and that was wonderful. I still make poi. My kids love to eat poi, raw fish, lomi salmon and lau-laus. And when I met my adopted mother, I learned more about that.

"All of those negative feelings I had when I was growing up are at peace now. I feel good about myself now. I'm glad I'm not blond and blue-eyed.

"I've had two husbands. My first husband is Italian and Scot, and he's the father of my children. And now I'm married to an Estonian Jew. I have no problems with the cultural differences. I like it all. I like all the food. I like all the people. I love my husband's Estonian relatives. It's marvelous. Now we're in a different age. It's great to look the way I look. It's great to be Asian, to be brown. It's exotic. It's a very positive thing, I wish I were twenty years younger. But ethnic background is a plus today. My kids love it. They're interested in it, and I open up to everything now.

"The irony of ironies is that when I grew up, my mother did not teach us to speak Hawaiian. She subverted her own Hawaiian background when I was growing up because she's tried very hard to mainstream us. Now, as a result of my coming to grips with my ethnic identity, she has gotten back into the Hawaiian thing. She is now a guru in a Hawaiian community in Southern California. She teaches Hawaiian, lei making, all the ethnic stuff and the folk lore. She's on radio and gives classes. She's founded a Hawaiian civic club. It's all very exciting. But none of that was happening the forties and fifties. That all happened in the sixties and seventies. It's all a product of civil rights. When black people decided they would go back to their roots, I think all the ethnic groups in the country took a cue from that and said, 'Hey, we've got roots too.' That's where we are.

"What I pass to my kids now is still California because I haven't been raised in the Islands. They don't speak Hawaiian, but I have taken them back to visit. One is living there now. I gave one of my children a Hawaiian name, and the others have asked for one as they've grown up. Their grandmother has given them one. They do identify with that even though they are only one-eighth Hawaiian. They're also one-eighth Chinese. They like it. They think it's terrific that they're six different things."

A Male Human Being

Phil Tajitsu Nash

Phil is in his mid-thirties and was born in the United States. His father is
Irish English and his mother is Japanese American.

"My dad is thirteenth generation, white–Anglo-Saxon Protestant. My
mother is a second generation Japanese American. People say, 'Did they
meet under the bridge at the River Kwai?' and I say 'No, the bridge at 160th
and Amsterdam.' It's a typical American romance except that one happens
to be of Japanese ancestry. My dad is from Massachusetts. He came to New
York after the war. My mom is from Seattle. She came to New York via
an internment camp in Idaho.

"I define myself as a male human being. I think it's society's need to
compartmentalize people that makes people call us half this or half that.
I think the word white should be abolished because it perpetuates the
notion that you can be this pure thing, and when your children are of European ancestry and something else, they are somehow seen as something
less. So I never use the word white unless I have to. I define myself as Asian
American because that is how I am perceived. The closest I've come to passing for an Asian is to have my middle name legally changed from Douglas
to Tajitsu. I was doing a lot of writing for Asian American papers, and
people were wondering why a white man was writing about these issues,
so I did it for that reason, and partly to honor the spirit of my mom's
family. That's the closest I've come to wanting more of an Asian identity,
and not having to explain all the time. I notice in some Asian American
papers names like Bill Blauvelt, or George Johnson — all these people I
know who are half Japanese, and half European American. Since I started
talking to George, he writes his name as George Toshio Johnson. Another
friend of mine, Steve Murphy, now calls himself Steve Shigematsu Murphy. Another friend of mine, Margaret Cornell, changed her name to
Michio Fukaiya, to Michio Cornell. It's an on-going question for a lot of
us who are of mixed ancestry.

"A lot of people are quizzical in a nice way. But it's unfortunate that we have to always be defining ourselves. People ask questions like, 'Do you know a good Chinese restaurant.' I went through a real militant phase where I asked them 'Well, you're French. Do you know a good French restaurant?' You know, the whole attitude that we should suddenly be experts on our cultures. I'm Japanese. Have I seen all of Kurosawa's movies? Well of course not. I like some of his stuff, but I'm not expected to know everything about his work. I was never really angry at myself or my parents. The anger was more towards others for forcing me into situations where I would have to define myself. You look at the Irish European who can say, 'Well, I'm a biologist. I'm not a black biologist.' Why do we always have to define ourselves? To that extent, I'm still a little bit indignant. I don't take it out on the average person who brings it up, because they just can't be expected to know. I'm at a more mellow place right now where I take it as it comes. I'm trying to define for myself where I want to go. Those Asian Americans that look more European can pass as such, and don't have to go through the anguish and soul searching that those of us, who look more Asian, do. But in some ways, my experience is no different than that of those whose parents are both of Asian ancestry. We're all treated according to stereotypes.

"I mean every time I walk up to the ticket counter and hand them my credit card that says Nash, in that person's mind, he must be thinking, he's really Nashiyama or he must have stolen this card. They look at me. For a woman it might make more sense; she might have married someone with the name. They're more used to that. But seeing someone like me with a European name must really throw people. And I don't think most people understand what it's like unless they put themselves in the mindset. It happens subliminally. They would look at the card, look at me, look at the card, and look at me again then put it in the machine. It's not that I'm a good looking woman, or something, so I know they're wondering. But then they decide that they can't turn down a Gold card. I sort of bought my way into a certain amount of respectability. I would say I don't experience prejudice, but I think that's because of my economic status. I'm a law professor, a public speaker. I don't sense it so much at this time. I sense prejudice does have a lot to do with money and appearance, because I can remember a traumatic experience one time when I tried to return some soda bottles. I was dressed grungy and hadn't shaved. I looked more Hispanic or like a street person. I walked into the grocery store, without the trappings of a professional person, so the supermarket manager said, 'Hey, Jose, get the hell out of here. We don't want these bottles.' Then I realized that that form of racial intolerance doesn't often happen to me because of my economic status, to a certain extent.

"Asians — say those who grew up here who are now in their thirties or forties – are probably a little more tolerant of white–Asian mixtures. Even older people are better although there is still some residual concern. For instance, in Japan, someone who is Japanese mixed with something else is called a 'love child,' and it has a pejorative meaning like your mother's a prostitute. At varying levels, depending on how much people know about the history of sexual exploitation of women, there is a certain amount of intolerance for mixtures of Asians with others. I would say that I have been fortunate to be Asian white, because if you are Asian black, such as my wife is, you face other types of pressures which are traditionally looking down at others. Look at all the bad words for blacks in Chinese.

"I was born in the Bronx, then moved out to Jersey when I was about two. I had a pretty traditional suburban upbringing, not coming in contact with very many Asians, not being heavily involved with Asian customs or rituals or anything. I was touched more by the Nash relatives. We would go to their house, and talk, and write letters. They were all teachers, and they would be interested in my studies.

"I would say my mother gave me certain values. She taught me to respect myself, and to respect others. We got together with relatives and had red rice for New Year's. We would also have sushi, and such. When I was ready to explore cultural things, my grandmother was there. I think things turned out well for me.

"I never really thought of myself as being different. The first time I really acknowledged the difference was in a high school class in tenth grade. I had just come back from Japan. My grandmother had arranged for me to go to the Boy Scout Jamboree, which happened to be in Japan in 1971. I studied Japanese with my grandmother before I went, and when I came back, I was very much into the Asian thing. So I distinctly remember writing the paper for my tenth grade comparative religion class. It's called Island Feudalism, comparing Japan and England, because they were both islands on the Eastern and Western end of the Euro-Asian land mass. I was sort of troubled and arrogant, because I was being taught by this former Jesuit priest who didn't know anything about Asian religions, so I said, 'I can teach this better than you,' so he said, 'Okay, why don't you teach the classes on Buddhism and Shintoism,' and so as a brash teenager I did all this research and presented my material. I ended writing about how Japan and England both went through these feudal eras and had indigenous animalistic religions, such as druidism and Shintoism.

"In college I took a class on the urban environment, and I wrote a paper on the Japanese internment camps as the precursor of modern prefabrication. How I got this topic, I have no idea. I went to the library and literally read thirty books. I read the entire Pearl Harbor Report which is twelve volumes. I just became so fascinated with the issue of internment. At the time no one was talking about it. This was 1975, and the beginning of the modern redress movement didn't begin until 1976. So I remember reading all this political stuff and being very hurt by it. My mom, like most nisei, never talked about it, and it was my grandmother who was very open. I went to law school, became very interested in this, and it sort of became the wedge I used for getting into academia and public interest groups.

"I'm proud of this country, but I'm not proud of all that has happened here. There is national chauvinism, things that are done in the name of this country that are not things I would do. Things are done in Hawaii, like annexation and racism. But I like the people. There is a basic goodness here. I'm not a blind patriot. I've travelled all around the world, and there are some good things here and there are some bad. My favorite quote is from Gandhi. Someone asked him what he thought of Western civilization, and he said, 'I'd love to see it.' I see myself as a patriot. I feel I belong here. I felt more of an American when I was in Paris. There, people would walk up to me and talk to me in French, so I could understand the feelings of an expatriate. And yet in this country, people walk up to you and say, 'Wow, you speak good English,' There is this presumption of foreignness that is really sort of irritating. I certainly am the most comfortable here, over other places. There is no other place I would call home.

"I don't think the identity issues is one that will ever be fully resolved. My wife is part Haitian and part Chinese. I sometimes consider what our children will be like. The geneticists will want to see all the variations that could come out of our two gene pools. Haitians by definition are so mixed up genetically that we have cousins who may have black curly hair, with a blonde, blue-eyed sister. That happens with Haitian families, so that literally could happen to us. My wife's father had red hair when he was younger. The recessive gene for blue eyes could happen to one of our kids, and we could have blue-eyed Asians without contact lenses. Or we could have someone who is very black looking. So I'm personally prepared for whatever happens. I think it will be interesting.

"I think a lot of my Asian derived friends go through life thinking they're white, and when they have kids, and the kids come home saying, 'Mommy, what's a chink?' they have to confront their identity for the first time.

"I imagine I'm going to be thinking about these issues for the rest of my life. The very knowledge that there is so much to think about has set me free. I know what I don't want to be called, and anything else if fine."

Eurasian

Joann Patricia Prosser

Joann is nineteen years old and was born and raised in the United States. Her mother is Chinese and her father is Irish German Welsh.

"Being Eurasian is something special. And I think I am a lot luckier than someone who doesn't have a mixed racial background. It makes me more tolerant of other people, and much more aware of the need for understanding among everyone in order to have a more understanding society. I love having my Oriental background. I love the food; I love the culture. It's very mystical because it's one of the oldest civilizations. I feel proud to be part of that.

"My mom was born in Canton, China, and my dad is Irish, German and Welsh. I consider myself a Eurasian — a mixture of the Western and Eastern blood. I consider myself a hybrid. That's what I tell my friends. I am not a mix, not a mutt; I am a hybrid.

"I've had a strange kind of background because I never lived near New York City where you would find a large population of Asians. And since I've lived in upstate New Jersey and eastern Pennsylvania, you don't normally find many Asians or Eurasians there. When I was in elementary school, it didn't dawn on me that much. I realized I was Chinese — that my mom was Chinese — and my friends liked my mom's cooking. That was kind of the extent of it, beyond going to my grandparent's house every weekend and eating the traditional Chinese food, and going on Chinese New Year's to watch the dragons and firecrackers in Chinatown. My grandparents would also celebrate all the Chinese holidays, like moon cake festival, and honor the ancestors. But beyond that, it was kind of hidden, or I really didn't think about it very much. When I was in the seventh grade, we moved out to the country in Pennsylvania. I've since found out that a lot of the people around here seem to be white supremists, and there seem to be a lot of KKK people who live around here, and there are a lot of very backward thinking people around here. Especially on the bus I had to take

220

to school. My bus was the rural bus that kind of picked up the leftovers —
the stranded people — out in the country. And when I went to school, every
single day, I hated taking the bus. It was the worst part of the day. I liked
going to school, but I liked being home a lot more. Every time I got on the
bus, they would make fun of me for being Chinese. And I would sit in the
front of the bus and really hated them for it because they were so ignorant.I
remember getting off the bus one time, and someone in the back of the bus
started chanting, 'chink-chink-chink--chink-chink' (in a sing-song kind of
way). I guess they thought it was Chinese music or something. I remember
getting off and being so upset, because I had normally not experienced that
before. Eventually the problem stopped when the kids got old enough to
drive, and they stopped taking the bus. I never told my mom about this.
Home was refuge. I didn't want to bring it home. I can't say the people who
rode my bus were representative of the entire school. These people were the
kind who would make fun of anyone. I would always sit at the front of the
bus. I would always read. I became a bookworm in seventh grade to isolate
myself from trying to make friends and being rebuffed. The people on the
bus didn't know my name and so they looked at me as something to make
fun of. Kids can be really cruel. But I wasn't scared of making friends
because I was Eurasian. It was just that I had transferred to a new school,
and in the seventh grade, kids can be real cliquish, and they seemed to all
have their groups of friends. I don't think they discriminated against me
because I was Eurasian.

"I think it was at the seventh grade, or just after that, that I developed
a sensitivity towards people who were treated poorly because they had
glasses, or braces, or because they were geeks. I got really mad and stuck
up for them because I had been there myself, and it really made me mad.
All that stuff is just ignorance. There is no difference inside.

"It's kind of weird. Some people will make fun of me; some people
won't think anything about the fact that I am Eurasian, and some people
will kind of regard me on a higher status because they think I am kind of
pretty because I have such a different mix. Some of my friends regard me
as almost better because they think the prettiest mixes are Asians and
Americans. Eurasian are the prettiest and most beautiful people. All my
friends who come here all think my mom is so cute. She's so tiny, so cute,
and so Chinese. And they love her cooking. They come to eat her cooking,
instead of seeing me. But I do know, I never really thought of being Chinese
that much, except when I went to Taiwan this summer.

"I don't speak any Chinese. When I was younger, my mom went back
to work on weekends to help my grandfather in the Chinese restuarant.
And we would spend weekends with my grandparents, and they would
speak Chinese. But they would always speak English to us. My mom speaks
Cantonese but my dad does not. So at we home would speak English. So

we never we never learned any Chinese. I feel cheated about that. I'm very upset because I feel that if I had learned Chinese when I was younger, it'd be much easier. And now I want to learn Chinese, but it's a lot harder. Because even though I've heard it spoken, it's very hard for me to pronounce the words, to hear the different tones. I really wish I could speak it."

A Summer in Taiwan: "I had a trip offered by the Taiwanese government. My Gung-Gung (Chinese term for maternal grandfather) helped to get me on that. That was a lot of fun. We were there for a month and a half, and the program had about eight hundred students. All the people were really, really interesting. I never realized there was such a diversity of Chinese around the world. I mean I met Chinese from Arizona, from the Dominican Republic, from Holland, Spain, from Canada. I mean from everywhere. I didn't anticipate finding them from so many places. There were about ten Eurasians in the school, and I met one guy from Arizona, whose father is Chinese, and his mother was Swedish, and we just had many of the same kinds of experiences growing up. And even in Taiwan, I was regarded as something different, because I was Eurasian and I wasn't Chinese. When we would be with a group of people eating and I would look around everyone would have Oriental faces — black hair, brown eyes, olive complexion. And they all looked alike. At first I didn't really consider myself different. I just assumed I was like them. But it was brought to my attention that I didn't look all Chinese.

"I would go out on the weekends with a friend of the family who took care of me, and we would ride the buses. Everyone on the bus would stare at me — not a mean stare — more out of curiosity, but a very, very bold type of stare. It was kind of weird. In fact, when we were at Sun Moon Lake (in Taiwan), to look at the various temples, there was a bunch of Taiwanese students there, and I felt really uncomfortable because this group of guys was just talking and looking at me. Eventually they approached my aunt and asked them if I would take a picture with them. And I thought that was really weird, so I obliged them. They said I was really pretty, and I supposed they hadn't seen very many Eurasions, or very many Westerners. I know they didn't think of me as Asian. But whether they made the distinction of me looking Eurasian or Western, I'm not sure.

"Before I went to Taiwan, I felt the same affinity towards being Irish, German and Chinese. It was like I was split in three's. I felt a third Chinese, as opposed to half. But after coming back, I feel much, much more Chinese, just because I was exposed to the origins of the country and understand more where my heritage came from. Whereas the German Irish culture, because my dad is third generation, is much more removed. Just being in Taiwan submersed me in the culture. They made a point of claiming the overseas Chinese as their own. I guess there is still that battle between mainland China and Taiwan. There was a lot of propaganda fed to us,

Joann Prosser and her sister, Diann Prosser. (Joann is on the right, wearing jeans.)

about us returning to the motherland. I found that to be rather amusing because I am American.

"I came back understanding my mother a lot more. I mean there are things my mother does that I can't understand from Western eyes. I didn't understand why she chose not to continue her career, and why she was always so devoted to my father, and to us (my sister and myself). She is so independent, and can stand on her own two feet easily. It was kind of hard for me to understand why she gave it all up to have a family, whereas a woman in the eighties in the U.S. would not do that. Another thing I've come to realize is how important the nucleus of the family is for the Chinese. My girlfriend pointed out to me that when the Chinese eat, they all share from the same dishes. I mean, we each get a bowl of rice, but then we pick up the vegetables and meat off the same plates with chopsticks. It's really different from Western style where everyone gets his own plate with everything in it. Something little like that can make a real difference in terms of sharing and togetherness."

How I Would Describe Myself: "Here in the United States I would describe myself as Eurasian. If people are aware of the different cultures, they would pick me out right away. But if they haven't been exposed to different cultures, they'd be confused. They might think I'm part Spanish, Italian or Hawaiian. They don't really know. They know I'm not German or Irish. They don't know what to make of me. But most people I've come into contact with—people I know here in town, or in school—basically know I'm Eurasian. Sometimes it enters in the conversation; sometimes it doesn't. It depends. If we're talking about family, they might make a comment as to my background. And I would explain to them that my mother was born in mainland China, and my father is German Irish Welsh. I guess they wouldn't be shocked to hear that, but pleasantly amazed.

"I do find a lot of people asking me if my mom is Vietnamese, as my dad was in the Vietnam War. I find a lot of middle aged people asking me that. Or when I tell them my mom was born in mainland China, I find a lot of them, if not openly asking me that, then at least wondering— especially if I mention that my father was in the Air Force. So I explain to them 'No, my mom came from Hong Kong, and had left China when the communists took over, and she was in New York City when she met my father.' I'm not sure that made a lot of difference, but I could sense that they were trying to figure out whether I was one of the mixed babies from the war. They wondered if my father was a good Christian or something, and brought me home. That kind of annoyed me a little because my mom's very independent and not like that at all. My mom is very independent. She's well educated. She's got a free spirit, and she's not at all tamed or domesticated into the servant type status that maybe the traditional Chinese had at one point."

Grandparents: "They're very special to me, especially my Gung-Gung. I love my Poar-Poar (maternal grandmother) very much too. But I've always admired my Gung-Gung. I probably admired him more because I lost my grandfather on my father's side nine years ago. My Gung-Gung has always seemed that much more courageous to me because he got his family out of China when the communists took over, and brought them to Hong Kong. Then he came to the U.S. to make enough money to have them brought over. And then he has always spoiled me, because I am the first grandchild and number one."

Asian Men: "Before I went to Taiwan, I used to think they were all thin, and a lot of them wore glasses, and that they weren't *really* geeks, but all were smart. I believed that none of them had good-looking bodies. I had never really met any Chinese guys before that I was interested in. The only Chinese boys I ever met were friends of the family, or my neighbor who is Eurasian, but he is younger than me. And I never grew up with any Chinese. So I basically had this image of Chinese men as geeks who would study very much and wear glasses and be very smart, studious and proper. I didn't think they were like a lot of my friends. What I found was there are very good-looking Chinese men around the world with incredible bodies. In fact, I met a guy, Danny Li from Texas, who has muscles from here to Arizona, I'm convinced. I never realized this because the ones I saw never had muscular bodies. I ended up coming home with a Chinese boyfriend. And I'm very happy.

"As for dating Asian men, it was never a topic of discussion with my parents because there just weren't any in this area. There was only one type to date. I mean even as far as blacks were concerned, there were only a handful in my high school. That was kind of a problem because during my senior year I went to the prom with my friend Carlton, who isn't very black, but he's a lighter skin black, but he's still considered black in our school. My father, which is kind of hard to understand, is prejudiced. He found the whole thing upsetting. I found that weird because he married an Asian woman. He told me I could go to the prom with this guy, but if I ever married a black person, I wouldn't inherit the land in the mountains which has been in his family for generations. I, of course, flew off the handle about that. I remember him telling me that my Gung-Gung was upset that I was seeing a black person. I do not know whether this was true or not. This was what I got from my father. I found it kind of funny in that I didn't care what my father thought, I was going to do it anyway. And Carlton wasn't my boyfriend; he was just a friend. I never thought of who I want to marry racially. I've always thought whoever I marry will be someone I love. It doesn't matter who they are."

Identity Crisis: "I can't say that I've ever really had an identity crisis that stemmed from being Eurasian. In this country I'm perfectly comfortable being what I am. When I was in Taiwan there were times when I wasn't comfortable until I learned to accept that people would look at me no matter where I went. I would hear them say the words, 'Piau Liang,' which means pretty, so I would be comfortable with that.

"I guess there have been moments when I wished I was something else, but that didn't have anything to do with my racial background. For instance, all little kids watch TV and want to be like Barbie with blond hair and blue eyes. And I remember there was a black family that lived down the road from us, and the little girl could braid her hair without rubber bands, and I thought that was the neatest thing in the world, so I wanted hair like that—black, kinky hair that would stay in braids without rubber bands. But I suppose I've received enough comments to be reassured that I am special. I love having black hair because everyone used to comment on my blue highlights. So I really like the way I am. I'm glad I'm Eurasian as opposed to pure Chinese or pure Western, because I like the mix.

"I've never differentiated the Orientals into Japanese, or Thai, or Korean, or Chinese, or Indian, or whatever. I've always thought of Orientals as Chinese. I mean I never thought of Orientals as Indians. Being Oriental means being Chinese. I find it hard to define to you what Eurasian is, except drawing upon my past experiences. But I can't define it, not in words. It's just a feeling. And I suppose that feeling, although it has many things in common with all Eurasians, there are also many things that differ because all Eurasians are different, depending upon what the other half is and how they've been brought up, and where they've been brought up.

"I guess I have experienced prejudice, but it hasn't been anywhere near the prejudice a black person might experience in my community which is a very small town. Most of my experiences have been positive. I haven't really experienced anything that has been harsh or has scarred me for life. I think it has strengthened me. It has made me understand more, given me insight."